Popular Art and the Avant-Garde

Popular Art and the Avant-Garde

Vincent van Gogh's Collection of Newspaper and Magazine Prints

Vincent Alessi

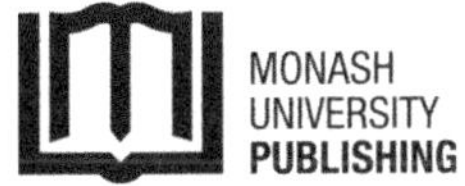

Popular Art and the Avant-Garde: Vincent van Gogh's Collection of Newspaper and Magazine Prints

Monash University Publishing
Matheson Library Annexe
40 Exhibition Walk
Monash University
Clayton, Victoria 3800, Australia
www.publishing.monash.edu

Monash University Publishing brings to the world publications which advance the best traditions of humane and enlightened thought.

Monash University Publishing titles pass through a rigorous process of independent peer review.

ISBN: 9781925495737 (paperback)

www.publishing.monash.edu/books/paag-9781925495737.html

Series: Art History

Series Editor: Luke Morgan

Design: Les Thomas

Cover image: Vincent van Gogh, *Gate in the Paris Ramparts*, 1887 (Van Gogh Museum, Amsterdam (Vincent van Gogh Foundation)).

A catalogue record for this book is available from the National Library of Australia.

CONTENTS

Dedicated to my loving and supportive parents,
Domenico and Concetta Alessi.

ACKNOWLEDGEMENTS

This book began life as my PhD thesis at La Trobe University many years ago. I was fortunate then to have a team of supervisors, each of whom took up the baton when required; Lucy Ellem, Dr Frank Heckes, Dr Richard Haese and particularly Associate Professor Adrian Jones, helped guide me towards its completion. These scholars took on the task with enthusiasm and commitment and have continued to offer support and encouragement, for which I remain indebted and grateful.

I am most grateful to Dr Nathan Hollier, Associate Professor Luke Morgan and Joanne Mullins from Monash University Publishing for taking on this project, and offering guidance and support throughout the journey to turn my manuscript into this publication. Thanks to Rachel Salmond for her meticulous editing and suggestions for further improvement.

Sincere thanks are extended to staff at institutions that made my research possible and enjoyable, in particular those at La Trobe University's Borchardt Library, the State Library of Victoria, the British Library, Monash University's Matheson Library and the Kröller-Müller Museum. A special mention to the staff at the Vincent van Gogh Museum who have always welcomed me and made me feel at home during my research trips and have been generous in answering many emails when I was far away. Sjraar van Heugten and Hans Luijten, who have always been generous with their time and knowledge whenever I have visited the Netherlands, agreed to read my work and gave me wonderful advice for its improvement.

I extend my sincere thanks to La Trobe University for giving me the opportunity to complete my PhD and, more recently, for supporting me in my research as a staff member. The University's recent financial assistance through a number of grants has been invaluable in enabling me to carry out the additional research required for this publication.

Thanks to the many of my family and friends who, over the course of this journey, have remained steadfast in their support and loyal with their friendship, even during long periods of silence. You offered sanity when required and stumped up a drink and laugh when I was in dire need. Thanks also to my academic colleagues, many of whom have become dear friends, whose wise words have helped me navigate the path to this book's completion.

I would not have succeeded in this undertaking without the support of those closest to me. Thanks to my brothers, Tony and Adrian, their partners

Daniella and Pauline, and my nephews and niece, and to my grandparents for watching from above – you are always close. I want to especially thank my partner Merideth Appleyard for listening, having faith and encouraging me when things got hard. I could not have achieved any of this without your support. I love you dearly.

Lastly, my thanks to my parents for years of support and encouragement – this book is for you. From a young age you instilled in me the value of a good work ethic and the need for respect and humility, and you made me aware that education is the door to knowledge and opportunity.

INTRODUCTION

And I've also acquired another ornament for my studio,
I got a great bargain on some splendid woodcuts from
The Graphic, some of them prints not of the clichés
but of the blocks themselves.
Just what I've been wanting for years.[1]

Writing to his brother Theo from The Hague in January 1882, Vincent van Gogh mentioned the beginning of a lengthy project. Already an avid collector of black-and-white illustrations, he had purchased an edition of *The Graphic Portfolio*, a selection of important works from the illustrated weekly newspaper *The Graphic* bound in a single volume. This acquisition would form the basis of what would become one of the most important collections van Gogh amassed during his lifetime. Over the next three years he would purchase, exchange, mount and file thousands of fine art engravings and prints cut from a variety of illustrated newspapers which would become an important visual aid and teaching resource – a bible to inspire him and a guide to what constituted art, shaping his burgeoning artistic practice.

Van Gogh became familiar with graphic works through his employment at Goupil & Cie., one of the leading art dealers in Europe, and through his uncles, Cor and Vincent, who were both successful art dealers and collectors in their own right. During this period van Gogh became attracted to graphic works that were reproductions of paintings by artists of the Barbizon and Hague schools and of works by a vast array of artists, such as Paul Delaroche, Ary Scheffer, Jean-Baptiste-Camille Corot and Jules Dupré. He wrote often about the works he had on his walls and would send prints as gifts to his family so that they too could enjoy similar black-and-white decorations in their own homes. At this time van Gogh's interest in these graphic works

---

1 Vincent van Gogh, *Vincent van Gogh: The Letters: The Complete Illustrated and Annotated Edition*, edited by Leo Jansen, Hans Luijten and Nienke Bakker (Brussels: Mercatorfonds, 2009), Letter 199, volume 2, 17.

Hereafter, quotations from van Gogh's letters will be from the English translations made available in the six-volume work cited in this footnote. All references to the letters will be abbreviated to the letter number (preceded by LT), volume and page numbers. The letters and their translations are also available online at http://vangoghletters.org/vg/.

was that of a consumer and artistic admirer. He collected, in the main, works produced as single-sheet prints, often after paintings exhibited in the French and English Salon exhibitions. After he had finally picked up his pencil in 1880 and began assembling his comprehensive collection, his interest and focus shifted. He began to collect as an artist intent on deep observation to assist him in his career ambitions, and turned the focus of his collecting towards works produced and distributed by the weekly newspapers. Hans Luijten notes that 'van Gogh rarely writes about old master prints or print-makers in his letters, focussing instead on contemporary works – and then only from a certain kind, namely illustrations from the weeklies'.[2] The prints in van Gogh's collection, unlike limited edition prints usually associated with high art, were produced in the thousands, appearing in newspapers either to illustrate news stories or as stand-alone works to be pinned up in the family home. Approximately 1,400 of these prints have survived in the collections of the Van Gogh Museum in Amsterdam.

The collection of popular black-and-white prints that van Gogh assembled between 1880–1884 is important in van Gogh scholarship because it shows a side of him that differs from that usually portrayed. His short artistic life, spanning only ten years, can be clearly defined by two distinct periods: the Dutch years, 1880–1885, which included a short stay early in 1881 in the Belgium Borinage mining district and Brussels; and the French years, 1886–1890. The works van Gogh produced during the French years are by far his most popular, as his art flourished under the influence of Japanese prints, the Impressionists and other avant-garde artists he met and befriended. From this later period has arisen the accepted view of van Gogh as an artistic revolutionary, a misunderstood genius, and a giant of late nineteenth-century art, while his output during the Dutch years has been considered as the precursor to his later blossoming. His time in the Netherlands, especially in the early years of his artistic development, should, however, be viewed differently. It was a period of transition, change and discovery. When van Gogh picked up his pencil and set out on his artistic career, he had no intention of becoming an avant-garde leader in the art world. His aims were rather humbler, being more centred on finding a career as a draughtsman earning a wage that would enable him to live within the middle-class norms prescribed and demanded by his family. After many years of drawing small scenes on his travels, van Gogh

---

2 Hans Luijten, 'Rummaging Among My Woodcuts – Van Gogh and the Graphic Arts', in Chris Stolwijk, Sjraar van Heugten, Leo Jansen and Andreas Blühm (eds), *Vincent's Choice: The Musée Imaginaire of van Gogh* (Amsterdam: Van Gogh Museum, 2003), 99.

had high hopes of becoming an illustrator for magazines and newspapers, from which he believed he could earn 100 French francs per month and live without any financial assistance from his family.

Familiar with newspaper illustrations from his time in England, van Gogh was keen to reacquaint himself with these works once he had decided to embark on an artistic path. During his three years of collecting, prints would at times dominate his thoughts, be the common denominator in the relationship with his peer Anthon van Rappard, and form one of the most important collections he amassed. Van Gogh's collection of black-and-white prints is unique, not least because he assembled it mostly on his own, in direct contrast to the other great collections he accumulated collaboratively with his brother Theo, such as of Japanese woodblock prints and of works by other artists.

Although the collection includes some works from German, Dutch, French and American sources, most of the prints in the collection are from English publications. While van Gogh accessed works from publications such as *Punch*, the *British Workman* and the *Pictorial News*, the bulk of his collection came from the two most popular English illustrated newspapers, *The Graphic* and *The Illustrated London News*, which he could purchase from local booksellers and second-hand dealers. Many, but not all, of the French, Dutch and German examples in the collection were collected with Theo's assistance.[3]

Illustrations from *The Graphic* and *The Illustrated London News* dominate van Gogh's collection for several reasons. Firstly, he had become familiar with both newspapers during his time in England, and their wide availability in Europe made it possible for him to find them when he returned to the Netherlands after his failed attempt to become a lay preacher. Secondly, the illustrations featured on at least every second page of these newspapers, often as full- or double-page works, which was not the case with many smaller publications. Thirdly, both publications, especially *The Graphic*, carried strong messages of social responsibility and their illustrations fitted within a wider social realist genre of art that appealed to van Gogh's sensibilities. The most important reason, however, was that the illustrations from *The Graphic* and *The Illustrated London News* were universally regarded as the best of their type.

A number of scholars and exhibitions have acknowledged the influence of black-and-white illustrations on van Gogh's work. English art historians Ronald Pickvance and Martin Bailey were leaders in identifying these illustrations as a key influence on the art of van Gogh. Their exhibitions and associated

---

3 Ronald Pickvance, *English Influences on Vincent van Gogh* (London: Arts Council of Great Britain, 1974), 28.

publications, *English Influences on Vincent van Gogh* and *Van Gogh in England: Portrait of the Artist as a Young Man*, were ground-breaking in shining a light on this collection.[4] Their work did not focus solely on the influence of the graphic arts. Pickvance's investigation, the first scholarly acknowledgement of the immense role English culture played in van Gogh's development, was much broader and included an analysis of van Gogh's time in London as an art dealer, his periods as a teacher and lay preacher, and his interest in English pictures, prints and literature. Pickvance describes van Gogh as a 'major Post-Impressionist whose being was steeped in English literature', and argues that van Gogh was the artist:

> who broke the narrow, chauvinistic, self-regarding barriers of French art of the 1880s; the one, who having lived in England for almost three years, having experienced the idiosyncrasies of its capital, its people, its painters, its illustrators and its novelists, was prone to re-assert those memories from his complex and multi-experienced consciousness.[5]

In confirming that his exhibition and publication was merely a starting point for the investigation of van Gogh's print collection, Pickvance cautioned 'in short, this exhibition is an appetiser, a small progress report on a fairly large and somewhat neglected subject. And generous though the number of illustrations may appear to be, they are but a fraction of those he knew'.[6] In addition to including 89 prints in the exhibition – the first time that so many of his collection had been exhibited – the value of Pickvance's investigation lies in his discovery of the dates van Gogh purchased the prints from *The Graphic*. Pickvance notes the limitations of his work, however, pointing out that it was possible and desirable to determine acquisition dates for prints from other publications, especially *The Illustrated London News*, but that it was too 'tedious to do so' for the purposes of the exhibition.[7]

Martin Bailey's work for the 1992 exhibition and publication have made a similarly important contribution to van Gogh scholarship.[8] In the foreword

---

4 Pickvance, *English Influences on Vincent van Gogh*; Martin Bailey (ed.), *Van Gogh in England: Portrait of the Artist as a Young Man* (London: Barbican Art Gallery, 1992).

5 Pickvance, *English Influences on Vincent van Gogh*, 11.

6 Pickvance, *English Influences on Vincent van Gogh*, 11.

7 Pickvance, *English Influences on Vincent van Gogh*, 34.

8 Bailey's other works relevant to this topic include: Martin Bailey, *Young Vincent: The Story of van Gogh's Years in England* (London: Allison and Busby, 1990); 'Van Gogh and *The Illustrated London News*', *The Illustrated London News*, Royal Issue (1990), 80–85; and 'Van Gogh in London', *The Antique Collector*, March (1992), 74–7.

to the 1992 catalogue, John Hoole and Jane Alison acknowledge the 'essential scholarly foundations' laid by Pickvance and outline the aim of their exhibition 'to show in an intriguing and accessible way the significance of van Gogh's personal experiences, his growing religious commitment and to set these within the context of English art and culture'.[9] The exhibition and catalogue, like the work of Pickvance, have components specifically dedicated to black-and-white illustrations, but lack a thorough and dedicated investigation of their significance.

Other exhibitions and publications, such as Florida State University Fine Arts Gallery's *Vincent van Gogh: The Influence of Nineteenth Century Illustrations* and the 2003 Van Gogh Museum exhibition, *The Musée Imaginaire of van Gogh,* held to mark the 150th anniversary of the artist's birth, have made important contributions. The latter exhibition provided new insights into how van Gogh thought of and used his collection in developing his artistic practice, and in its catalogue Luijten asserts that 'it is almost impossible to overestimate the importance of the graphic arts for Vincent van Gogh. He wrote repeatedly about the engravings he had seen, collected, hung, traded or copied'.[10] Luijten was referring to the whole gamut of graphic works of which van Gogh was aware, including prints reproduced after paintings, religious engravings, Japanese prints and illustrations from French, German and Dutch journals. Luijten's essay analyses van Gogh's development and response to his prints in the context of his extensive collection and includes examples of van Gogh's appropriation of figures from the prints into his own work, thus reinforcing the argument that van Gogh's collection was a teaching resource as much as it was simply a visual one. He also touches on van Gogh's aim to become a draughtsman, which is an area that needs to be investigated in greater depth.

Although scholars have consistently acknowledged van Gogh's collection of black-and-white prints, there has to date been no thorough investigation of the print collection itself or deeply focussed analysis of its influence across van Gogh's artistic oeuvre. A study of the constitution and composition of the collection, its thematic structure and recurring motifs is needed. The influence of these prints on both the themes and style of van Gogh's work also needs further attention. Indeed, the question of why van Gogh collected these prints in the first place has never been fully explored. The central aim of this book is to fill these knowledge gaps comprehensively and thereby add

9 Bailey, *Van Gogh in England*, 7.

10 Luijten, 'Rummaging Among My Woodcuts', 99.

to existing scholarship regarding the influence of black-and-white graphic works on van Gogh's practice and artistic aspirations.

Chapter 1 touches on the history of wood engraving and the development of the craft in the context of illustrated newspapers. It traces the development of illustrated journalism, a revolution of Victorian society, assessing the aims of newspapers of the period and analysing how the public received them, while also examining their influence on van Gogh. It also considers how these developments were in effect a response to and reflection of a quickly changing and modernising society.

Chapter 2 views the nineteenth century through the eyes of the young van Gogh. It focuses on the developments and reality of Victorian England and van Gogh's perception of this reality. It highlights the limitations of his experience and subsequent knowledge of the developments in England and the complexities of a metropolis such as London. It assesses how his view of Victorian society, especially its negative aspects, was coloured by his reading of socially focused novels by writers such as Charles Dickens. This chapter also considers the technological advancements arising from the Industrial Revolution that led to extensive change in working and living conditions and to population migration. It reviews the social transformation of the age and considers its impact on van Gogh's years, in an attempt to place the production of popular prints within its social context.

Chapter 3 analyses van Gogh's collection of black-and-white prints, offering for the first time a timeline for his acquisition of the illustrations cut from *The Illustrated London News*, thus creating a more thorough picture of the development of his collection when considered alongside the similar work completed by Pickvance. Furthermore, the analysis of the collection in this chapter offers a clearer understanding of its thematic and stylistic structure. We can begin to understand what images van Gogh chose to collect and why he collected them, establishing a context in which to investigate how they shaped his career aims and subsequent process, style and technique.

Chapter 4 assesses van Gogh's early ambitions to become an illustrator. It acknowledges Theo's role in pursuing this career path and argues that, contrary to popular belief, van Gogh never aspired to lead the art world's avant-garde. It considers how his aim to become a draughtsman encouraged his illustration collecting and shaped the collection's development. It studies the role of van Gogh's print collection during the early years of his artistic career and its fundamental effect on his artistic language and style.

The final chapter presents three case studies demonstrating the influence of black-and-white illustrations on van Gogh's practice. The first focuses predominantly on the Dutch years and investigates van Gogh's use of the collection to resolve problems of composition. It views early single studies copied from figures in the collection and assesses how van Gogh resolved complex issues by studying intently the work of the illustrators he collected. The second study looks at van Gogh's efforts to develop his own version of the *The Graphic*'s 'Heads of the People' series. It examines his early attempts to replicate a body of work worthy of such a title, before assessing how the 'Heads of the People' series shaped his approach to portraiture throughout the rest of his career. The final case study argues that a legacy of the prints was van Gogh's consistent practice of creating a series of drawings on a specific theme with the capacity to narrate a larger story in pictures.

In this book I aim to shine a spotlight on a collection that has in the past been acknowledged but never fully recognised for its impact. While van Gogh's reputation has been rightly based on his later master works, I argue that the black-and-white prints in his collection were fundamental in his development and had a long-lasting effect on his practice – stylistically, thematically and conceptually. They reveal another side of van Gogh and underpin his initial attempts to become a draftsman, which were an essential stepping-stone on his path towards the long-lasting artistic reverence in which he is held. They helped shape his aims, gave focus to his subject matter, and ultimately played a role in creating his unique visual voice. Without his print collection the van Gogh who dominates popular consciousness around the world could not have been possible; it reveals a different side to van Gogh that we need to acknowledge if we are to fully understand his career.

Chapter 1

THE RISE OF THE POPULAR PRINT

Mirror to a Changing Society

By the late nineteenth century, Europe, particularly England, was coming to the end of a period of great transformation. The Industrial Revolution, the length and nature of which had varied across Europe and within each country, had brought changes to society that fundamentally reshaped every aspect of people's existence, especially in large cities like Paris, London, Manchester and Birmingham.[1] The rise of capitalism as the predominant economic model had brought a new kind of money that was distributed more widely and accumulated in larger amounts. Individual success predominated over past notions of communal well-being and paternalistic responsibility, and social orders were replaced by social classes. More populist and evangelical forms of religion played a new role in defining moral standards. Rapid economic growth gave rise to new forms of poverty and degradation, in which the gap between the haves and have-nots increased, fostering the growth of slums and the spread of disease. People migrated from the countryside in droves seeking new prosperous lives in the growing industrialised cities. Harnessing the power of steam underpinned the growth of shipping and rail networks and aided the burgeoning growth of factories. These urban and industrial developments opened the way for a new modern visual culture. Social, technical, economic and other changes, both positive and negative, were embraced,

---

1 Although many scholars argue that the Industrial Revolution was not confined to the nineteenth century, the period 1760–1840 is seen as particularly relevant in England's economic development. Melvin Kranzberg suggested that we regard the Industrial Revolution 'more as a *progress* than a distinct period of time' (Melvin Kranzberg & C.W. Pursell Jnr. (eds), *Technology in Western Civilisation*, vol. 1 (New York: Oxford University Press, 1967), 217).

discussed, criticised, applauded and, most importantly, illustrated in the growing print media of the time. Although newspapers had a long tradition, it was not until the nineteenth century that illustrations became central to their modus operandi and aesthetic. Magazines and newspapers, such as *The Penny Magazine*, *The Illustrated London News*, *The Graphic*, *L'Illustration*, *Harper's Weekly*, and even satirical magazines like *Punch* and its French-based inspiration *Le Charivari*, were all part of the visual communication explosion of the nineteenth century.

New technologies, such as the steam engine and the use of boxwood as an alternative to expensive metals in engraving, made the mass production of illustrations viable and affordable. Papermaking was mechanised in England from 1803, the first steam-powered printing press arrived in 1814, and cylinder presses that used stereotyping processes enabled inexpensive and rapid production from the late 1820s. In 1851 one of the pioneer illustrated newspapers, *The Illustrated London News*, demonstrated a further advance in printing technology – its custom-built Applegath Vertical Press – at the Great Exhibition, celebrating it in the pages of its weekly supplement of 31 May 1851.[2] These developments were complemented by the introduction of boxwood as a material for the plates for the illustrations. Although relief printing had been practised since the mid-fifteenth century, its use had declined almost to the point of extinction until it was revived and revolutionised by Newcastle engraver Thomas Bewick. His success with using boxwood for wood engraving encouraged book publishers and newspaper editors to turn to wood engraving as the preferred method for illustrating their publications. These technological advances allowed for the mass production of high-quality images at an affordable price that made them instantly available to a mass audience, appealing to readers and collectors such as van Gogh.

The popularity of the new form of communication was central to breaking down barriers in the fine arts. As black-and-white illustrations rose in popularity, what had traditionally been considered high art, and hence the domain of the upper class, became instantly accessible to the lower classes. The audience had changed and become 'a new mass audience embracing heterogeneities of class, education, gender and economic means'.[3] It had become possible for workers

2 For further information about the Applegath Printing Press see *Illustrated London News*, 31 May 1851, 31–32; Paul Fyfe, "A Great Exhibition of Printing: *The Illustrated London News* Supplement Sheet (1851), *Cahiers Victoriens & Édouardiens*, Issue 84 (Autumn 2016), 1–16.

3 Julie F. Codell, 'The Aura of Mechanical Reproduction: Victorian Art and the Press', *Victorian Periodical Review*, 24/1 (1991), 4.

to have an artwork hanging in their home or workplace, which helped change in perception of what could be considered worthy artistic subjects. Artists, such as those of the Barbizon school, were already depicting the rural class; the new mass-produced newspaper prints reinforced the relevance of such classes as subject matter; newspapers were central in promoting depictions of the urban poor as both acceptable and relevant.

This chapter traces the development of illustrated journalism and the rise of mass-produced prints, revealing how their growth during the nineteenth century was made possible by groundwork laid by their predecessors in previous centuries. It reveals the shift in the power of illustrations in journalism from a subordinate position of merely accompanying text to a position of artistic quality and integrity that differed from the approach taken by earlier newspapers. As illustrated newspapers and magazines became widely available they reminded their readers of the positives in an increasingly troubled society, while at the same time reflecting on the plight of the disenfranchised and of the many problems that plagued their changing society. They played a key role in reinforcing notions of community in a world increasingly focused on the individual. Their black-and-white illustrations helped move printmaking beyond a traditional high-art medium to something more democratic and socialist. For van Gogh this was evidence of a new direction for art – one of the people for the people.

In the early nineteenth century illustrations were included in many forms of popular literature, including religious publications, cheap fiction and newspapers. The increasing regularity of their appearance in newspapers was, according to Allan Ellenius, 'a veritable explosion'. The proliferation of visual information was, he argued, an indication of the 'new and revolutionary importance of the mass-produced image'.[4] None of this would have been possible, however, without the revival of wood engraving, which enabled a transition from costly and time-consuming etching on metal plates. Almost all of the illustrations in newspapers in the nineteenth century were printed from wood blocks. Unlike earlier illustrations, which had little in the way of texture and chiaroscuro, Bewick's experiments and developments in working with boxwood made it possible to achieve the fine detail previously only feasible with metal plates.[5] New technology made it possible to produce images

4 Allan Ellenius, 'Reproducing Art as a Paradigm of Communication: The Case of the Nineteenth Century Illustrated Magazines', *Figura*, 21 (1984), 70.

5 Wood engraving was done on the very hard end grain of the wood, enabling the rendering of fine details and complexity of an original drawing. This was in contrast to works made using the softer side grain of the wood, which was cut into rather than finely engraved.

without a defined border, which was a radical development in black-and-white illustration. Douglas Bliss refers to Bewick's new method of wood engraving as

> the antithesis of Woodcutting proper [in which] you cut away the surface of the block so as to leave islanded in relief the *black lines* which form the design…[Y]ou use the plain surface of the block (considered as though already covered with ink) as a black ground upon which you make your design with the graver in the form of white lines.[6]

A limitation that Bewick and his followers encountered was the size of each block – usually no larger than 20 x 15cm – which did not allow for large images that were possible using other techniques. In 1860 Charles Wells devised a system of riveting small blocks of boxwood together to produce images of any size. Designs were transferred onto the joined blocks, which were then separated and distributed to multiple engravers to complete, and reassembled when they were finished, with the edges refined by a master engraver to eliminate any visible joins. The developments achieved by Bewick and Wells, together with the cost advantage of wood over metal, ensured it was relatively easy and inexpensive to reproduce designs of almost any size. Wood engraving became the preferred option for mass-produced illustrations as newspaper and magazine proprietors looked for cheap and efficient practices to complement other rapidly developing production techniques.

In 1861, at the beginning of the decade that would become the apogee of black-and-white illustration, John Jackson wrote his treatise on wood engraving, an important text that serves to this day as a history of the art as well as a manual for its practice. Jackson's advice covered areas from the appearance of 'healthy' blocks to a warning against chewing small pieces of boxwood. He offered advice on tools, techniques and procedures, described the range of effects available to the engraver, and demonstrated how it was possible to enable complex and rich designs by combining several techniques. By its very nature, wood engraving was an art of line, and the most important of these, as Jackson emphasised, was the outline.[7] Even as developments allowed for more complex compositions, outline formed the basis for the use of all other effects. It is a defining aesthetic trait in many of the works that van Gogh gravitated towards and added to his collection. It was to become a feature evident in his own drawings and paintings, especially in his early output

---

6 Douglas P. Bliss, *A History of Wood Engraving* (London: Spring Books, 1964), 5.

7 William A. Chatto & John Jackson, *A Treatise on Wood Engraving: Historical and Practical* (London: Henry G. Bohn, 1861), 587.

when he was primarily concerned with mastering his craft so that he could find employment as a draughtsman.

The need to learn and master the multitude of effects available to engravers soon led to the formation of engraving workshops, the establishment of professional engravers, who often served long apprenticeships, and a clear demarcation between engravers and artists. Jackson commented:

> When, with the age of Bewick, wood-engraving began to reassume its importance for book illustration, both designing and engraving were generally performed by the same hand; but, in the present day, the professions are becoming too important to be joined, and those who … commenced by practising both, now, recognising the modern policy of a division of labour, confine themselves with few exceptions to one.[8]

The distinction between draughtsman and engraver also fuelled a heated battle between the creative mind and the technical. Many draughtsmen saw the engraver as little more than a tradesperson, often accusing them of not following the designs presented and, therefore, not conveying the feeling and expression intended. Many distinguished engravers disagreed, including Gilbert Dalziel, son of one of the well-regarded Dalziel brothers. Gilbert wrote passionately in defence of not only his father and uncles but also of the many other accomplished engravers: 'To interpret faithfully the *intention* of the designer was the aim of all the competent wood-engravers and their brains had to be used just as much as those of the artist'.[9] Dalziel argued for a higher place in history for engravers:

> My view is that the book illustrations of the sixties and thereabout were the joint work of two brains – the artist's and the wood-engraver's; also, that the excellence attained was due to that happy collaboration. Call it "trade", call it "art", call it anything you please: the fact remains that the old wood-engravers of last century played their part and played it well; also, that to-day they are fully entitled to share equal honours with the artists of a glorious period that will ever stand out as being remarkable for the beauty and refinement of its book and magazine illustration.[10]

8 Chatto & Jackson, *A Treatise on Wood Engraving*, 549.

9 Gilbert Dalziel, 'Wood-Engraving in the "Sixties" and Some Criticism of To-day', *Print Collectors' Quarterly*, 15 (1928), 82.

10 Dalziel, 'Wood-Engraving in the "Sixties"', 84.

Hubert Herkomer, one of the finest illustrators and painters of the period, disagreed. He believed that the engraver was afforded too much prestige and importance and that mass-produced illustrations had become mere showpieces for the technological advancements of the engraver rather than the skill of the artist. He disputed this publicly in 1882, writing 'the most modern work ... is done to show the skill of the engraver rather than the art of the draughtsman. I do not hesitate to say that this is the first sign of a decadence'. Herkomer berated both the engraver and the supportive stance taken by some newspaper editors: 'you marvel at the handling of the engraver, and forget the artist. Correct or honest drawing is no longer wanted; complete designs are no longer in request; a "bit", just covering an awkward corner of the page, is all that is required'. Herkomer preferred to equate engravers with musicians arguing they were just interpreters who used the composition of others to showcase tricks they had learnt: 'accepting the engraver as an interpreter, we have only to look back in order to see that all interpreters, no matter what their art, have at times allowed their cleverness to mar the dignity of their mission'.[11]

It is to be expected, of course, that engravers and artists would heap praise on their respective professions and blame any shortcomings on the other. In truth, black-and-white illustration relied on the skill of both arts at all times; without the engraver translating the image as faithfully as possible, artists' illustrations and reproductions of paintings would not have been disseminated so effectively to the population at large. Their collaboration was essential in the production of a new mass visual culture, in which citizens anywhere were able to read newspapers and view the accompanying illustrations in the comfort of their own homes, workplaces, libraries and other public spaces. Moreover, it was a telling example of the growing division of labour in a modernising society, as specifically defined professions within industry came to be the norm rather than the exception.

The rising sales of newspapers and magazines in the late nineteenth century were due to the fact that people could read a newspaper almost anytime, anywhere.[12] People read as they travelled on trains, for instance, a practice seen in E.R. King's illustration *The Workman's Train* (Figure 1).

---

11 Hubert Herkomer, 'Drawing and Engraving on Wood', *The Art Journal* (1882), 167.

12 For an analysis of sales figures and numbers of newspaper titles, see Joanne Shattock & Michael Wolff (eds), *The Victorian Periodical Press: Samplings and Soundings* (Leicester: Leicester University Press, 1982), xiii; Aled Jones (ed.), *Powers of the Press: Newspapers, Power and the Public in Nineteenth-century England* (Aldershot: Scolar Press, 1996), 49; Hannah Barker, *Newspapers, Politics and English Society, 1695–1855*

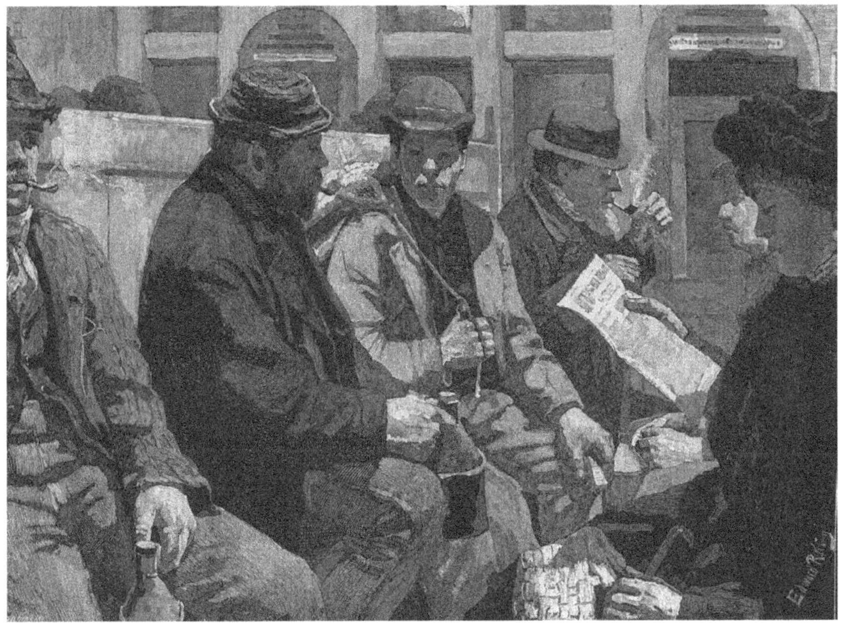

Figure 1. E.R. King, *The Workman's Train* (*The Illustrated London News*, 14 April 1883)

Working people who could not afford their own copy of a newspaper could read them at workingmen's clubs, mechanics institutes, public houses, weavers' huts, barber shops, taverns, tobacconists and coffeehouses. Newspapers were also available in places the middle and upper classes visited: parlours, drawing rooms, lobbies of Parliament and clubrooms. Unlike the lower classes, however, who used newspapers primarily for information and entertainment, the emerging middle class and the upper classes turned to newspapers for 'progress and self-improvement' opportunities.[13] A further option for the poor and the middle class was to combine their finances to purchase a newspaper to share. Individuals would read the paper and pass it on, or the content would be read out aloud at a public meeting, a regular occurrence among illiterate working-class people. The explosion of illustrated newspapers helped address illiteracy in a way that had not been thought possible. One of England's earliest illustrated weekly papers, the *British Workman*, included quality images and

(Harlow: Longman, 2000), 29–30; I. Asquith, 'The Structure, Ownership and Control of the Press, 1780–1855' in George Boyce, J. Curran & P. Wingate (eds), *Newspaper History from the 17th Century to the Present* (London, Constable, 1978), 99.

13 Paul Hogarth, *The Artist as Reporter* (London: Gordon Fraser, 1986), 24.

many visual aids, such as alphabet boards, intended to help the illiterate if they were hung in homes. Its editor, Thomas Bywater Smithies, proclaimed that 'the people must have pictures, and the pictures must be good',[14] as he directed his focus towards the city's slums which he perceived to be 'inhabited by his more reluctant scholars'.[15] Through the *British Workman*, which reached its sales peak of 250,000 in 1862, Smithies and others involved with the newspaper took up as their mission to help the unfortunate and to contribute to reform, including raising the literacy levels of the lower classes. The illiterate could follow stories not just by listening, but also by seeing; they could pick up the newspaper and begin to make sense of the stories reported by referring to the illustrations. All classes could share the pleasure of reading a newspaper and marvel at the masterful illustrations.

The Penny Magazine, launched in England in 1832, was one of the first publications to use a large number of wood engravings for journalistic purposes. Its founder, Charles Knight, developed his illustrated newspaper believing that working people wanted access to quality images like those found in art galleries, museums and more expensive books. He declared:

> As the public encouragement enabled the conductors to make greater exertions to give permanency to the success which the 'Penny Magazine' had attained, it became necessary to engage artists of eminence, both as draughtsman and wood-engravers to gratify a proper curiosity, and cultivate an increasing taste, by giving representations of the finest Works of Art, of Monuments of Antiquity, and of subjects of Natural History, in a style that had been previously considered to belong only to expensive books.[16]

The example set by *The Penny Magazine* and embraced enthusiastically by many publications around the world, led to the rise of illustrations serving as more than mere accompaniments to texts. Illustrations informed readers of the many medical and scientific discoveries that were everyday occurrences throughout the period. They served to highlight for the reader the content of an article, just as photos do today. They began to enhance serialised fictional stories, many of which ran for many months, thus helping to maintain interest

14 Peter R. Mountjoy, 'Thomas Bywater Smithies, Editor of the *British Workman*', *Victorian Periodicals Review*, 18/ 2 (1985), 46 (quoting G. Stringer Rowe, *T.B. Smithies: A Memoir* (London, 1884), 49).

15 Mountjoy, 'Thomas Bywater Smithies', 46.

16 *The Penny Magazine of the Society of the Diffusion of Useful Knowledge*, vol. I (London: Charles Knight, 1832), preface.

and links across issues, and preparing 'the reader for some significant moment in each instalment's action, signalling what important development in the story's action he may expect this week, and making it possible through each memorable dumb-show for the reader to keep track of a complex action over a five-month period'.[17] For van Gogh, an avid reader, these illustrations enhanced his experience and confirmed the possible relationship between literature and the visual arts.[18] The explosion in the use of illustrations in newspapers made it possible for all people to be educated to some degree in almost all areas.

More a weekly magazine than a newspaper, *The Penny Magazine* created a new demand for artists and engravers. Kenneth Lindley has acknowledged it as the first of many publications that 'brought fame to their artists and fortune to their proprietors'.[19] The illustrations, like the written text, covered a wide range of subjects, including diagrams of scientific and mechanical devices, images of foreign lands, plants and animals, religious monuments, contemporary architecture, ancient monuments and cities, portraits of famous people and reproductions of art works.[20] Knight believed that illustrations were often more instructive than words and were definitely more enjoyable. He also saw the venture as a 'mission into the field of popular education', which included both factual instruction and the promotion of higher-order values.[21] Writing in the first issue he declared:

> we shall endeavour to prepare a useful and entertaining weekly Magazine, that may be taken up and laid down without requiring any considerable

17 Philip V. Allingham, 'Robert Barnes' Illustrations for Thomas Hardy's *The Mayor of Casterbridge* as Serialised in *The Graphic*', *Victorian Periodical Review*, 28/1 (1995), 38.

18 For an analysis of the influence of literature on van Gogh, see Wouter van der Veen, *Van Gogh: A Literary Mind* (Zwolle: Waanders, 2009) and Judy Sund, *True to Temperament: Van Gogh and French Naturalist Literature* (Cambridge; New York: Cambridge University Press, 1992).

19 Kenneth Lindley, *The Woodblock Engravers* (Newton Abbot: David & Charles, 1970), 43.

20 The Preface to the first volume stated: 'the subjects which have uniformly been treated have been of the broadest and simplest character. Striking points of Natural History – Accounts of the Great Works of Art in Sculpture and Painting – Descriptions of such Antiquities as possess historical interest – Personal Narratives of Travellers – Biographies of Men who have had a permanent influence on the condition of the world – Elementary Principles of Language and Numbers – established facts in Statistics and Political Economy – these have supplied the materials for exciting the curiosities of a million of readers' (*The Penny Magazine of the Society of the Diffusion of Useful Knowledge*, vol. 1 (1832)).

21 Patricia Anderson, '"A Revolution in Popular Art": Pictorial Magazines and the Making of a Mass Visual Culture in England 1832–1860', *Journal of Newspaper and Pictorial History*, 7 (1991), 53.

> effort; and that may tend to fix the mind upon calmer, and, it may be, purer subjects of thought than the violence of party discussion, or the stimulating details of crime and suffering.[22]

He believed his *Penny Magazine* could improve the standards of all levels of society, as he expressed in his hope that 'our *Penny Magazine* will be to *all* classes – a universal convenience and enjoyment'.[23]

Following the success of *The Penny Magazine*, the production of illustrated newspapers increased, although many of them were short-lived. The most successful and one of the longest running was Henry Ingram's *The Illustrated London News*. Launched on 14 May 1842, 26,000 copies of the first issue were sold, and by the year's end weekly circulation had reached 60,000. The newspaper's circulation figures continued to grow, reaching a peak of 300,000 copies per week by 1863.[24] It was the first newspaper to have news and illustrations on the front page, rather than advertisements, which James Bishop has claimed to be 'a publishing revolution'.[25] The newspaper was even bolder in its declarations, proclaiming that art had become the bride of literature. Arthur Bryant concurred a century later, placing the newspaper's achievements on the highest of pedestals: 'viewed in their entirety the bound volumes of the *ILN* constitute what is probably the most important single pictorial source for the social history of any age or country'.[26] The newspaper was notable for its dedication to and promotion of illustrations as an integral part of reporting news stories. In its early days, however, it was committed to using stock-images, as Henry Vizetelly, the paper's first printer, confirmed when he recalled Ingram's idea that engravings of certain subjects 'could easily enough be prepared in advance'.[27] Such an approach was problematic, as images were often inaccurate or not fit-for-purpose – Vizetelly gave the example of an illustration of Prince Albert wearing a string of pearls rather than a tiara.[28] Another problem for these illustrated papers was their capac-

22 *The Penny Magazine*, 31 March 1832, 1.

23 Anderson, '"A Revolution in Popular Art"', 1.

24 Christopher Hibbert, *The Illustrated London News: Social History of Victorian Britain* (London: Angus and Robertson, 1975), 13.

25 James Bishop, 'The Story of *The Illustrated London News*', *The Illustrated London News*, 30 May 1992, 30.

26 Leonard de Vries (ed.) *Panorama 1842–1865: The World of the Early Victorians as Seen Through the Eyes of The Illustrated London News* (London: John Murray, 1967), 5.

27 Henry Vizetelly, *Glances Back Through Seventy Years* (London: Kegan Paul, Trench, Trübner and Co., 1893), 224.

28 Vizetelly, *Glances Back Through Seventy Years*, 232.

ity to respond accurately to events at short notice. A few days before the first issue of *The Illustrated London News* was released, Ingram and his associates learnt of a fire that had devastated the city of Hamburg. The newspaper had no artists on site, so had to prepare a design sourced from references to hand. Vizetelly recollected that the image was constructed from a print of Hamburg held in the British Museum:

> The view of the city was engraved by one of my assistants and was copied, I remember, from a print in the British Museum, the artist, in drawing the subject upon wood, having added the necessary flames and volumes of smoke, as well as the crowd of people, in boats and on the river bank, supposed to have been attracted by the conflagration.[29]

This practice was in direct contradiction of the promise made by the newspaper that the pencil would not lie. Vizetelly later confirmed the hypocrisy, declaring that the first issue did not have one engraving from an authentic source.[30] However, as the newspaper grew and technology made the printing process speedier and more efficient, it began to employ 'special artists' – a term first used by *The Illustrated London News* during the reporting of the Crimean War (1853–56) – who could record scenes accurately and quickly on location.

Although it was the aim of many draughtsmen to establish a reputation as an oil painter, one outcome of the growth of illustrated newspapers and magazines was the emergence of the special artist, employed specifically for newspaper illustration. Peter Sinnema categorises these artists into three distinct groups. The first was the artist as reporter who travelled to different locations and scenes to record information just as photographers do today; the second was the foreign correspondent who was based in a particular country and commissioned to report on events in that country; and the third was the local artist who was given snippets of current news and asked to prepare illustrations from a written source. These three types of artists were bound together by their special role in newspaper illustration: 'all three must provide newsworthy pictures, which implies not only (a) a truth-function, the picture's basis in fact, but also (b) the ability to attract a readership through the capacity to excite, entertain, shock'.[31] The skill set required by these special artists, except perhaps the local artist, differed from the skill set of those

29 Vizetelly, *Glances Back Through Seventy Years*, 233–4.

30 Vizetelly, *Glances Back Through Seventy Years*, 237.

31 Peter W. Sinnema, *Dynamics of the Pictured Page: Representing the Nation in The Illustrated London News* (London: Ashgate, 1998), 69–70.

preparing designs in their studios; the special artists were required to make rapid drawings on location, completing their work regardless of conditions. Like journalists, they also had to assess the situation, choose what represented it best and develop a strong intuition so that they could reach locations before situations occurred. While the reporting of wars formed the bulk of a special artist's work, they were also employed in other contexts, including coverage of scientific expeditions, foreign lands and local news. Artists were recruited from all artistic spheres, and, according to Hogarth, 'whatever their background, most seem to have found being a Special Artist a congenial occupation'.[32] It was not unusual, therefore, for some of those employed as special artists to remain as such for their entire career. Hogarth writes that 'nowhere is the essential restless spirit of the artist revealed more graphically than in the role of reporter', and it is not surprising that such an occupation lured both the young and adventurous at heart.[33]

In this context one can begin to appreciate van Gogh's interest in drawing for newspapers. He had an adventurous spirit and was comfortable with the prospect of becoming an artist as reporter. In a letter to his brother Theo, he articulated his belief that he could become a special artist based in Holland: 'now I think to myself that if The Graphic and Harper send their draughtsmen to Holland, they wouldn't be unwilling to take on a Dutch draughtsman if he could supply them with something good for not too much money'. Van Gogh continued, all but stating that he is a special artist, 'I believe that it isn't every day that the managers of illustrated magazines find someone who regards those magazines as his special goal'.[34] Although van Gogh never found the job he coveted, he was acutely aware of the role the artist played in print media, particularly in documenting the contemporary world and environment and in making art available to the broadest possible audience.

Even though the reporting of wars, revolutions and royal events required many special artists and assisted in selling a greater number of copies, newspaper editors could not always rely on reportage of such events to fill the pages of their papers each week. A list of the regular columns in *The Illustrated London News* exemplifies the varied content of newspapers of the time, regardless of their format, frequency and origin: Foreign Intelligence; Imperial Parliament; The Court and Haut Tan; Theatres and Theatrical Portraits; Sporting Intelligence; Naval and Military Intelligence; Chess; Literature;

---

32 Hogarth *The Artist as Reporter*, 30.

33 Hogarth *The Artist as Reporter*, 7.

34 LT 348, Volume 2, p. 343.

Provincial and Police. Although the preface of the first volume claimed it was welcomed into 'the popular heart', the above list of regular columns and the words from the preface to the second volume offer a more accurate indication of the target audience of *The Illustrated London News*: 'For the sake of our real, faithful, and influential patrons – the RESPECTABLE FAMILIES OF ENGLAND – we have kept the purity of our columns inviolate and supreme'.[35] The 'respectable families' were the middle classes; as Sinnema emphasised, 'at 6d. the *ILN* of the mid-nineteenth century was significantly more expensive than the *Penny Magazine* and well out of reach of the working and even lower classes'.[36] The lack of illustrations reflecting contemporary life accurately and a concerted effort to be politically correct reinforced the notion that the newspaper was not targeting the majority of the population. For example, the London it so often presented – busy, prosperous, comfortable and clean – was not the only London. Charles Knight, who showed the vulgarity and poverty of urban life in his *Penny Magazine* often criticised the idyllic images in *The Illustrated London News*. Smaller and less successful newspapers, such as the *Pictorial Times*, supported Knight's ideals and 'insisted on digging deeper and bringing to light the inadequacies and iniquities of the new Poor Law'.[37] *The Illustrated London News*' conservative response to damning inquiries and sensitive stories further emphasised that its target audience was not the working class, which was most affected by the poor conditions in mines and factories. Their middle-class target audience was happy to 'avoid facing anything radically new, startling, or threatening in the city'.[38] Even when *The Illustrated London News*' artists began in the 1870s to illustrate the homes of the urban poor, they did not depict them accurately, but as clean and with well-fed inhabitants, contrary to the reality of their situation.[39]

---

35 *The Illustrated London News*, volume 2, 7 January–24 June 1843, preface.

36 Sinnema, *Dynamics of the Pictured Page*, 16.

37 Michael Wolff & C. Fox, 'Pictures from the Magazines', in Harold James Dyos & Michael Wolff (eds), *The Victorian City: Images and Realities* (London: Routledge and Kegan Paul, 1973), 574.

38 Wolff & Fox, 'Pictures from the Magazines', 565.

39 Wolff & Fox (p. 573) give an example of the contrast between *The Illustrated London News*' representation of such scenes and that of a competitor: 'When *The Illustrated London News* ventured timidly inside a workman's home, it showed the head of the family dandling a robust infant on his lap or the mother putting a bonnet on a little girl; when the *Illustrated Times* traced a lost child back to its home in Lincoln Court, Drury Lane, mother was delousing the hair of a rather more bedraggled urchin. The reporters and illustrators on the *Illustrated Times* were informed by a desire to go and look for themselves'.

Nevertheless, throughout its early years *The Illustrated London News* continued to promote itself as a paper for the masses and emphasised its close relationship with its readers, as evidenced in the preface to its third volume in which the editors claim: '[*The Illustrated London News*] and the public became friends – close friends – warm friends – and, as we hope and believe, friends not easily to be parted'.[40] This relationship was undoubtedly based on the high moral values that the newspaper proclaimed it promoted. The editors believed that the breadth of their illustrations acted not only as an agent for upholding social and moral standards, but also as a record of contemporary history:

> We may take up the tone serious to describe, if they were not indescribable, the pride and gratification we experienced, in being thus, for the third time, in a condition to be *put on the shelf* – not shelved as we use the word despisingly, but in the sense of treasure-trove – picked up, garnished, and bound together as a fair ornament for the place we occupy – as a familiar friend – a library oracle to be consulted and referred to – for wisdom and history, for entertainment, intelligence and art![41]

The editors went beyond merely stating that the volumes acted only as an 'oracle' of Victorian history, further asserting that the reader may enjoy the illustrations in the volumes as art.

This notion of the illustrations being artworks was a consistent theme in the early volumes of *The Illustrated London News* and through those of its competitors and peers. The second volume of *The Illustrated London News* boldly declared: 'Yes, these tomes are little monuments of Art, which we are building up on the broad lands of the community'.[42] The illustrations are again emphasised as a key quality in volume four: 'there is one gem of knowledge and interest in this volume to which we point with pride. It is to the Illustrated History of the Art, by which we have risen into fame, power, and popularity – the Art of the Engraving upon Wood'.[43] And in volume five the editors took the liberty of promoting their deeds in verse:

> How Art hath reared its triumphs in our tomes! –
> How it hath ploughed, and tilled, and cropped our field,
> It hath gone into a million homes! –

40 *The Illustrated London News*, volume 3, 1843, preface.

41 *The Illustrated London News*, volume 3, 1843, preface.

42 *The Illustrated London News*, volume 2, 1843, preface.

43 *The Illustrated London News*, volume 4, 1844, preface.

With what a glorious impress hath it sealed
Year after year of fate! – as TIME rolls on
We form its picture-gallery of the mind,
For many after years to gaze upon
Through the dim Past at what it left behind!
And as it peers the wondrous vista through,
Dwell on the glories we have brought to view![44]

The overwhelming success of *The Illustrated London News* spawned a plethora of illustrated newspapers and magazines in England, Europe and America.[45] It was not until the birth of *The Graphic*, however, that *The Illustrated London News* faced its only true challenger.[46]

The Graphic was the newspaper that set the benchmark for illustrations as works of art in their own right. Its first issue was published by engraver William Luson Thomas on 4 December 1869. According to Thomas, a student of renowned wood-engraver W.J. Linton, the new publication was 'eagerly sought for by the public – out of curiosity, no doubt'.[47] It had many similarities with its well-established rival, including its size, large engravings that covered the bottom two-thirds of the cover page, a bold masthead, and the claim of being a 'formal catalogue' to be bound and preserved as an artistic record of the period. *The Graphic*, which ultimately provided van Gogh with the bulk of the illustrations in his collection, differed from many of its peers, however, and especially from *The Illustrated London News.* Unlike other publications whose illustrations suffered from inferior composition, poor figure drawing and character observation, the sacrifice of originality and accuracy for speed and topicality, and a lack of sympathy for their subjects, *The Graphic* elevated its illustrations and its artists to a level of merit that paralleled 'high-art'. It did not rely on stock designs, which were reused for many subjects and shared amongst newspapers; rather, it commissioned new works on a weekly basis

44 *The Illustrated London News*, volume 5, 1845, 'Our Prefatory Poem to Vol. V'.

45 Examples of this new 'Art-instruction' in America are *Frank Leslie's Illustrated Newspaper* (New York 1855) and *Harper's Weekly* (New York 1857). The rise of *L'Illustration* (Paris 1843), *Illustrirte Zeitung* (Leipzig 1843), *La Illustracion* (Madrid 1849), *Le Monde Illustré* (Paris 1857) and *Vsemirnaya Illyustratziya* (St. Petersburg 1869) in Europe can also be attributed to the style and success of *The Illustrated London News*; see Hogarth, *The Artist as Reporter*, 24.

46 Mason Jackson, *The Pictorial Press: Its Origins and Progress* (London: Hurst and Blackett, 1885), 311.

47 William Luson Thomas, 'The Making of *The Graphic*', *Universal Review*, 2/5 (1888), 82.

from serious artists interested in doing serious work. *The Graphic* published full- and double-page illustrations independent of any text other than the title, which were viewed as independent works of art and were the output of a practice not embraced by other newspapers at the time. Subjects included the depiction of topical contemporary stories, moralising works that addressed issues of poverty and inequality, a trait common in Victorian narrative and social realist painting, and black-and-white reproductions after paintings, often those shown at the Royal Academy and the French Salon. These single- and double-page illustrations, rather than the often smaller illustrations accompanying news stories that were embedded in pages of text, established *The Graphic*'s reputation and attracted the eye of van Gogh.

The birth and rise of *The Graphic* and, soon after, of other illustrated publications in England, America and Europe prompted a shift in the regard in which artists and their works were held. The pioneering *Illustrated London News* did not initially attract quality artists, as Jackson confirmed in 1885: 'with the exception of the drawings by [Sir John] Gilbert most of the illustrations in these first six numbers are of an inferior character, and show that the conductors of the paper had not yet obtained the best artistic help'.[48] A few years later, C.N. Williamson also commented on the poor artistic quality of the newspaper's early illustrations, suggesting it was because artists and quality draughtsmen had such a low opinion of news illustration:

> The idea of applying art to the production of illustrated papers was even yet but the glimmering in the minds of men. Accordingly, we find all the early numbers of *The Illustrated London News* were very poorly illustrated. Most of the cuts were crudely designed, and engraved by mere journeymen wood-choppers. Artists and engravers of note, while freely employing their talents in book-illustration, had not yet come to think it worth their while to draw for the "picture-papers".[49]

It was not until the birth of *The Graphic* that quality artists were attracted to illustrated journalism in any number. As noted above, there was little regard for honesty in the designs of the early illustrations in *The Illustrated London News*; not one image in the first issue was from an original source. In contrast, Thomas of *The Graphic* wanted veracity in his newspaper and its illustrations, recalling: 'the originality of the scheme consisted in establishing a weekly

48 Jackson, *The Pictorial Press*, 295.

49 Charles Norris Williamson, 'Illustrated Journalism in England: Its Developments – 1', *Magazine of Art*, 13, (1889–90), 300.

illustrated journal open to all artists, whatever their method, instead of confining my staff to draughtsmen on wood as had been hitherto the general custom'.[50] Furthermore, Thomas insisted on the work being honest and true, quoting renowned British artist Sir Joshua Reynolds to emphasise his point: 'the natural taste or appetite of the human mind is for truth', and claimed that 'it was this artistic truth, this swift and imaginative and convincing rendering of the appearance of things' that his artists 'revealed to the public eye'.[51]

The Graphic's success was based on a sound artistic policy and the confidence that Thomas instilled in his artists, to whom he showed great respect. He praised his artists publicly and gave them the kudos, rather than the engraver, whom he saw as a mere cipher for their creativity. Thomas remained intimately involved with the artistic side of the newspaper, setting high standards, commissioning work and even engraving some illustrations himself.[52] Unlike its main rivals, *The Graphic* attracted quality artists and illustrators from the outset, as evidenced in the list of its contributing artists. Many were, or would become, members of the Royal Academy – the highest recognition for artists in Britain. Contributors included William Powell Frith, Sir John Everett Millais, George Frederick Watts, Sir Arthur Boyd Houghton, George John Pinwell, Charles Green, Luke Fildes, Frank Holl, and Sir Hubert Herkomer, the last three of which were among van Gogh's favourite black-and-white artists. Alongside this corps of great visual artists were influential literary contributors, including Charles Dickens and Anthony Trollope. The fusion of great artists, quality illustrations and highly regarded writers set *The Graphic* apart from its competitors, giving it an overall air of artistic superiority. As such it set the benchmark for art produced by newspapers and demanded by the public, gave artists an opportunity to pursue their artistic careers beyond the established realm of the official salons, and confirmed black-and-white popular illustration as a valid art form, which could be enjoyed by sections of the community that had previously been excluded from art appreciation and connoisseurship.

Thomas' attitude towards his artists not only helped ensure the success of *The Graphic*, but also had many positive outcomes for the artists. Preparing illustrations for newspapers provided a constant income and an arena in which an artist could refine their talent. Illustrated publications 'were the organs which enabled them to make a living... [and] springboards to the better

---

50 Thomas, 'The Making of *The Graphic*', 81.

51 Thomas, 'The Making of *The Graphic*'. 87.

52 Julian Treuherz (ed.), *Hard Times: Social Realism in Victorian Art* (Manchester: Manchester City Art Galleries, 1987), 54.

paid and higher status occupation of oil painting'.[53] Many of the great artists contributing to *The Graphic* followed the path of illustrator to oil painter. Herkomer, whose painting *The Last Muster: Sunday in the Royal Hospital, Chelsea* established him as one of the great Victorian painters, first published part of this painting as an illustration in *The Graphic.* Frank Holl, another of *The Graphic*'s successful illustrators, also benefited from his time contributing to the newspaper, which according to his daughter, 'artistically and morally ... helped him: to steady his aim, to concentrate his forces, fix his purpose, and enable him to *finish and carry right through that which he began*...It also gave him, indirectly, stability, self-confidence, courage and concentration – invaluable and essential assets'.[54] Thomas, one of the most authoritative voices in the history of black-and-white illustration, reinforced this view:

> An illustrated paper must necessarily, in its turn, emphasise and dwell upon the gifts of rapid insight and effective execution rather than on the more delicate and matured intentions of art. Yet so many of the men who began with us have achieved lasting success in their profession that I may well be permitted to question if the qualities of speed and vigour of accuracy, exacted by the circumstances of working for a publication like ours, have not contributed materially to their present eminence.[55]

Thomas stressed that being an illustrator for *The Graphic* was not a consequence of lacking the skill and potential to be a successful oil painter, arguing that 'you might as well enter a cab-horse for a steeplechase!'[56] Rather, the limited timeframe in which artists had to work when preparing drawings for the newspapers forced them to be focussed, as Holl Reynolds observed of her father. Special artists had to make instant decisions for their illustrations; they had to go with what they saw. Preparing drawings in their studios, artists were often facing publishing deadlines. Furthermore, they had to simplify their drawings as best as they could for a medium that was completely different from painting, even though most aspired to be painters.

The Graphic not only set the standards for artistic quality; it also introduced to the public new subjects that were often outside the domain of both newspapers and high art. The newspaper and many of its artists have often been

53 Paul Goldman, *Victorian Illustration: The Pre-Raphaelites, the Idyllic School and the High Victorians* (Aldershot: Scolar Press, 1996), 264.

54 Ada Holl Reynolds, *The Life and Work of Frank Holl* (London: Methuen, 1912), 97–8.

55 Thomas, 'The Making of the *Graphic*'. 87.

56 Thomas, 'The Making of the *Graphic*'. 87.

categorised as 'social realists' because of the focus of many of the single- and double-paged illustrations on working-class life, the poor and the destitute. The newspaper worked towards documenting the negative aspects of the Industrial Revolution, in direct contrast to the more refined and conservative *Illustrated London News*; *The Graphic*'s illustrations were intended to be discomforting to the reader. Hogarth contends that Thomas considered his artists...

> a vital instrument to remind the reading public that, as Christians, they had a moral duty to be concerned at the plight of the less fortunate ... he favoured pictures that told a story, and believed art should be enjoyed as much for its closeness to life and truth as for any aesthetic qualities it may possess.[57]

He maintains that Thomas' religious beliefs influenced the newspaper's content and choice of illustrations; his newspaper preached 'such evangelical Liberalism, ... [it] pontificated on the social evils of the day, and demanded reforms. It set out to shock and to enlighten its middle-class readers'. Thomas did not, however, demand specific images from his artists, asking instead that they simply be of 'universal concern'.[58]

Luke Fildes' contribution to the first issue of *The Graphic* is a fine example of the newspaper's social realist theme. *Houseless and Hungry* (Figure 7) depicts a group of street people waiting for admission into the casual ward of a workhouse. *The Graphic* described the figures as 'portraits of real people ... [with] nothing in common except hunger, destitution, and rags'.[59] The illustration is composed so that the figures dominate, being placed close to the picture plane and commanding the entire horizontal line. The only figures of authority or indication of a higher social class are the two policemen tucked away in a doorway in the back-left corner. It conveys an overall feeling of desolation and coldness, together with a sense of desperation. The illustration makes no criticism of the poor; the homeless are not meant to be despised. Instead, the viewer is made to feel sympathy for their plight and to ruminate on societal developments that had led them to their desperate situation. It depicts a reality of the progress of the Industrial Revolution and its associated modernising project.

Fildes' colleague Frank Holl, who was often criticised for constantly working on themes of the poor and destitute, was likewise driven to record the plight

57 Hogarth, *The Artist as Reporter*, 56.

58 Hogarth, *The Artist as Reporter*, 56.

59 *The Graphic Portfolio*, 1876.

of the less fortunate, not voyeuristically, but out of genuine concern for raising public awareness of what was happening in the newly industrialised society. He often travelled to the seedier sides of the city to experience what he wished to depict, which left a lasting impression on him, according to his daughter:

> These rambles in the very poorest quarters of London brought my father face to face with many terrible scenes of misery and poverty, and even crime. It was scarcely a morbid attraction for the seamy side which led him forth upon these unsavoury peregrinations, but rather, I take it, a latent idea that, by depicting them forcibly and poignantly in his own work, he might bring home to the indifferent eyes and hearts of the public the wretched and iniquitous state of affairs which lies close to our own doors. This may have been the reason he so nearly always took for his subjects some story of poverty, of sorrow, or of crime.[60]

For Holl, Fildes and *The Graphic*, the message they sought to preach was always the same: the poor should not be forgotten and society should do everything possible to bring about reform to assist those in need. They achieved this by producing illustrations that drew attention to increasing levels of inequality, but also by engendering empathy for and positively commenting on the systems put in place to assist the poor, such as the establishment of workhouses (depicted in Fildes' *Houseless and Hungry* – see Figure 7), which provided food and shelter even if for one night only. *The Graphic* was presenting contemporary problems, exposing many of the evils that beset a changing society, but commenting on and supporting possible solutions. It encouraged its readers in private contemplation, reflection and, desirably, action in response to new challenges. It also appealed for charity donations from its middle-class readers, thus creating an atmosphere of social responsibility. The newspaper was not the first to focus on the darker sides of society, but it was the first to present them in images in single- and double-page formats and the first to place emphasis on human interest, setting an agenda and establishing a platform, ultimately endorsed by van Gogh, for many other newspapers to follow.

Illustrated newspapers came to the fore in the mid-nineteenth century and played multiple roles. On the one hand, they demonstrate the possibilities and positives of the new technologies of the age – the mass production of paper, the printing of text and images simultaneously, the quick transfer of news and illustrations, the far-reaching distribution of newspapers, and new divisions of labour. On the other hand, they serve as illustrated diaries of development

60 Holl Reynolds, *The Life and Work of Frank Holl*, 108–9.

and change in society, enabling later generations to view their content, both literary and visual, as bound volumes of the history of the period. These newspapers and magazines were simultaneously ambassadors and agitators. They revealed all that was good in society and, especially in the case of papers like *The Graphic*, they ensured that the negative aspects of society were also exposed. Most importantly, they gave credence to the depiction of society's underbelly as a valid artistic subject. It was this type of image that was of greatest interest to van Gogh. They encouraged him to collect, pointed him in the direction of becoming an illustrator, and ultimately assisted in shaping his artistic practice – stylistically, technically and thematically. But perhaps the most important aspect of the rise of illustrated newspapers and magazines was that they assisted in the evolution of black-and-white illustration and brought prestige to them as an art form. They transformed a traditionally high-art form into a more democratic and socialist art form; they brought art from the gallery into people's homes. It was an art form of the people for the people, a creed that van Gogh would almost make his own. The illustrations came to be used by artists, like van Gogh, who found in them a guide for their own artistic practice. They offered instruction on technique, composition, and sometimes subject matter. Occasionally, as they did for van Gogh, they stimulated in the artist the idea of becoming a draughtsman.

Chapter 2

VAN GOGH IN NINETEENTH-CENTURY ENGLAND

The Making of an Evangelical Mindset

On 17 March 1873 van Gogh wrote to Theo, 'you'll have heard that I am going to London, and probably very soon'.[1] He told him of his transfer to the London office of Goupil & Cie. with enthusiasm and a sense of apprehension: 'it will be very different for me', but he was 'looking forward to seeing London very much'.[2] Van Gogh's knowledge of the greatest metropolis in the world was limited and shaped predominantly by his reading. He was an avid admirer of Charles Dickens and George Eliot and may well have read and seen Doré's images in the newly published illustrated travelogue, *London, a Pilgrimage* before arriving in London.[3] His admiration for both Eliot and Dickens is evident in his constant encouragement to family and friends to read their works with serious intent. He urged Theo in 1878, for instance, to 'make sure somehow you get hold of and read the books by Eliot, you won't be sorry' and when he had time he would soon 'read them again'.[4] He told

---

1 LT 5, volume 1, 25.

2 LT 5, volume 1, 25.

3 Blanchard Jerrold & Gustave Doré, *London, a Pilgrimage* (London, 1872). While van Gogh was definitely aware of Doré's illustrations, as he commented on them in later letters to both Theo and van Rappard, he does not mention seeing or reading this book until after his return from England (see letters 129, 162, 234, 263, 267 and 854). Van Gogh may have seen it, though, through his friendship with the Van Stockum family of publishers. If he had seen it, his knowledge of London would have been shaped by Doré's masterful illustrations and Jerrold's colourful writing.

4 LT 142, volume 1, 220–1.

van Rappard in March 1883 that he found '*all* of Dickens beautiful' and that he had reread Dickens' *A Christmas Carol* and *The Haunted Man* 'almost every year since I was a boy'.[5] In the same letter he offered his French edition of Dickens to van Rappard, who was struggling to read them in English, as he planned to buy the complete English Household Edition, thus indicating that he had read Dickens in at least two languages. Dickens' texts provided van Gogh with an idea of what to expect of London in the 1870s. Through the eyes of Dickens, he viewed London as a heaving industrial city that was at once extravagant and rundown and troubled by the social ills caused by rapid industrialisation. He became aware of the working poor and downtrodden, whom Dickens so admired and supported. He learnt about England's rural heartland and its political and social engagement with London through Eliot's rural realism. While these literary depictions were essentially realist and to an extent accurate, the complexity and nuances of a city like London, which had changed so drastically and quickly, could never be fully understood until the city had been experienced.

So, what were the times that Dickens and Eliot, Jerrold and Doré described like? There was change across all spectrums of life – social, economic, cultural and political.[6] One dramatic change was the shift in Britain's population from being predominantly rural to city- and industry-based.[7] At the beginning of the nineteenth century one-fifth of the population lived in cities and towns; by the end of the 1880s three-quarters of the population had relocated to a city.[8] Van Gogh was fully aware of shifting populations. He had been raised as a youngster in the Dutch countryside before leaving the family home to work in cities. Unlike many who worked the land but left it to look for work in industry, he left the parsonage in Zundert in 1869 to work in the rapidly expanding world of art dealing, thus experiencing the contrast between rural and city life in a slightly exceptional way. He wrote to Theo from London in November 1873: 'I cannot tell you how interesting it is to see London and English business and the way of life, which differs so much from ours'.[9]

---

5 LT 325, volume 2, 300.

6 Melvin Kranzberg & C.W. Pursell Jnr. (eds), *Technology in Western Civilisation*, vol. 1 (New York: Oxford University Press, 1967), 219.

7 Although industry was changing to incorporate technological developments of the time, traditional methods persisted in many parts of the country.

8 Harold James Dyos & Michael Wolff (eds), *The Victorian City: Images and Realities* (London: Routledge and Kegan Paul, 1973).

9 LT 12, volume 1, 17.

London experienced one of the greatest population booms in history. Between 1801 and 1881 the population of London increased from one million to more than four million, and by the early 1900s had swelled to over seven million. The most rapid expansion was between 1841 and 1851, when about 40 per cent of the increase occurred.[10] After 1851 London's growth slowed to the extent that migration levels into central London had begun to reverse by the end of the 1880s for a number of factors. Cheaper rail travel made it possible for people to travel daily to and from work in the city.[11] The middle and upper classes wanted to escape the vices, threats and dirtiness of the growing slums in the city and to control their workers from a safe distance. They sought refuge in the new expanding suburbs. Eventually, the working class joined their wealthier fellow-citizens, once a new economic model was in place that brought independence and prosperity to the working classes and enabled a form of social mobility previously unknown.[12] This cycle of the wealthy and more advantaged moving to the suburbs of London encouraged a new divide between rich and poor, putting in place a constant gap that was almost impossible for most residing in the slums to bridge. Land further from the city was cheaper, but only suited people with regular employment. Consequently, the lower classes remained in the overpopulated areas of the city, so that they were at hand to take advantage of the limited employment opportunities.[13] E.R. Dewsnup offered his view of class difference in 1907, along with his justification as to why the poor, at least for a short period, should remain separated. Confirmed slummers, he argued:

> might be compelled to live in barrack dwellings under the strictest sanitary supervision, at least until they learned how to live decently in decent houses: in their cases, a restriction of the liberty of the individual is desirable both for their own sake and for that of other citizens.[14]

---

10 Anthony Wohl, 'The History of the Working Class in London, 1815–1914', in Stanley Chapman (ed.), *The History of Working Class Housing* (Newton Abbot: David & Charles, 1971), 15.

11 Dyos & Wolff, *The Victorian City*, 13.

12 Eric Lampard refers to this as 'social–structural differentiation' – that is, upward social mobility, made possible by the extension of all and enabling the attainment of 'middle class' status (Eric Lampard, 'The Social Impact of the Industrial Revolution', in Kranzberg & Purcell, *Technology in Western Civilisation*, 310).

13 Gareth Stedman Jones, *Outcast London* (Oxford: Clarendon Press, 1971), 159.

14 Ernest Ritson Dewsnup, *The Housing Problem in England: Its Statistics, Legislation and Policy* (Manchester: University of Manchester, 1907), 232.

It is hard not to read these words as the view of someone belonging to the upper and middle classes, who felt threatened by the unknown and preferred to see the separation of classes as existing for his own personal benefit.

Van Gogh was aware of the exodus from the city into the suburbs and its demographic. He wrote to his friends that 'many people who have their businesses in London live in some village or other outside London and come to the city every day by train'.[15] It was in the suburbs – the home of the middle and upper classes – that van Gogh lived when he first arrived in London. As already noted, it is unclear whether van Gogh was aware of Jerrold's travelogue, but his descriptions of the landscape outside of London were remarkably similar. Jerrold described the changing view from his train window as he rode out of central London: 'we are getting away from London houses, London smoke, and London commerce. We are almost quit of the black barges. There are bits of greenery. The air is clearer'.[16] In an early letter from London, van Gogh's description of his new abode expresses similar sentiments: 'Here where I live it's a quiet, convivial, nice-looking neighbourhood, in this I've really been fortunate'.[17] At the same time, in writing to his friends, the van Stockum-Haanebeek family, he described his neighbourhood as 'very pretty, and so peaceful and convivial that one almost forgets one is in London'.[18] He even paints a picture in words of the streetscape for his friends: 'in front of every house there is a small garden with flowers or a couple of trees, and many houses are built very tastefully in a sort of Gothic style'.[19] Although in later years van Gogh was to associate more closely with the poor, in his early years in London (1872–74) he saw himself as belonging to the middle class, as was reflected not only in where he lived but also in how he presented himself.

As well as dressing like those in the middle class – van Gogh's parents wrote to Theo of how he had bought a top hat and of how he was 'gradually turning into a true cosmopolitan' – he began to enjoy many of their leisurely pursuits.[20] 'I am not at all in a hurry to go and see everything', he informed friends in August 1873, 'for the time being I have enough with the museums,

15 LT 12, volume 1, 35.

16 Jerrold & Doré, *London, a Pilgrimage*, 44.

17 LT 11, volume 1, 32.

18 LT 10, volume 1, 31.

19 LT 10, volume 1, 31.

20 Letter from Reverend van Gogh to Theo van Gogh, 31 May 1873, *Van Gogh's letters*, at http://webexhibits.org/vangogh/letter/2/etc-fam-1873.htm, accessed 15 August 2019.

parks, &c., which attract me more'.[21] Of the parks he visited he wrote fondly of Rotten Row in Hyde Park 'where hundreds of ladies and gentlemen go riding', an activity more upper class than middle class.[22] When he was collating his collection of prints in The Hague, he found a double-page illustration of this scene and wrote to van Rappard: 'please look and see whether you got a large wood engraving from me in the past, with no draughtsman's name below it, depicting gentlemen and ladies riding in a park'.[23] Other prints in van Gogh's collection illustrating the middle and upper classes making use of the parks include George du Maurier's *Battledoor and Shuttlecock*, which shows a group of well-dressed middle-class women enjoying a game of shuttlecock and J.D. Linton's *Curds and Whey in St. James's Park* (Figure 2), which depicts a lazy Sunday afternoon in one of the grand new public areas.[24] Although van Gogh collected these illustrations years after he had left London, they were reminders of the time he had spent there which would no doubt have influenced what he chose for his collection.

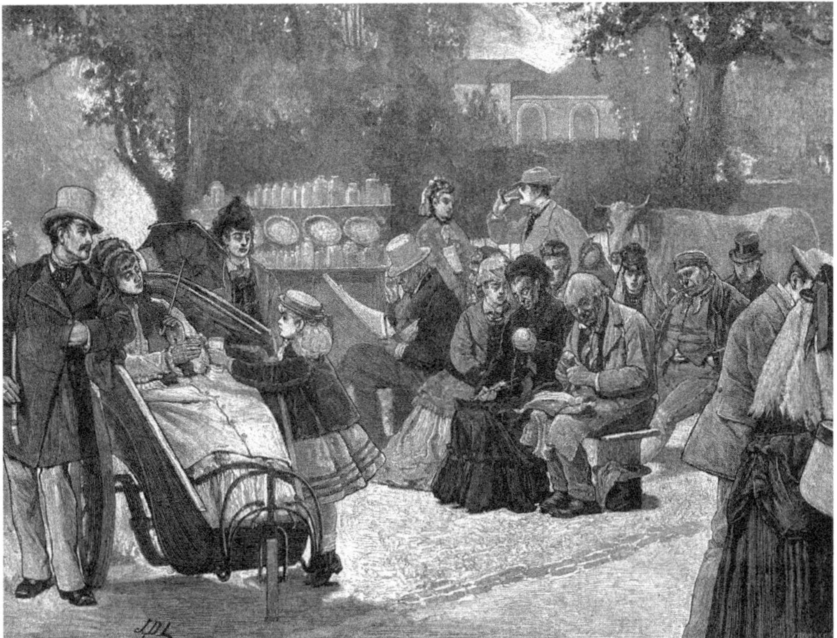

Figure 2. J.D. Linton, *Curds and Whey in St. James's Park* (*The Graphic*, 14 June 1873).

21 LT 12, volume 1, 35.

22 LT 10, volume 1, 31.

23 LT 273, volume 2, 174.

24 G. du Maurier, *Battledoor and Shuttlecock* (*The Graphic*, 13 May 1871).

During his years in London, van Gogh's views of the city came to be shaped by his increasing religious zeal, offering an insight into his understanding of the darker side of society during the late Industrial Revolution. He was aware of the plight of the working class, commenting to Theo in 1876 that he had 'tended to associate, especially in Paris and London, with people from the poorer classes and foreigners'.[25] By the middle of 1876, van Gogh's focus on his religion had led to his eventual dismissal from Goupil & Cie after which he turned his attention towards a new career as a lay preacher, missionary or teacher, so that he could work more closely and share his growing empathy with the poor in London and its outer reaches.

Van Gogh's sympathy for the working and lower classes is evident in three letters written between April 1882 and October 1883 – long after he had left London and was truly on his artistic path. To Theo he revealed his own experience of sleeping on the streets of London amongst the poor and the lasting effect it had on his appearance and personality:

> ... and if Mauve imitates and parrots me, saying 'that's the face you pull', this is how you talk, I'll reply: My dear fellow, if you had spent damp nights in the streets of London or cold nights in the Borinage as I have done, hungry, roofless, feverish, perhaps you'd also have the occasional ugly tic, and something in your voice, to show for it.[26]

In another he equates nature to poverty: 'a row of pollard willows sometimes resembles a procession of orphan men', and 'the grass trodden down at the side of a road looks tired and dusty like the inhabitants of a poor quarter'.[27] Although van Gogh does not link these descriptions to a particular city, they could easily be drawn from what he saw and experienced in London and the English Sunday schools and ministries he worked at. The third letter, written to his parents from Drenthe, highlights the difference van Gogh saw between country people and city people:

> Well, if I compare the population of a city and these people, I don't hesitate for one moment in saying that these heathland people or peat workers seem better to me. Yes, the difference seems to me to be enormous, even if they cheat one another no less than on Het Heike, although I don't say that they do, I don't know yet.

25 LT 85, volume 1, 104.

26 LT 221, volume 2, 61.

27 LT 292, volume 2, 218.

> I recently spoke about something of the kind to the man I lodge with, who also farms – by chance, because he asked me what it was like in London, he'd heard so much about it. I told him that, to me, a simple peasant who *worked and thought while he was working* was the civilized man – that this has always been so, will always remain so, that here and there in the country one sees someone in whom one sees what that is, and in the city one finds a few among the very, very rare excellent people who are almost exactly as noble in a very different way. But that in my view it goes no further, and that generally speaking one has more chance of meeting a reasonable human being in the country than in the city. And also that I thought that the more one went to the big cities, the more one went into the darkness of *un*civilization and stupidity and wickedness. He said that it actually appeared the same to him.[28]

Such negative views of the city, as Raymond Williams notes, 'formed a large part of the visitor's or middle-class observer's sense' of London.[29] It was common to view the country as 'a natural way of life: of peace, innocence, and simple virtue', in contrast to the city which was 'a place of noise, worldliness and ambition'.[30] Van Gogh's thoughts about the distinction between the city and the rural areas, between the poor and those of means, as he expressed them in his letters, are similar. Furthermore, the letters inform us of van Gogh's experience and perceptions of the negative consequences of the rapid change taking place in England, especially in London. They reveal that he was of the opinion that many of the ailments plaguing the underprivileged arose from the rapid growth of towns and industry, which did not allow for any parallel development in living standards, nutrition, housing, clothing and medical care. His views were shared and framed not only by his own experience but also by the authors such as Eliot, Dickens and Jerrold.

Williams argues that nineteenth-century authors, such as Eliot and Dickens, 'provide some of the most vivid descriptions of life in an unsettled industrial society'.[31] Michael Irwin claims the novels of these writers are 'full of attempts to make the reader *see* what is taking place'.[32] For van Gogh, whose

28 LT 399, volume 3, 50.

29 Raymond Williams, *The Country and the City* (London: Chatto & Windus, 1973), 144.

30 Williams, *The Country and the City*, 1.

31 Raymond Williams, *Culture and Society 1780–1950* (Harmondsworth: Penguin Books, 1963), 99.

32 Michael Irwin, *Picturing: Description and Illusion in the Nineteenth-Century Novel* (London: George Allen & Unwin, 1979), 2.

experience of England was in the main limited to London and its surrounds, these writers offered a window on parts of the country he never visited. He refers continually to Dickens in his letters, admiring the author and evincing sympathy for his characters. He found in Dickens and other authors he admired 'characters with whom he identified: often alone against the world, oppressed, sensitive, touching and misunderstood'.[33] One of van Gogh's favourite novels was Dickens' *Hard Times*, which was attacked for its 'sullen socialism' and its critique of social conditions in Victorian England, but at the same time praised for its importance as a chronicle of Victorian industrial society.[34] The novel is not set in London, but in the fictitious Northern England town of Coketown, and based in part on Dickens' experience of witnessing a major workers' strike in Preston. It tells the story of the struggles of the working class, the refinement and politics of the wealthy built upon those struggles, the organisation of contemporary class society, and the potential for individuals to move within this structure. Early in the novel, Dickens gives a vivid description of Coketown's characteristics – features that were the same in many of the industrial cities spreading throughout England.

> It was a town of red brick, or of brick that would have been red if the smoke and ashes had allowed it; but as matters stood it was a town of unnatural red and black like the painted face of a savage.
>
> It was a town of machinery and tall chimneys, out of which interminable serpents of smoke trailed themselves for ever and ever, and never got uncoiled.
>
> It had a black canal in it, and a river that ran purple with ill-smelling dye, and vast piles of buildings full of windows where there was a rattling and a trembling all day long, and where the piston of the steam-engine worked monotonously up and down, like the head of an elephant in a state of melancholy madness. It contained several large streets all very like one another, and many small streets still more like one another. Inhabited by people equally like one another, who all went in and out at the same hours, with the same sound upon the same pavements, to do the same work, and to whom every day was the same as yesterday and tomorrow, and every year the counterpart of the last and the next.[35]

---

33 Wouter van der Veen, *Van Gogh: A Literary Mind* (Zwolle: Waanders, 2009), 227.

34 Charles Dickens, *Hard Times* (Ware, Herts: Wordsworth Classics, 1995), introduction.

35 Dickens, *Hard Times*, 18.

These images can be traced to Dickens' report from his trip to Preston, where he describes arriving in the town and being confronted by 'the cold smokeless factory chimneys'.[36] He also wrote that Chadwick's Orchard in Preston, where an open-air meeting was held, 'blossoms in nothing but red bricks'.[37] He described the maze of laneways he negotiated to attend a meeting of the strikers as 'tolerably crowded by the lower sort of working people'.[38] Dickens damned the consequences of industrialisation and the environmental impact and conditions that workers faced every day in the factories and mines. He offered readers, who, like van Gogh, had never travelled to any of the industrial cities like Birmingham, Manchester or Sheffield, their only experience of industrial towns.

The characteristics of the protagonists in Dickens' novels also mirror those of the workers in many of England's industrial towns and cities. Stephen Blackpool, a character in *Hard Times*, was much admired by Van Gogh, who described him as a worker 'who's well portrayed and extremely likeable'.[39] Blackpool is a power-loom weaver who is wrongly accused of robbing the town bank and, towards the end of the novel, is injured after falling down an old mineshaft. On a stretcher after his rescue, and close to death, he relates his feelings about the terrible experience; the poignant prose reflects Dickens' views on the dangers of industrial work.

> I ha' fell into as pit that ha' been wi' th' Fire-damp crueller than battle. I ha' read on 't in the public petition, as onny one may read, fro' the men that works in pits, in which they ha' pray'n and pray'n the lawmakers for Christ's sake not to let their work be murder to 'em, but to spare 'em for th' wives and children that they loves as well as gentlefolk loves theirs. When it were in work, it killed wi'out need; when 'tis let alone, it kills wi'out need. See how we die an no need, one way an another – in a muddle – every day![40]

These words would have resonated with van Gogh who witnessed similar accidents while living in the Borinage from December 1878 to October 1880. They would also echo the sentiment of a number of prints depicting mining accidents and the experience of those left behind that entered his collection

36 Charles Dickens, 'On Strike', in Charles Dickens, *The Works of Charles Dickens, volume XIX*, (London: The Gresham Publishing Co., 1854), 236.

37 Dickens, 'On Strike', 243.

38 Dickens, 'On Strike', 239.

39 LT 153, volume 1, 243.

40 Charles Dickens, *Hard Times*, 209.

years later. C.J. Staniland's *The Risca Colliery Explosion – The Two Widows, 1860 and 1880* (FIGURE 3) is an example, in which two women are being consoled after hearing of the death of their husbands, while in the background a crowd surrounds a mineshaft, frantically attempting to save others trapped after a colliery explosion. For van Gogh, both Staniland and Dickens focus poetically on human experience and overtly suggest that regardless of class, all people remain equal.

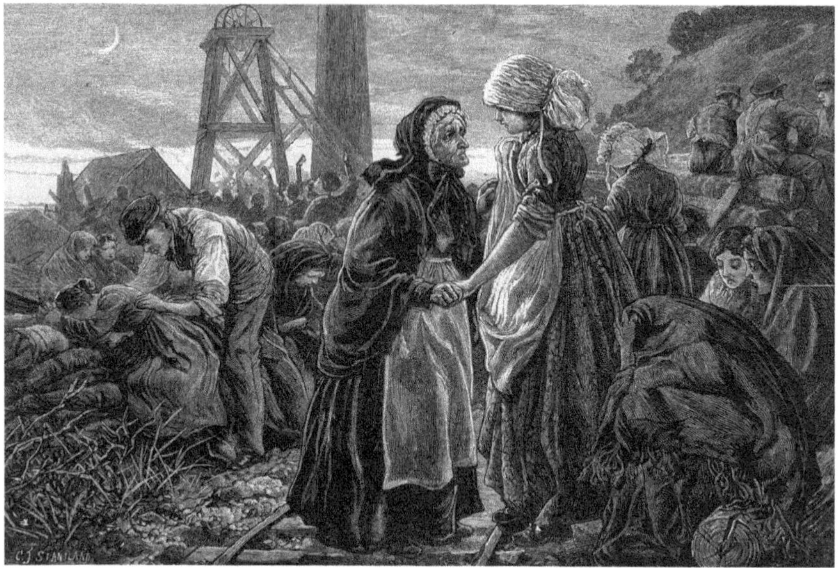

Figure 3. C.J. Staniland's *The Risca Colliery Explosion – The Two Widows, 1860 and 1880* (*The Graphic*, 31 July 1880).

The industrial towns Dickens portrayed in his novels were partly a product of the belief that the Industrial Revolution encouraged men to 'use the resources of nature and to master her'.[41] The most obvious example of such mastery, and the one with the greatest impact, was the evolution of the steam engine. The steam age developed during the first thirty years of the nineteenth century, but had its greatest triumphs in the 1840s and 1850s, as more industries realised the potential of steam and application to a wide array of machinery. As Carroll Pursell put it, 'previous decades had witnessed the birth of the Industrial Revolution, and subsequent generations were to live with the logic

41 Kranzberg & Pursell, *Technology in Western Civilization*, 219.

of mechanisation'.[42] The most celebrated application of steam power was in the development of the steam train and the expansion of the railways, which greatly benefited van Gogh as he travelled around first England and then across Europe, when he lived in the Netherlands and in France.

After the first railway line opened in 1830, track available for public use in England expanded from thirty to a staggering 9,000 miles by the mid-1850s, which meant that people could travel for leisure and work. By the end of the nineteenth century cheaper train travel allowed most people, regardless of their wealth, to use the immense rail network. However, the train system, perpetuated the discrimination inherent in the class-based society in which it operated. Many of the railway companies, such as the Great Western Railway Company, would limit the use of their services by the extreme poor and working class by scheduling few or no cheap train services in the early morning.[43] Carriages were divided into first, second and third class, with varying levels of comfort and price; third-class carriages had neither roof nor seats; second-class passengers had a seat without cushions; first-class travellers had all the comforts technology could provide. For a time, those with the financial means could even travel in their own carriage – the ultimate in exclusive comfort. Passenger lists reflected the dynamics and variety of people who used the system, and where they were most likely to be found in the hierarchy of comfort. Country gentlemen, clergymen and military officers were usually found resting in first class, while typical second-class travellers included surveyors, solicitors, respectable tradesmen and gentlemen's servants. Third-class passengers were mainly workers, as depicted in one of van Gogh's favourite illustrations, Edward King's *The Workman's Train* (Figure 1), in which the central figure looks forlorn and exhausted, with his work-bag slung over his shoulder. He shares a crowded hard bench with his fellow commuters, with no room to stretch or place their meagre belongings. In contrast to the top hats and finely-made suits of first-class passengers, these figures wear heavy workers' coats and carry flagons of wine, hinting at the roughness and uncouthness of third-class passengers.

Large numbers of working-class people were displaced by the steam train and the expansion of the railways. At the time their displacement was considered a condition of scientific and social progress rather than a denial of community.[44] Many so-called leaders also saw it as a solution to the dark stain

---

42 Kranzberg & Pursell, *Technology in Western Civilization*, 392–3.

43 Harold Perkin, *The Age of the Railway* (London: Panther Books, 1970), 257.

44 Francis Klingender, *Art and the Industrial Revolution* (New York: Augustus M. Kelley, 1968), 119.

of the slums. Railway companies were often lauded for solving the housing question, as they made it possible to demolish slum areas and whisk those who dwelt there to other parts of the city or out to new suburbs.[45] In reality, though, railway companies did very little to provide alternative housing for the people they displaced. It was not until 1885 that railway companies were forced by law to contribute to the relocation of people their infrastructure had displaced.[46] This did not, of course, eradicate slum areas. Many of the poorer inhabitants could afford neither the dearer housing nor the cost of travel out to the cities' perimeter. Instead, they retreated to small pockets of unused land or moved into larger homes that the middle classes had vacated, which had become cheap, shoddily converted, shared flats, that became filthy and overcrowded.[47] Other factors contributing to the gap between classes were the increase in workers being laid off from their employment and the need for workers to reside in poor housing close to their places of employment. Dock developments, the building of warehouses, the conversion of houses into workshops, urban improvement and street clearances all contributed further to the dreadful problems of the poor.[48]

One of the main reasons for the working class living in crowded urban conditions and slums was the major change in conditions, roles and structures of employment. People no longer lived exclusively in small communities on the land; they migrated to the city looking for employment or any other means of survival, whether through crime, prostitution or begging. New employment opportunities were to be found in factories, mines, service industries, and, in London, finishing companies.[49] Many of these places of employment expected their workers to work long hours, starting and finishing at scheduled times, with few breaks, all of which was in direct contrast with agricultural labour for whom time was governed by the sun and the seasons. Industrial cities and towns were governed by the clock in a system described as 'disciplined

45 Wohl, 'The History of the Working Class in London', 18.

46 Dewsnup, *The Housing Problem in England*, 19.

47 Harold Dyos argues that one cause of slums developing in London was uncontrolled town planning. Because the city had no rectilinear grid, there were many dead-end streets and backwaters which were ideal places for the criminal classes that made up a portion of the slums (Harold James Dyos, 'The Slums of Victorian London', *Victorian Studies*, 11 (1967–8), 25–6).

48 For an overview of all contributing factors, see Jones, *Outcast London*, 162–9.

49 Jones notes that in the second half of the 19th century London was mainly a finishing centre for many products. This was partly because of London's geographical position, which would have made the manufacturing of primary goods, such as steel and iron, expensive. London factories in these industries could not compete with factories in places such as Newcastle and Liverpool (Jones, *Outcast London*, 27–9).

industrial capitalism' where emphasis was placed on 'the time-sheet, the time-keeper, the informer and the fines'.[50] Workers became part of a machine that produced goods rapidly and constantly, sometimes over a never-ending 24-hour period. Steam and its machinery were 'a weapon with which to discipline the workers and subject them to the will of the employers'.[51] While many employees embraced the development of workplace machinery as a way of improving living standards, they were exposed to the new economic reality of boom and bust cycles, which increased the possibility of unemployment and predominantly affected casual labourers living in the slums near the factories.

As nineteenth-century Britain experienced one of history's most rapid modernisation projects, religion remained a constant in the changing society. England was where van Gogh's own pilgrimage towards becoming a preacher began. After his dismissal as an art dealer he returned to England in April 1876, working for a short time as a teacher in a Congregational boys' school and then assisting in the Richmond Methodist parish, where in late 1876 he gave his first sermon at the Wesleyan Methodist Church. At this time he experienced England's multi-denominational faith-based society and developed his own religious view, founded explicitly on following the teaching and acts of Jesus Christ.[52] In October 1876 he told Theo about coming across churches of different dominations: 'I rode past Mr Jones's little church and saw another in the distance where light was still burning so late. I headed for it and found it to be a very beautiful little Roman Catholic church in which a couple of women were praying'.[53] Van Gogh was very open-minded in his approach to Christianity, as his roommate Paulus Coenraad Görlitz confirmed in his recollection of van Gogh's religious observance on a Sunday when they both lived in Dordrecht in early 1877.

> When Sunday came van Gogh would go to church three times, either to the Roman Catholic Church, or to the Protestant or Old Episcopal church, which was commonly called the Jansenist church. When once we made the remark, "But, my dear van Gogh, how is it possible that you can go to three churches of such divergent creeds?" he said, "Well, in every

50 Edward Palmer Thompson, 'Time, Work-Discipline, and Industrial Capitalism', *Past and Present*, 38/1 (1967), 82.

51 Klingender, *Art and the Industrial Revolution*, 112.

52 The Van Gogh family's religious background was rooted in the Dutch Reformed Church, but van Gogh was well aware of the three main Christian groups in England: Anglicans (the establishment Church of England); Nonconformists (principally Congregationalists, Presbyterians and Methodists); and Roman Catholics.

53 LT 93, volume 1, 121.

> church I see God, and it's all the same to me whether a Protestant pastor or a Roman Catholic priest preaches; it is not really a matter of dogma, but of the spirit of the Gospel, and I find this spirit in all churches.[54]

Van Gogh's practice of attending different churches was unusual at a time when adherence to one's own church was all but absolute.[55] Each faith not only had its own theological focus and direction for its congregation, but also a particular demographic, divided along lines of class, wealth and, in some cases, ethnicity. The Roman Catholic Church continued under the Vatican's direction and its faithful were poor Irish migrants who had left Ireland during the Potato Famine. Catholics were mainly centred in London, Liverpool and Birmingham, which had a high proportion of Irish immigrants among their populations.[56] There were also some Catholics among the aristocracy of northern England, whose adherence to Catholicism stretched back to before the Reformation. The Roman Catholic Church also attracted new converts, usually intellectuals who appreciated the aesthetics of the Latin ritual.[57] The state church – the Church of England – was divided into three major groups. The first was the evangelical or 'low' church, which emphasised personal piety, Bible reading (especially at home), strong moral values, social reform and philanthropy, and encouraged Sunday school attendance. At the other end of the spectrum was the Anglo-Catholic or 'high' church, which was more traditional than the low church and emphasised priestly authority, indulged in elaborate altars and richly decorated vestments, and funded the restoration of churches back to their Gothic splendour. The third group was the Broad Church, which had no single central doctrine and was open to anyone with Christian belief. They were more liberal, promoted social reform, and remained more open to intellectual and scientific inquiry. By the early twentieth century they had become the most popular of the three groups. Nonconformists, usually strongest in towns and cities, shared the Anglican evangelicals' belief in the authority of the Bible and in developing a personal

---

54 Vincent van Gogh, *The Complete Letters of Vincent van Gogh*, (Boston: Bulfinch Press, 2000), Letter A7, 596–7.

55 After van Gogh had left England and returned to The Netherlands, he continued to attend English churches, such as the English Reformed Church in Amsterdam's Begijnhof (see Martin Bailey (ed.), *Van Gogh in England: Portrait of the Artist as a Young Man* (London: Barbican Art Gallery, 1992)). 67, and van Gogh's letters 144, 152, 160 and 162).

56 Owen Chadwick, *The Victorian Church* (London: Adam & Charles Black, 1970), vol. 2, 401.

57 Sally Mitchell, *Daily Life in Victorian England* (Westport, CT: Greenwood Press, 1996), 246.

relationship with God. They tended to have lower social status, which was confirmed by the trend towards baptising children into the Church of England as families became wealthier.[58]

Texts such as *Paradise Lost*, *The Pilgrim's Progress* and the Bible were widely read by Victorian readers. Van Gogh was fascinated and strongly influenced by *The Pilgrim's Progress*, in spite of its antipathy towards Roman Catholicism.[59] He wrote to Theo, 'If you can ever get Bunyan's Pilgrim's progress, it's very worthwhile reading. For my part I love it with heart and soul'.[60] His belief in leading a life as close as possible to that of Jesus Christ, which is why he was not deterred by the nuances of and differences between the major Christian denominations, was founded on Bunyan's text.[61] In addition to his devotional reading of Bunyan, van Gogh also read many other texts, including the Bible, which advances in printing techniques for mass production of books enabled wide circulation and ensured that there was a Bible in most homes.[62]

58 Mitchell, *Daily Life in Victorian England*, 242–4.

59 For discussion of the Protestant overtones of Bunyan's text, see Linda Colley, *Britons: Forging the Nation 1707–1837* (London: Vintage, 1996), 28–9.

60 LT 99, volume 1, 133.

61 In his recollections of van Gogh, Dr M.B. Mendes da Costa (van Gogh's Latin and Greek teacher) recalled the influence of Bunyan's *The Pilgrim's Progress* on van Gogh: 'So far everything went well, including mathematics, which he had begun studying with another master in the meantime; but after a short time the Greek verbs became too much for him. However, I might set about it, whatever trick I might invent to enliven the lessons, it was no use. "Mendes," he would say – we did not mister each other any more – "Mendes, do you seriously believe that such horrors are indispensable to a man who wants to do what I want to do: give peace to poor creatures and reconcile them to their existence here on earth?" And I, who as his master naturally could not agree, but who felt in my heart of hearts that he – mind, I say *he*, Vincent van Gogh! – was quite right, I put up the most formidable defense I was capable of; but it was no use. "John Bunyan's *Pilgrim's Progress* is of much more use to me, and Thomas à Kempis and a translation of the Bible; and I don't want anything more." I really do not know how many times he told me this, nor how many times I went to the Reverend Mr. Stricker to discuss the matter, after which it was decided again and again that Vincent ought to have another try' (Letter from Mendes da Costa to *Het Algemeen Handelsblad*, Amsterdam, 2 December 1910, in *Van Gogh's letters*, at http://webexhibits.org/vangogh/letter/6/etc-122a.htm, accessed 16 August 2019).

62 For an introduction to the influences of religion and religious texts on van Gogh, see Tsukasa Kodera, *Vincent van Gogh: Christianity versus Nature* (Amsterdam: J. Benjamins Publishing, 1990); Tsukasa Kodera, 'Van Gogh and the Dutch Theological Culture of the Nineteenth Century', in *Vincent Van Gogh, International Symposium* (Tokyo: Tokyo Shimbun, 1988), 141–70; Tsukasa Kodera, *Vincent van Gogh from Dutch collections: Religion – Humanity – Nature* (Osaka: National Museum of Art, 1986); Tsukasa Kodera & Yvette Rosenberg (eds), *The Mythology of Vincent van Gogh*, Amsterdam: John Benjamins Publishing, 1993); Cliff Edwards, *Van Gogh and God: A Creative Spiritual Quest* (Chicago: Loyola University Press, 1989);

Organisations such as the Religious Tract Society and the British and Foreign Bible Society disseminated the Bible vigorously from the beginning of the nineteenth century. The British and Foreign Bible Society alone issued more than two and a half million copies between 1804 and 1819, increasing this number to six million by the middle of the century.[63] The domestic circulation of such a very large number of Bibles was due to the Victorian belief in living an enlightened life; Bible reading, according to Richard Altick, was 'practiced less as a conscious exercise of the intellect than as a ritual which was an end in itself'.[64]

One of van Gogh's favourite illustrations depicts an agricultural labourer engaging in this very practice (see Figure 37). *The Graphic*'s description of the image praised the farm labourer, the noble task of farming, and the importance of regular reading of the Bible:

> With books, it may be admitted, the old generation of rural poor are but scantily acquainted. If, however, such a patriarch as is here represented can read, we may be pretty sure that he spends some of his well-earned leisure over the well-worn pages of the family Bible, and that poor and humble as his lot may be, he derives thence lessons and cheerfulness and contentment, as well as a foretaste of the happy future which awaits him in the next state of being.[65]

Van Gogh would have agreed with *The Graphic*'s promotion of regular Bible-reading and the suggested association between the noble work of farm labourers and religious piety. The increased availability of religious reading material throughout the nineteenth century and this romantic vision of farm labourers reading the Bible are key factors in the religious revival of the time. While church attendance was higher in rural villages than in the cities, religion generally remained important to most Victorians. This was evident from

---

Kathleen Powers Erickson, *At Eternity's Gate: The Spiritual Vision of Vincent van Gogh* (Grand Rapids, MI: W.B. Eerdmans Publishing, 1998); Thomas Buser, 'Van Gogh as a Religious Artist', *Gazette des Beaux Arts*, 114 (1989), 41–50; W. Fowlie, 'The Religious Experience of van Gogh', *College Art Journal*, 9/3 (1950), 317–324.

63 Richard Altick, *The English Common Reader: A Social History of the Mass Reading Public 1800–1900* (Chicago: University of Chicago Press, 1967), 101.

64 Altick, *The English Common Reader*, 99–100. An analysis of newly published texts from the end of the nineteenth century confirms the standing of religious reading material in England. 811 new books on religion were published in 1870, compared to 381 novels and 366 works of drama and poetry. By 1886 the trend had altered slightly with new novels eclipsing religious reading material 969 to 752 (see Robert Ensor, *England 1870–1914* (London: Oxford University Press, 1936), 159–60).

65 *The Graphic*, 9 October 1875, 350.

the continuous building of churches and chapels as the population spread, the mass availability of devotional texts and the Bible, and a social reform agenda with origins partly in evangelical philanthropy and in the fundamental teachings of all denominations. Owen Chadwick argues that the population felt 'a moral and social need for religion', regardless of whether they attended church regularly or not.[66]

One of the major shifts in relation to religion and the denominations that proliferated during this period was a focus on promoting and upholding moral values. The Industrial Revolution brought many social evils and it was left partly to religious institutions to provide solutions and benefits for those who had suffered under its relentless progress. Evangelicals worked tirelessly, especially in the first fifty years of the nineteenth century, to assist all members of society. They worked with the upper and middle classes, and at the same time concentrated much of their resources in converting the working class and poor. They set up institutions like the London City Mission 'to extend the knowledge of the Gospel among the inhabitants of London and its vicinity – especially the poor'.[67] This evangelical spirit shaped Van Gogh's religious zeal in fundamental ways, eventually influencing the kind of work he produced as an artist. Before taking up his pencil, he intended to work with the London poor, as he explained to Theo: 'should I find anything it will probably be a situation somewhere between minister and missionary, in the suburbs of London among working folk'.[68] Although he never stated it, he must have been fully aware of the work of the Evangelicals, especially those associated with the London City Mission who went among the destitute in London's rough areas, visiting in gin palaces, public houses, railways stations, all-night coffee stalls, and even refuge dumps.[69] In July 1876 van Gogh curiously ponders such a role, indicating a possibility that he might join their ranks:

> Being a London missionary is rather special, I believe; one has to go around among the workers and the poor spreading God's word and, if one has some experience, speak to them, track down and seek to help foreigners looking for work, or other people who are in some sort of difficulty, etc. etc. Last week I was in London a couple of times to

66 Chadwick *The Victorian Church*, vol. 2, 472.

67 Ian Bradley, *The Call to Seriousness: The Evangelical Impact on the Victorians* (London: Jonathan Cape, 1976), 46.

68 LT 84, volume 1, 103.

69 Bradley, *The Call to Seriousness*, 46.

> find out if there's a possibility of my becoming one. Because I speak various languages and have tended to associate, especially in Paris and London, with people from the poorer classes and foreigners, and being a foreigner myself, I may well be suited to this, and could become so more and more.[70]

Three months later van Gogh expanded on his evangelical philosophy and the significance placed on Sundays. Walking the streets of London, he observed: 'oh, those Sundays and how much is done and striven for on those Sundays, it's such a relief to those poor neighbourhoods and busy streets'.[71] He may have been referring to the establishment of Sunday Schools, which Ian Bradley considers 'the most successful of the agencies which the Evangelicals devised to convert the working classes'.[72]

Another organisation working to assist the poor and destitute was the Salvation Army, established in 1878. Although different from the more conventional religious institutions that van Gogh had experienced, the Salvation Army aimed to assist the poor within a radical religious framework.[73] Of his Army's approach, General William Booth wrote:

> I have boldly asserted that whatever his peculiar character or circumstances might be, if the prodigal would come home to his Heavenly Father, he would find enough and to spare in the Father's house to supply all his need both for this world and the next; and I have known thousands, nay, I can say tens of thousands, who have literally proved this to be true, having, with little or no temporal assistance, come out of the darkest depths of destitution, vice and crime, to be happy and honest citizens and true sons and servants of God.[74]

Booth outlines his solutions for many of the social problems that had arisen from rapid industrialisation, including unemployment, homelessness, crime and destitution. Essential to his plan was the need to change the moral character of the fallen.

---

70 LT 85, volume 1, 104.

71 LT 93, volume 1, 121.

72 Bradley, *The Call to Seriousness*, 44.

73 William Booth argued against the perception of the Salvation Army by conventional churches as a 'spiritual despot' (William Booth, *In Darkest England and the Way Out* (London: International Headquarters of the Salvation Army, 1890), 242–3).

74 Booth, *In Darkest England and the Way Out*, preface.

> In all cases where a man's own character and defects constitute the reasons for his fall, that character must be changed and that conduct altered if any permanent beneficial results are to be attained. If he is a drunkard, he must be made sober; if idle, he must be made industrious; if criminal, he must be made honest; if impure, he must be made clean; and if he is so deep down in vice, and has been there so long that he has lost all heart, and hope, and power to help himself, and absolutely refuses to move, he must be inspired with hope and have created within him the ambition to rise; otherwise he will never get out of the horrible pit.[75]

The programs that organisations like the Salvation Army and the Evangelicals put in place made available financial assistance, recreation opportunities, study groups, excursions into the country, and Sunday schools; all of these were intended to offer guidance and address morality, the absence of which was believed to underpin many of the evils plaguing the destitute and poor. Van Gogh's religious charitable spirit seems to have been informed by the new practices of many of these groups, especially the Evangelicals.

Van Gogh was part of a wave of people who migrated from country areas to the ever-expanding metropolises, such as London, looking for wealth and employment. His experience of England during his two stints there, from May 1873 to May 1875 and from April to December 1876, was limited in the main to London and its surroundings. He never visited England's north, nor did he venture south of London. His knowledge of England beyond London was shaped not by personal experience, but by his reading of authors such as Dickens and Eliot, and possibly by Jerrold and Doré's illustrated travelogue. As already noted his time in England had a lasting effect on him, shaping both his art and his views of life and moral convictions. Initially he found a place in London's middle class, living in their suburbs, dressing as they did and enjoying their leisure activities. Eventually he became more attuned to the differences between those living a simple rural life, as he had in the past and as some of his family continued to live, and those living in the larger cities, both cosmopolitan people and the ever-increasing poor. This dichotomy would eventually find expression in his black-and-white print collection. As religion became the focus in van Gogh's life, he left the sanctuary of his middle-class world to work with those less fortunate. Although his decision to follow such a path was not based entirely on his experience in London and the growing importance of religion in a rapidly and radically changing society, these two factors undoubtedly influenced his humanitarian attitude.

75 Booth, *In Darkest England and the Way Out*, 85.

He witnessed first-hand the negative changes in society: the rise of slums; vices such as public bars and prostitution; the rapid growth of people living on the streets; and the desperation of the unemployed. He became a champion of the people affected by these changes, first as a lay preacher, and later as an artist and collector of popular black-and-white prints. The depiction in art of the poor and their struggles appealed to van Gogh. He firmly believed they were worthy subjects that had a place in the canon of fine art, and it was his experience of London and his exposure to the many downsides of the Industrial Revolution that engendered his belief. While van Gogh was aware of and rallied against many of the negative outcomes of industrialisation, one aspect of technological change proved to be of immense benefit to him in the early years of his artistic development – the birth of a mass visual culture. One of industrial England's greatest triumphs, it gave rise to the weekly illustrated newspapers whose images formed the basis of van Gogh's vast collection of black-and-white prints and became central to his early artistic direction, helping shape both his visual and conceptual voice.

Chapter 3

'A KIND OF BIBLE'[1]

Van Gogh's Collection of Popular Prints

During his first years in England van Gogh accumulated a few illustrations to decorate his room and for scrapbooks to send to his brother Theo and sister Wil. He sent others as gifts to family and friends. The illustrations were from illustrated magazines and mass-produced prints, such as those sold by his employer Goupil & Cie, one of Europe's leading producers and sellers of such works. Van Gogh gained his knowledge of these works during his employment with Goupil & Cie, as well as from his uncles, Vincent and Cor van Gogh, both successful dealers in black-and-white reproductions with significant collections. Writing to Theo soon after he had arrived in Amsterdam in early January 1878, van Gogh said he had seen 'a great many good drawings at Uncle Cor's'.[2] He was also well aware of the popular prints in mass-produced illustrated magazines and newspapers. In 1877 he encouraged Theo to subscribe to *Katholieke Illustratie* which had reproduced 'Dore's prints of London – the wharves of the Thames, Westminster, Whitechapel, the Underground railway'.[3] He was familiar with the *The Illustrated London News* and *The Graphic* in England, recalling to van Rappard years later:

> More than 10 years ago I used to go every week to the display case of the printer of The Graphic and London News in London to see the weekly publications. The impressions I gained there on the spot were so strong that the drawings have remained clear and bright in my mind, despite everything that has since gone through my head.[4]

1 LT 311, volume 2, 266.

2 LT 139, volume 1, 214.

3 LT 101, volume 1, 138.

4 LT 307, volume 2, 255.

The first image that van Gogh is known to have collected from one of these English publications dates back to 1874, long before he entertained the idea of becoming an artist. He advised Theo that 'today I'm enclosing that little book for you in the crate to be sent … and also a portrait of Corot from the London News, which I also have hanging in my room'.[5] Van Gogh was not yet an avid collector, but his modest collection at the time was an indication that he saw artistic value in the art form and saw its merit for educating and inspiring a modest man, and decorating the walls of his home. It was not until the early 1880s that van Gogh began to collect black-and-white prints seriously. At the peak of his collecting, he had amassed close to two thousand sheets, among them illustrations from the two English newspapers mentioned above, as well as from French publications such as *L'Illustration, La Vie Moderne* and *Le Monde Illustré*, the American *Harper's Weekly*, and other small now forgotten newspapers. These were complemented by what are best described as fine-art mass-produced prints, such as those produced and sold by Goupil & Cie.

Since Pickvance's 1974 exhibition and the publication of its catalogue, *English Influences on Vincent van Gogh*, many texts have acknowledged the influence of popular prints on van Gogh's art. Pickvance's work focused on the English prints in van Gogh's collection and paid attention to *The Graphic*, especially in constructing an acquisition timeline. However, little has been done to rebuild the collection or to complete a timeline of acquisition for the sheets from *The Illustrated London News*, the second most represented illustrated newspaper in van Gogh's collection. Pickvance acknowledged this gap, suggesting that 'a pattern of his acquisitions from *The Illustrated London News* can be worked out', but that 'it would be tedious to do so here'.[6] Furthermore, there has been no thorough analysis of the collection – what was collected, why it was collected, and whether it had a thematic structure. This chapter addresses this lacuna in van Gogh studies.

Most of van Gogh's black-and-white illustrations came from the pages of *The Graphic* because of his good fortune in locating and purchasing a complete set of volumes dating from 1870 to 1880. He expressed his enthusiasm about the purchase to van Rappard: 'I now have The Graphics in my possession. I sat looking at them until deep into the night'.[7] This complete set of volumes

5 LT 30, volume 1, 54. The portrait was by Achille Isidore Gilbert and appeared in *The Illustrated London News* (27 February 1875).

6 Ronald Pickvance, *English Influences on Vincent van Gogh* (London: Arts Council of Great Britain, 1974), 34.

7 LT 303, volume 2, 238.

has made it relatively easy to identify when prints from *The Graphic* entered van Gogh's collection,[8] but it is more difficult to establish when he acquired prints culled from myriad other publications, including *The Illustrated London News*. One of the difficulties in constructing a timeline is that there seems to be no evidence of a systematic approach in van Gogh's collecting. As Luijten has pointed out:

> Van Gogh was always on the lookout for reproductions, and he must have acquired many works on mere impulse ... His purchases were at least partly determined by what was available at the local booksellers, who often bought up auction remainders or dealt in second-hand books, among them copies from lending libraries.[9]

The diversity of publications from which van Gogh collected is also broad, thus adding to the problem. Luijten notes that during the 1880s, when van Gogh was most actively building the collection, he sourced works mainly from *The Graphic*, *The Illustrated London News*, *Harper's Weekly*, *L'Illustration*, *Le Monde Illustré*, *L'Univers Illustré* and *La Vie Moderne*. While prints from these publications constitute the bulk of the collection, others are from lesser known magazines such as *De Hollandsche Illustratie* and *Illustrirte Zeitung*.[10]

While constructing an accurate timeline would be difficult for the reasons given above, the prints still present in the collection and van Gogh's letters can assist in creating a picture of when key works from *The Illustrated London News* were added to the collection, thus complementing Pickvance's work on the holdings of English prints. Nevertheless, even with this information there remain gaps in our knowledge. While van Gogh often listed prints he admired, those that informed his work, or those he intended to send to friends and peers, such as van Rappard, he does not always provide detailed information about when he acquired them. Van Gogh tended to reference prints that were already in his possession rather than those he had recently purchased. For example, when he wrote to van Rappard that: 'Caton Woodville is extraordinarily clever – I see that more and more – in addition to what you have, Nightly visit, I have more large things from Ireland by him, which form

8 See Pickvance, *English Influences on Vincent van Gogh*, 33–4.

9 Hans Luijten, 'Rummaging Among My Woodcuts – Van Gogh and the Graphic Arts', in Chris Stolwijk, Sjraar van Heugten, Leo Jansen and Andreas Blühm (eds), *Vincent's Choice: The Musée Imaginaire of van Gogh* (Amsterdam: Van Gogh Museum, 2003), 102.

10 Luijten, 'Rummaging Among My Woodcuts', 102.

a series together with other sheets by O'Kelly and Gregory and Dadd'.[11] Sometimes, however, van Gogh does mention recently found prints by name or description, as in January 1883 when he advised van Rappard: 'I found a girl's head by Percy Macquoid, that's wonderfully fine, a woodcut *after a painting* by him'.[12] On occasion, as in this letter to van Rappard, van Gogh also gave extensive lists of recently acquired prints, invaluable for creating a timeline:

> Other fine prints I've found since include
>
> | | |
> |---|---|
> | B. Constant | Sick fellahs beside the Nile |
> | Julien Dupré | Herdswoman |
> | Smith | A street in South Lambeth |
> | Ridley | Boat race |
> | Robinson | ditto |
> | Green | Street in Whitechapel |
> | Régamey | Prison in New York |
> | Thulsptrup | Workroom in Sailors' hospital or home |
> | Abbey | Winter girl |
> | " | Peter Stuyvesandt |
> | Reinhardt | Fishermen |
> | Barnard | 6 sheets |
> | Ed. Frère | Wood gatherers |
> | Buckman | donkeys on Hampstead Heath |
> | " | Gathering poppies |
> | Walker | Tip girls (Miners)[13] |

Of the approximately 1400 prints still in the collection, just over 200 are from *The Illustrated London News*. In addition, of more than 500 references to black-and-white prints in van Gogh's letters, almost a fifth can be confidently ascribed to works from that newspaper. By combining this information, it is possible to construct a picture of which issues of *The Illustrated London News* van Gogh accessed. Two conclusions can be drawn from this data. Firstly, van Gogh never possessed any complete volumes of *The Illustrated London News*, as he did of *The Graphic*. Although his collected prints cluster around the years 1872, 1874 and 1880, many weekly issues of the newspaper are not represented, which indicates that he either received prints and swapped them

11 LT 275, volume 2, 182.

12 LT 302, volume 2, 235.

13 LT 302, volume 2, 236.

with van Rappard or purchased single weekly issues of the newspaper from which he culled images. For example, references in van Gogh's letters and an analysis of the current print collection show that he accessed only 32 of *The Illustrated London News*' 52 issues for 1880. Prints collected from issues published in 1872 and 1874 reveal even lower access ratios; from 1872 he accessed 15 of 52 issues, and from 1874 27 of 52. The second point of note is the sporadic nature of the collection. For many years prints from only a single issue appear in the collection; for example: 1847, 1849, 1855, 1861, 1877 and 1879. This can be attributed to two main facts: firstly, unlike *The Graphic*, it was more difficult to find a complete run of *The Illustrated London News*, and secondly, van Gogh exchanged some of the prints with van Rappard, as confirmed in several letters, such as his February 1883 letter to van Rappard: 'I've just received the roll of woodcuts. Many thanks for them',[14] which contained a number of works from *The Illustrated London News.*

Van Gogh seems to have acquired prints from *The Illustrated London News* over six periods of time. The two main periods of acquisition were between January and October 1882 and between January and February 1883. Four shorter periods – May 1883, July 1883, February 1884, and September 1884 – yielded smaller numbers of works for his collection. Van Gogh undoubtedly acquired prints at other times through exchanges and by constant rummaging in art dealers and bookshops, but most likely only in very small numbers.

Although in the early part of 1882 van Gogh's letters to Theo were dominated by discussions about his progress, appearance and problems with peers, family and friends, including his parents and Anton Mauve, there are indications of his burgeoning print collection. In January 1882, in a letter to Theo with a twelve-point response to criticism levelled at him, van Gogh dedicated the second half of the letter to his practice and his print collection, mentioning an important bulk purchase of prints:

> And I've also acquired another ornament for my studio, I got a great bargain on some splendid woodcuts from The Graphic, some of them prints not of the clichés but of the blocks themselves. Just what I've been wanting for years ... I bought them from Blok, the Jewish bookseller, and chose the best from an enormous pile of Graphics and London News for five guilders.[15]

14 LT 311, volume 2, 265.

15 LT 199, volume 2, 17–18.

Giving only a hint of what he had purchased, the passage confirms that there were illustrations from *The Illustrated London News* among them. It also suggests the quality of prints with which he began his collection. Prints 'not from the clichés' were those found in *The Graphic Portfolio*, a selection of that newspaper's best illustrations in one bound volume. That he chose 'the best from an enormous pile' suggests that those from *The Illustrated London News* were similar in quality to those from *The Graphic*, most likely double-page illustrations.[16]

The growing size of van Gogh's collection was confirmed a few months later, in March 1882, when he declared that he had enough prints to mount a changing presentation over two nights at Pulchri, an artists' society in The Hague.[17] By June of that year he was proudly claiming that the collection comprised of over 1,000 sheets.[18] In his next letter van Gogh listed the seventeen folios by which he had catalogued and sorted his collection.[19] This list of folios, although not specifically identifying individual prints from *The Illustrated London News*, provides an insight into what was already in the collection. A folio for the works of illustrator Fred Barnard, for instance, seems to have included prints from the years 1874–76, 1880 and 1882. Van Gogh mentions acquiring further prints by this artist, all from 1872, in a letter to van Rappard dated 3 July 1883.[20] A folio dedicated in part to Charles Green is similarly noteworthy. Van Gogh mentions acquiring two works by Green, also from 1872, in his July letter to van Rappard. Therefore, all other known prints of this key artist must have been in the collection by mid 1882, including works from 1866 and 1879.

Between January and October 1882, van Gogh's letters were full of lists and discussion of his growing collection and possible exchanges with van Rappard. Many of the works referenced, however, were from *The Graphic* and other publications rather than from *The Illustrated London News*. It is

16 Although there are no double-page illustrations in the current collection held by the Van Gogh Museum, they did form an important part of van Gogh's holdings. This is evident in his mention of a folio dedicated to double-page illustrations in a letter to Theo (LT 235, volume 2, 90).

17 'Blommers has asked me to give a talk one evening at Pulchri about my collection of woodcuts after Herkomer, Frank Holl, Du Maurier &c. I'd very much like to do it, I have enough for two evenings if necessary' (LT 213, volume 2, 45).

18 'I must also tell you that all goes well with my collection of woodcuts, which I think as belonging to you although I have use of them. I now have at least a thousand prints, English (especially SWAINS'S), American and French' (LT 234, volume 2, 85).

19 LT 235, volume 2, 89–90.

20 LT 359, volume 2, 369.

not until September 1882 that van Gogh discussed prints from *The Illustrated London News*. He had sent a selection of prints with a letter to van Rappard, in which he told his friend that the folds in many of the illustrations were caused, not by the forwarding but 'because they were kept for so long in a subscription library'.[21] He continued, 'I may be able to add some more later, since the Jew told me he still had more of that jumble of magazines at home (from which I took these and my own) ... When I have time I'm going to look through his jumble'.[22] Amongst this jumble were prints from *The Illustrated London News*. Van Gogh mentions *Reflections* by Percy Macquoid, which appeared in the 1874 Christmas edition, which he described as 'a girl in white leaning against a tree'.[23] He also identified Alfred Edward Emslie's *A Colliery Explosion: Volunteers to the Rescue*, a work that he intended to emulate in the future and which he referenced again a month later, indicating its importance in his collection.[24] In subsequent letters he continued to list woodcuts that he had just found in various issues of *The Illustrated London News*, such as, *Deserted* (21 December 1872) by Samuel Read, *The Rising of the Waters* (17 December 1881) also by Emslie, *A Midsummer Night's Dream: A Sketch in a London Park* (8 July 1882) by Harry Furniss, *The East London Hospital For Children* (27 April 1872) by Matthew W. Ridley, and Caton Woodville's *Turf-Market at Westport, County Mayo* (6 March 1880).[25]

Van Gogh did not write about acquiring further prints from *The Illustrated London News* until January 1883, at the same time he purchased the twenty-one volumes of *The Graphic*.[26] Although advising van Rappard that he had

21 LT 263, volume 2, 152.

22 LT 263, volume 2, 152.

23 LT 263, volume 2, 152.

24 'I made a big effort to get things with miners – this and an English one of an accident are the best – such subjects are rarely handled, by the way. I would like to do studies of them myself sooner or later" (LT 263, volume 2, 152); 'As it happens, I have another one by an English draughtsman, Emslie, in which the subject is men going into the mine to help the casualties of an accident if possible, while the women stand and wait' (LT 272, volume 2, 171).

25 'Among other things by Read I have an autumn effect and a moonlight and a snow which are very beautiful' (LT 273, volume 2, 174); 'I found a beautiful print by Emslie, *The rising of the waters*, a peasant woman with 2 children on a half-flooded pasture with pollard willows' (LT 276, volume 2, 186); 'Do you know Harry Furniss, *A midsummer night's dream*, depicting various characters – an old man, a street urchin, a drunkard &c. – who spend the night on a bench under a chestnut tree in the park?' (LT 276, volume 2, 186); 'Or take another print by Ridley, the children's ward of a hospital, which I have, soberly and austerely engraved by Swain' (LT 279, volume 2, 190); 'But Herkomer wouldn't reject, for example, the distribution of turf tickets in Ireland by Caton Woodville' (LT 279, volume 2, 190).

26 See LT 302, volume 2, 235–7.

not yet received *The Graphics*, he confirmed having with him prints from *The Illustrated London News*: 'I have found a girl's head by Percy Macquoid', he wrote, describing *Girl of Pont Aven* (30 December 1876).[27] He continued listing other prints he had recently found from *The Illustrated London News* such as Smith's *Sunday Morning in the New Cut, Lambeth* (27 January 1872), Robinson's *A Sketch at the International Boat-Race* (15 June 1872), a collection of works from Régamey's series focusing on Blackwells Island Penitentiary in New York – *Dining Room* (all from 1876), Frère's *Gathering Wood* (22 January 1876), Buckman's *For the London Market* (12 June 1875) and Walker's *Group of Tip Girls* (27 February 1875).[28] Although only short, the list indicates that copies of *The Illustrated London News*, most likely loose issues, were available from local booksellers. It also suggests that, even though the ten volumes of *The Graphic* were of utmost importance, van Gogh retained an interest in acquiring the best from whatever copies of *The Illustrated London News* and other publications he could get his hands on.

In a number of letters from February 1883 van Gogh wrote at length, as expected, about the prints from *The Graphic*, which had become his focus as he trawled through the ten years of issues he had acquired. He continued to mention, however, prints from *The Illustrated London News* sporadically, often duplicates, indicating that, although they were new finds, he had accessed copies of the same issues in previous years.[29] Many of these duplicates were intended for van Rappard's collection, as van Gogh told him:

> Come soon and collect the remainder. I know of no better way of determining which duplicates you have than for you to sort through them yourself, for listing the titles would be too laborious. But if you think you won't be able to visit for the time being, and if you long to have them, I can make up a package with everything that I have in duplicate. I could send it to you and then you could keep what you don't yet have and return the rest.[30]

27 See LT 302, volume 2, 235.

28 LT 302, volume 2, 236. Van Gogh does not always give the correct title of the work but rather a description of the work or an abbreviated title. For instance he lists the works as: Macquoid 'Head of a Little Girl'; Smith 'A Street in South Lambert'; Robinson 'Boat Race'; Régamey 'Prison in New York'; Frère 'Wood gatherers'; Buckman 'Gathering Poppies'; Walker 'Tip Girls (Miners)'.

29 One of these was E. Frère's *Snowballing* (19 February 1876). Van Gogh asked van Rappard 'Do you have *Snowballing*, a large sheet from London News by E. Frère, a school playground with boys? I just got a duplicate' (LT 311, volume 2, 266).

30 LT 321, volume 2, 283.

Van Gogh mentioned a number of duplicate prints that he had either sent or intended to send, providing evidence of the issues of *The Illustrated London News* he had in his possession. They were predominantly from 1872, with others from 1875, 1876, 1881, as well as several Christmas numbers. Prints listed from 1872 included Arthur Hopkins' *The Boat Race and The Weather: 'Oh Dear, What a Disappointment'* (30 March 1872), George du Maurier's *The First Warm Day* (20 April 1872), Patrick Michael Fitzgerald's *The Poor Irish Scholar* (27 January 1872), Robert Barnes' *Good Friday* (30 March 1872), and the split image *Arch's Cottage, Barford* and *A Labourer's Home at Whitnash* (13 April 1872) by an unknown artist. Prints from 1875, 1876 and 1881 included Achille Isidore Gilbert's portrait of Corot (27 February 1875), Félix Régamey's *American Sketches – Prison Life on Blackwell's Island – No. 1 Returning from Work* (19 February 1876), *Christmas Eve* by Heywood Hardy (23 December 1876) and Frank Holl's *Home Again* (3 September 1881). Works sourced from Christmas issues included Henry Robert Robertson's *Christmas on the 'Wave'* (Christmas number 1874), Charles Robinson's *The Romance of (a Rescue)* (Christmas number 1875), *Nearing Home* by Emslie (Christmas 1880) and *Hopes and Fears* by William Overend (Christmas number 1881).

In February 1883, van Gogh told van Rappard that he had mounted his woodcuts from *The Graphic* on card, a project that in due course would include the mounting of prints from other publications.[31] He used several types of card, varying in colour, texture and weight, with fifteen distinguishable variations. In total, ninety-nine prints from *The Illustrated London News* in the collection are mounted. Thirty-five prints from 1880 issues are mounted, twenty-four of which are on the most frequently used card, with the remainder attached to two other types of card. Another nineteen sheets from 1872 issues are mounted on seven different types of card, and eleven more from 1873, again mounted on several types of card including the most commonly used. There are ten sheets from 1875, a further eight sheets from 1874, five from 1881 and four each from 1876 and 1882. These years correlate with the prints in the collection that van Gogh reveals in his correspondence. It is possible, therefore, to conclude that by early February 1883, the end of van Gogh's two main periods of acquisition, he had collected prints from 1872, 1874, 1875, 1876, 1880, 1881 and 1882 issues of *The Illustrated London News*.

Although his collecting slowed after March 1883, van Gogh continued to collect further prints when the opportunity presented. In May he advised

31 'I've finished mounting and cutting out The Graphic woodcuts. They look much better now that they're arranged in order' (LT 321, volume 2, 284).

van Rappard, 'I took an issue of London News for the sake of a sheet by King – Workmen in a wagon of the Underground Railway' (see FIGURE 1).[32] Van Gogh had recently formed the view that the best illustrations had appeared in the 1870s when *The Graphic* was launched to challenge the dominance of *The Illustrated London News*, which explains why he chose to purchase single issues, seeking an illustration of strength and quality, rather than buying contemporary issues in bulk or on a regular basis. Although he was critical of the work from later years, by which time he had already amassed a sizeable collection, his collecting pattern indicates that he continued to leaf through newer issues on the off chance that something worthwhile would appear. Seemingly content with his collection, van Gogh wrote of no further acquisitions until early July 1883.

Of the new prints discussed, thirteen were from *The Illustrated London News*. However, unlike the print by Edward King that he had acquired in May, he found them in older issues. It is unlikely that they were found in a bound volume, as van Gogh would have been inclined to write about such a treasure. Rather, they were likely from piles of old issues that van Gogh rummaged through. He was still able to find prints from 1872, mostly from the second half of the year.[33] The remainder of the prints were from earlier issues and included Read's *Emigrants from the Isle of Skye* (15 January 1853), Birken Forster's *Christmas – The Cottage Door* (24 December 1859), John Everett Millais' *Christmas Story Telling* (20 December 1862) and Palmer's *The Sheffield Steel Manufacturers – Hall of the Fork Grinders* (18 March 1866). Van Gogh described these newly found sheets as 'all beautiful things', declaring them 'valuable additions' to his collection.[34] He echoed these sentiments to Theo, describing his collection as 'the hundred masterpieces of modern wood engravings' – a comparison to the exhibition Exposition de Peinture that included works by Corot, Delacroix, Millet, and a selection of Old Masters that Theo had seen and written about.[35] Van Gogh emphasised the importance

32 LT 341, volume 2, 331.

33 Van Gogh lists the following prints from the second half of 1872; T. Green's *Sunday at the Foundling Hospital* (7 December) and *A City Church Congregation* (5 October), Ridley's *London Bridge* (16 November), Barnard's *The First to Come* (21 December) and *The Last to Go* (21 December), Hopkins' *The Paddling Steamer* (3 August), Régamey's *The Diamond Diggers, South Africa* (31 August). Prints from the first half of 1872 included J.M.L.R.'s *The Ascent of Mount Vesuvius: Tourists at the Foot of the Cone* (1 June) and *The Easter Monday Volunteer Review at Brighton: Deploying the Line* (6 April) and Barnard's *Hampstead Heath on a Holiday* (25 May) (LT 359, volume 2, 366–70).

34 LT 359, volume 2, 369.

35 LT 358, volume 2, 364.

of the recently discovered prints in the context of his collection, declaring 'I had already had some last year, but what I've found since goes far beyond my expectations'.[36] His excitement and subsequent reverential discussion reveals the importance of the find, even if it paled in comparison with his earlier raids, and that he remained an avid collector.

One reason that van Gogh acquired fewer prints after his July 1883 find was that he moved from the artistic hub of The Hague to the rural province of Drenthe in September and then to the remote village of Nuenen in December. The only opportunity for discovering more prints in such places were chance finds of recent issues. In February 1884 van Gogh confirmed the scarcity of illustrated publications and his luck in finding new sheets: 'I haven't got much more in the way of woodcuts this winter – even so, one very fine print by O'Kelly, Irish emigrants – and a cotton spinning mill by Emslie, and then the print from the Xmas issue of The Graphic, For those in peril upon the sea'.[37] The prints by O'Kelly and Emslie were both from *The Illustrated London News*, appearing on 21 July 1883 and 25 August 1883 respectively.[38] It is most likely, therefore, that other prints in van Gogh's collection from 1883 (except King's *The Workman's Train* acquired in May 1883) were also found at this time. These additional prints, of which there are only three, date from about the same time.[39]

The last period in which van Gogh acquired further prints from *The Illustrated London News* was September 1884. Again, he reported the scarcity of newspapers in Nuenen, advising that he found works in the larger city of Utrecht.[40] The two prints – Frank Holl's *Ordered Off* and Gordon Thompson's *The Shepherd* – were both from 1884 and confirm van Gogh's continuing interest in the illustrated newspapers. These two prints, along with a further two, comprise the full representation from all 1884 issues of *The Illustrated London News*. It is likely, therefore, that they were all collected during van Gogh's short visit to Utrecht. After September 1884, there are no further references in van Gogh's correspondence to any new acquisitions. Numerous

---

36 LT 358, volume 2, 364.

37 LT 431, volume 3, 111.

38 O'Kelly, *Departure of Irish Emigrants at Clifden, County Galway* (21 July 1883); Emslie, *At Work in a Woollen Factory* (25 August 1883).

39 A.M. Emslie, *Seaside Sketches: The Luxury of Idleness* (18 August 1883); W.H. Overend, *Her Mother was Standing in the Balcony* (16 June 1883); unknown, *The Exhibition of the Royal Society of Painters in Water Colour* (23 June 1883).

40 'Tell me, do you know ORDERED OFF by *Frank Holl* from the London News? I brought it with me from Utrecht, at the same time as a shepherd by Thompson' (LT 461, volume 3, 173).

factors may have contributed to this halt, financial reasons and his location being the most significant. What is certain, however, is that among the prints in the existing collection there are none dated after 1884. If van Gogh acquired works from *The Illustrated London News* after this period, they may have been lost during his travels.

Thematic Analysis of the Collection

Although the Van Gogh Museum retains a significant portion of van Gogh's collection of prints and many of its gaps can be filled in by reference to his letters, any investigation of the collection's thematic structure should begin with the consideration of what van Gogh chose not to collect. Writing to Theo about his prospects of drawing for the illustrated newspapers, van Gogh revealed subjects that were of no interest to him:

> Current events – that's what they wanted. If by that they meant things like illuminations for the king's birthday, say, that would give me precious little enjoyment. But if it pleased the gentlemen to include under current events scenes from the everyday life of the people, I'd have nothing against doing my very best for those.[41]

Many of the publications whose prints van Gogh collected, especially the two prominent English newspapers, *The Graphic* and *The Illustrated London News*, covered 'current events'. This content included, as van Gogh suggested, news of the Royal Family (celebrations, trips, revelations of their daily lives), of tragic events (train accidents and murders), of social, economic and technological developments, of the colonies, of fashion, and of sport. Quite often, as expected, news and current affairs stories had illustrations published alongside them. Because such illustrations needed to be supplied expeditiously, they were frequently simple line drawings, rather than large-scale tonal works that paralleled a high-art aesthetic. That there are none of these simple illustrations either in van Gogh's extant collection or referred to in his correspondence confirms his interest in works with more weight, both in subject and appearance.

The collection's thematic structure is initially indicated in a letter in which van Gogh lists the seventeen folios into which he had sorted and filed his collection.[42] In these folios were prints from many of the mass-produced,

---

41 LT 324, volume 2, 292.

42 LT 235, volume 2, 89–90.

widely available illustrated newspapers and magazines, as well as from smaller English, French, Dutch and German publications, together with reproductions produced and distributed by companies such as Goupil & Cie. The folios reveal the subjects van Gogh deemed important and which shaped his collection. They also hint at what van Gogh wanted to illustrate were he to join the ranks of his draughtsmen heroes. While some of the folios contained illustrations of specific subjects, such as portraits, miners, factory workers and farmers, others were for the artists he most admired, such as Luke Fildes, Gustave Doré and George du Maurier.

Several broad themes can be identified across the seventeen folios: workers; landscapes; animals; portraits; ship scenes; military sketches; and city scenes. For some of these categories van Gogh kept separate folios, such for portraiture, which he said contained '*Heads of the people* by Herkomer, supplemented with drawings by others and by portraits'.[43] Others, however, such as those for individual artists, or another containing double-page illustrations, included images from a number of the broad thematic categories that defined his collection.

One of the most significant themes was of workers, which included images of rural, industrial and city workers, revealing van Gogh's holistic view of labour in an increasingly industrialised society. The first folio van Gogh listed for Theo included many of these types – miners, fishermen and factory workers – together with drawings after Irish characters, including illustrations of farmers and rural workers. There were also images of workers in the folios for individual artists. That dedicated to Jean-François Millet, for instance, contained Millet's series *Les Travaux des Champs* – drawings illustrating agricultural workers during different seasons and times of the day. Van Gogh would return to these images in 1889, translating the black-and-white originals into a series of golden-yellow and blue paintings. The folio dedicated in part to Charles Green contained images of industry, such as *Sketches at a Manchester Cotton Factory*, an illustration in three parts showing life on the factory floor.[44] The theme of city-based workers, whom van Gogh witnessed first-hand during his time in England, Amsterdam, The Hague and Paris, also crossed a number of folios. Similarly, the folio that held mostly illustrations of London life, which was described by van Gogh as containing everything 'from the opium smokers and Whitechapel and The Seven Dials to the most elegant ladies and Rotten Row or Westminster Park', would have

43 LT 235, volume 2, 90.

44 C. Green, *Sketches at a Manchester Cotton Factory* (*The Graphic*, 26 October 1872).

contained images of the new city worker enjoying both the virtues and vices of the growing metropolis.[45]

Two further thematic groupings were landscapes and animals, which van Gogh placed together in a single folio, and which he told Theo included examples by Karl Bodmer, Hector Giacomelli and Auguste Lançon.[46] A work by Lançon, *Lionne à l'affut*, showing a tiger crouched low, preparing to pounce on its prey, and Bodmer's, *Le cerf mort*, depicting a dead stag in a clearing, give a sense of the diversity of animal images in this folio.[47] While there are no longer any works by Giacomelli in the collection, van Gogh describes a double-page illustration after the artist of crows in flight as splendid.[48] Discussing Bodmer, an artist he had admired from earlier days as an art dealer, van Gogh declares him to be an artist whose prints are finished like paintings, citing a number of works – lithographs and illustrations from *L'Illustration* and *Le Monde Illustré* – including the dark tonal print *Combat de cerfs, Forêt de Fontainebleau* from 1861.[49] In the letter discussing Giacomelli's crows, van Gogh refers to van Rappard's copy of Bodmer's *Assemblée de grand-ducs*, admitting that he himself did not yet own a copy, but that he had at least seen and remembered the work. English artists, such as Macquoid, George H. Thomas, John MacWhirter and William Small, whose work van Gogh knew and collected, depicted a wide range of animals, from working animals to domestic and prize animals.[50] While van Gogh rarely discussed images of animals at length, comparing his admiration for the work of Bodmer and his criticism of a work such as Macquoid's *A Disarrangement in Blue* reveals what interested him most.[51] He decried Macquoid's drawing of two dogs wrestling with draperies on a fallen mannequin, which 'satisfies me less, I find it a little pedantic and too refined'.[52]

45 LT 235, volume 2, 90.

46 LT 235, volume 2, 90.

47 A. Lançon, *Lionne à l'affut* (*Le Musée Universal*, date not known); K. Bodmer, *Le cerf mort* (*L'Illustration*, 2 March 1872).

48 LT 321, volume 2, 284.

49 LT 333, volume 2, 318.

50 Some examples are: P. Macquoid, *Sketches at the Mule and Donkey Show at the Crystal Palace* (*The Illustrated London News*, 16 May 1874) and *A Disarrangement in Blue* (*The Graphic*, 13 November 1880); G.H. Thomas, *The Last Lot* (*The Illustrated London News*, 15 February 1868); J. MacWhirter, *Spindrift* (*The Graphic*, 30 September 1876) and *A Great While Ago the World Began…* (*The Graphic*, 5 August 1871); W. Small, *The Cattle Show at the Agricultural Hall – Judging the Herefords* (*The Graphic*, 18 December 1875).

51 P. Macquoid, *A Disarrangement in Blue*, *The Graphic* (13 November 1880).

52 LT 304, volume 2, 250.

In contrast he found Bodmer's intense study of nature to be of the highest order, as he told Theo in September 1889, years after his enthusiasm for collecting prints had waned:

> Let's take good Bodmer for example. Was he not able to study nature as a hunter, a savage, did he not love it and know it with experience of an entire long manly life… I'm *always* an admirer of Bodmer, but I admire and I like the man who knew all the forest of Fontainebleau, from the insect to the wild boar and from the stag to the lark. From the tall oak and the lump of rock to the fern and the blade of grass.[53]

Images of animals were not a priority for van Gogh, and there are only a few in the estate and scattered references to such images in letters, but he did collect some. He was attracted, as his reference to Bodmer indicates, to those that interrogated and depicted the animal kingdom with sympathy, reverence and honesty and within what can best be described as a Romantic construct, where nature was powerful and sublime.

The theme of landscape in this folio is somewhat ambiguous. Many images in the collection show figures in the landscape, such as workers in the fields, the middle class enjoying public parks, or people walking through the landscape. However, this folio most likely contained images of scenes similar to the paintings of artists and movements of which van Gogh was likely to have been aware – The Hague painters, European Romanticism, and the old Dutch masters. *The Western Highlands, Connemara – Lough Gill* is one such example (Figure 4).

In this majestic print from *The Graphic*, the landscape is viewed from an elevated position, down towards hills and a lake beneath a moody sky. In the bottom right-hand corner a young man stands on a ledge admiring the view. Dwarfed by the expansive landscape, the positioning of the diminutive figure before such a majestic view can be traced back to Romanticism, in which nature was seen as awe-inspiring and sublime, almost in a religions sense. Edward Duncan's *A Winter's Morning*, which appeared in *The Illustrated London News*, is similar in sentiment,[54] although its view across pastoral lands is more akin to the work of English artists, such as John Constable, whose work van Gogh encountered while living in England.[55]

---

53 LT 798, volume 5, 76.

54 E. Duncan, *A Winter's Morning* (*The Illustrated London News*, 10 June 1854).

55 '…among the old painters, Constable, a landscape painter who lived about 30 years ago, whose work is splendid, something like Diaz and Daubigny' (LT 11, volume 1, 32).

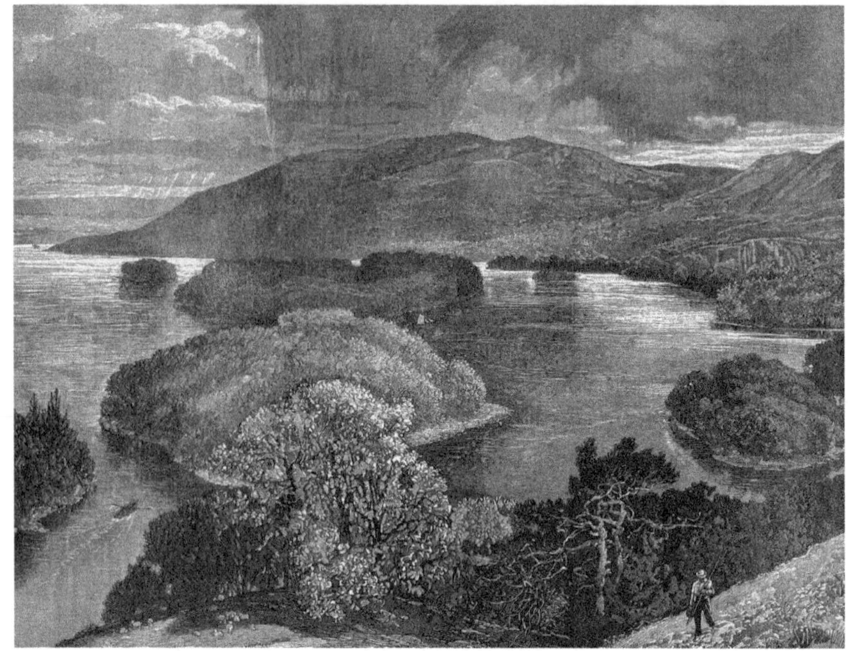

Figure 4. *The Western Highlands, Connemara – Lough Gill*
(*The Graphic*, 19 August 1871).

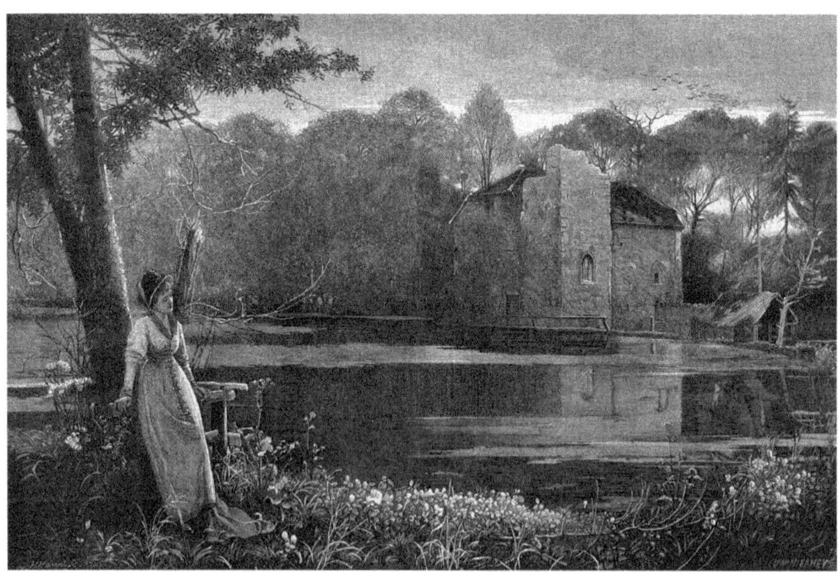

Figure 5. Edward Henry Fahey, '*He Never Came*'
(*The Graphic*, 17 June 1876).

Many other illustrations include a dominant singular figure, standing in awe of a powerful and vast landscape, and should be considered as part of van Gogh's portfolio of landscapes, as it is the landscape that predominates conceptually and thematically. Edward Henry Fahey's *'He Never Came'* (Figure 5) and Macquoid's *Reflections*, both depicting young ladies leaning against a tree in contemplation, are two such examples.[56]

In Fahey's print, a figure to the far left leads the viewer towards the centre of the composition, directing the gaze towards the still body of water and cottage in the distance. The tranquillity of the landscape, the reflection off the still water, the poetry of a flock of birds rising above the tree canopy dominate the image and seduce the viewer. In Macquoid's print, a woman also leans against a tree, contemplating the still water, disturbed slightly by two small birds, and the surrounding forest. Here, the landscape is presented as a beauteous scene and sublime in the Romantic sense. Van Gogh was aware of this artistic tradition and undoubtedly wanted to instil a similar sentiment in his own works; thus it would make sense that a folio of animals and landscape would include an eclectic mix of images. Images of animals and landscapes do not dominate his collection and cannot be identified as an overarching theme. Nevertheless, having illustrations of landscapes and animals filed away in his collection gave him easy access to images that could help him solve problems of composition, perspective, and sentiment, amongst other things when producing his own works.

In the folios containing portraits and city scenes were a greater number of prints that could assist him with his own artistic output. At the centre of his portraits' folio was *The Graphic*'s 'Heads of the People' series, a collection of prints depicting types of people, particularly members from the working and lower classes, rather than individuals. To complement this significant series, van Gogh added illustrations of eminent people, such as the Archbishop of Westminster, the Reverend Henry Edward Manning, and Prime Minister William Gladstone.[57] There were also portraits of historians, such as François Guizot, and composers, including Richard Wagner.[58] Van Gogh may have also included portraits from other series, such as Randolph Caldecott's 1875 illustrations for Washington Irving's *Old Christmas* (1820), a selection of small

---

56 E.H. Fahey, *'He Never Came'* (*The Graphic*, 17 June 1876) and P. Macquoid, *Reflections* (*The Illustrated London News*, Christmas edition 1874).

57 C. Roberts, *The Most Reverend Henry Edward Manning, D.D.; Roman Catholic Archbishop of Westminster* (*The Graphic*, 11 July 1874); H.S. Uhlrich, *The Right Hon. W.E. Gladstone M.P.* (*The Graphic*, 24 April 1880).

58 Ch. Reutlinger, *François Pierre Guillaume Guizot* (*The Graphic*, 19 September 1874); F. Hanfstaengl, *Richard Wagner – Musical Composer* (*The Graphic*, 30 August 1873).

line drawings which included portraits, ten of which appeared in *The Graphic* in 1875.[59] This portraits' folio was of upmost importance to van Gogh. When he began drawing in 1881 he told Theo that he felt 'confident of succeeding in becoming more or less capable of working in magazine or book illustration' and that he would 'probably also succeed in being able to do portraits'.[60] Years later, as he became a more confident draughtsman, he indicated that not only could he excel as a portraitist, but that he could begin to earn enough money not to have to rely on Theo's financial assistance:

> And then – there's more and more demand for portraits – and there aren't so very many who can do that, and I want to try to learn to render a head with character. I've become particularly keen on this recently because my grasp of colour is becoming sounder.[61]

Given his expressed aims, his reasons for dedicating a complete folio to portraits were clear. Similarly, it is understandable why his collection of portraits was so diverse, ranging from depictions of the working class to images of politicians and composers of renown. If van Gogh was going to become a portrait painter, he needed a wide range of examples to study.

Like portraiture, the broad theme of city scenes is obvious in van Gogh's collection. He spent a major part of his adult life in cities of various sizes, including The Hague, Brussels, Amsterdam, Paris and London. It was here that van Gogh experienced the diversity of characters and settings that defined the new metropolises. The city could be at once cosmopolitan and rich, and cruel and full of hardship. A gentleman wearing a top hat could stand alongside a factory worker or beggar. A walk through the slums could follow a delightful stroll through a city park. Van Gogh was aware of the contradictions of the city and collected images that represented its diversity, because they were familiar to him and reflected his empathy with city-dwellers and because they assisted him in his own creative endeavours.

---

59 *The Graphic*, 25 December 1875, title-page. Although, van Gogh owned two picture books by Caldecott, including *Old Christmas*, it is unlikely that he would have removed the images from the books to include in his print collection. He was more likely to have collected the images printed in *The Graphic*. He discussed these illustrations with van Rappard, further supporting this likelihood: 'I don't remember whether I've already written to you about *Old Christmas* [and *Bracebridge Hall*] from Washington Irving's *Sketchbook*, ill. by Caldecott. Two books at sixpence apiece, published by Macmillan & Co., London. In each a *hundred* small drawings, which are by Caldecott, but are sometimes so beautiful that one thinks of Menzel' (LT 309, volume 2, 260).

60 LT 162, volume 1, 263.

61 LT 470, volume 3, 188.

Although the folios are a wonderful introduction to the analysis of van Gogh's collection, they only provide a limited amount of information. Some themes definitely stand out above others – workers, peasants, miners and city scenes, for example. He was, however more eclectic in his collecting. Subjects range from social realist images to those depicting people viewing artworks at London's Royal Academy of Art. Likewise, even though van Gogh declared his disinclination to produce illustrations of current events, it did not prevent him from collecting images of Britain's Royal Family for example.[62] To complete a comprehensive analysis of its thematic structure, a broader view of van Gogh's collection needs to be embraced.

Social realism looms large as a theme in van Gogh's collection. As a movement within the context of the visual arts it was central to artistic endeavour in Victorian England. It was very much a theme of the time, arising out of the Industrial Revolution and its many outcomes. As Julian Treuherz has commented:

> In the nineteenth century, painters sought to bring into their art the new social and political concerns of the age of industrialization and democracy. Poor people were taken as subject matter for a new kind of art, in which social conscience was combined with a documentary interest in accurate recording. Realism was an art, which sought not just to represent things naturalistically, but also to depict the lowly and commonplace, correcting the historical bias in art towards the grand and spectacular; and social realism sought to do both in relation to modern social problems.[63]

The development of this movement in England was consistent with its rise in continental Europe. The work of English artists parallels the concerns of Europeans such as Jean-François Millet, Gustave Courbet, Honoré Daumier, Anton Mauve, Jozef Israëls and Jules Bastien-Lepage, all of whom van Gogh admired and held works by in his collection of black-and-white prints. Van Gogh aspired to recreate sentiments similar to those expressed by these artists in his own work, so he collected their prints to aid him in his work.

Artists such as Millet and Bastien-Lepage were painters, first and foremost, whose paintings were reproduced as black-and-white prints for a mass market. Millet's *The Sower*, for example, which van Gogh copied at the start of his artistic

62 W. Small, *The Prince of Wales in Ceylon: The Princes Highland* (*The Graphic*, 13 January 1876) remains in van Gogh's collection at the Van Gogh Museum.

63 Julian Treuherz (ed.), *Hard Times: Social Realism in Victorian Art* (Manchester: Manchester City Art Galleries, 1987), 9.

career, was painted in 1851, with a black-and-white reproduction engraved by Paul Edmé Lerat appearing two decades later, in 1873. In Victorian England, however, the social realist artistic movement centred on the work of artists contributing to illustrated newspapers such as *The Graphic* and *The Illustrated London News*. When *The Graphic* was launched in London in 1869, it had a major influence on the development of social realism. Artists such as Holl, Fildes and Herkomer, all favourites of van Gogh, were central to this growth. In contrast to their European counterparts, many of these artists produced black-and-white illustrations before attempting to render them as full-scale oil paintings, quite often for the annual Royal Academy exhibition. They often manipulated the image in the original print to make it more palatable for a painting-viewing public. Treuherz notes that 'what was acceptable on the page of a magazine was less so hanging on a wall'.[64] For example, in the painting *Eventide – A Scene in the Westminster Union* (1878), which was based on the illustration *Old Age – A Study at the Westminster Union*, Herkomer altered the facial expressions to a more cheerful disposition and added a vase of flowers to the composition to make the image more palatable.[65] Nevertheless, even though this was a deliberate sterilisation of images for a high-art context, the original black-and-white illustrations served the important purpose of introducing difficult subjects to the masses; they prepared the public to accept these paintings as works of art. Van Gogh's collection is populated with many such 'pre-painting' illustrations, including Herkomer's *At Death's Door* and *Sunday at Chelsea Hospital* (Figure 10) which, as noted by van Gogh, was first drawn for *The Graphic* but initially rejected, and Holl's two works *At a Railway Station – A Study*, *London Sketches: The Foundling* and *I am the Resurrection and the Life*.[66]

Perhaps the most famous illustration to go on to become a monumental painting was Fildes' *Houseless and Hungry* (Figure 7). It first appeared in the

64 Treuherz, *Hard Times*, 11.

65 H. Herkomer, *Eventide – A Scene in the Westminster Union*, 1878 (Walker Art Gallery, Liverpool) and *Old Age – A Study at the Westminster Union* (*The Graphic*, 1 April 1877).

66 H. Herkomer, *At Death's Door* (*The Graphic*, 26 August 1876), reproduced as the painting *At Death's Door*, 1876 (private collection); *Sunday at Chelsea Hospital* (*The Graphic*, 18 February 1871), reproduced as the painting *The Last Muster*, 1875 (National Museums and Galleries on Merseyside). Van Gogh possessed both the first 'rough sketch' of the final painting and the cropped image of the two old men, which was reproduced in *The Graphic* in 1875 (LT R20, Volume 3, p. 350). F. Holl, *London Sketches: The Foundling* (*The Graphic*, 26 April 1873), reproduced as the painting *Deserted*, 1874 (private collection); *At a Railway Station – A Study* (*The Graphic*, 10 February 1872), reproduced as the painting *Leaving Home*, 1873 (private collection); *I am the Resurrection and the Life* (*The Graphic*, 17 August 1872), reproduced as the painting *I am the Resurrection and the Life*, 1872 (location unknown).

inaugural issue of *The Graphic* and was realised as a painting almost five years later. Subsequently titled *Applicant for Admission to a Casual Ward* (1874), the painting was deemed so controversial when it was first exhibited that it had to be surrounded by a barrier and patrolled by policemen; the confronting subject matter, the coarseness of its execution and the dominant figure of a homeless mother and child ensured a rowdy response.[67]

The practice of artists, such as Holl, Herkomer, Fildes, Small, Walker, Doré, Gavarni, Green, Fitzgerald, and many others, contributing to illustrated newspapers was steeped in a social realist conceptual paradigm. They tackled subjects that were often the outcomes of industrialisation. As champions of public campaigns and philanthropic action, the newspapers were voices highlighting the social problems depicted by their artists. *The Graphic* was established with the stated aim of encouraging the presentation of social realist images by true artists at the highest level attainable. Fildes' *Houseless and Hungry* (Figure 7) is a case in point. It depicts a crowd of poor homeless wretches looking for accommodation on a cold London night. It was a popular theme in the visual arts, as were those focusing on the effects of alcoholism, sweatshops, crime, childhood sickness, illness and mortality, poverty, unemployment, emigration, death in the workplace, and the documentation of a changing way of life. All of these subjects appear frequently in van Gogh's collection, to the extent that it can be suggested that social realism was the umbrella concept informing his print collecting. However, to conclude that it is the thematic mainstay of the collection would not explain fully van Gogh's choices. Many illustrations in the newspapers were not social realist in nature. Why, then, are there so few of these images in the collection? We need to view the collection through van Gogh's eyes, rather than from the newspaper editors' perspective to refine further the overarching themes of van Gogh's collection.

Two key themes beyond social realism influenced van Gogh's choices and define his print collection. The first is the rural–urban dichotomy, which was not only a significant factor in society at the time but also a reflection of van Gogh's life experience. The second theme reflects van Gogh's moral ideals, established in his youth and firmly entrenched by the time he took up his pencil. His experience as the son of a pastor and his years of religious enthusiasm, including his unsuccessful attempt to join the clergy, were crucial to his choices in developing the collection.

---

67 L. Fildes, *Applicant for Admission to a Casual Ward*, 1874 (Royal Holloway College, University of London, Egham, Surrey).

The rural–urban dichotomy was more apparent during the late nineteenth century than it is today and was most pronounced in countries like England and France, where thousands migrated from the country to the burgeoning metropolises of London and Paris, with far-reaching consequences. One consequence was increasing poverty, and another, the growth of the slums in the city. Conversely, there was a great rise in wealth and in popular leisure and pastimes, with parks emerging in cities and more theatres opening. Forms of employment also changed; for example, office workers began to populate the city. Differences in fashion between city dwellers and their rural counterparts became more pronounced and identifiable. Perhaps the greatest difference, though, was not so much physical, but a difference in perception of the city and the country. The country was viewed as peaceful, cleaner and morally superior, whereas cities were viewed as busy and chaotic, crime-ridden and morally corrupt. People living in the country were considered in almost religious terms, while city folk were seen as seduced by excess and indulging in vice. The views of van Gogh, who had first-hand experience of this dichotomy, conformed to this perception. Writing to Theo on his arrival in London in November 1873, he identified the difference between the city and the country: 'I can't tell you how interesting it is to see London and the trade and the way of life here, which are so very different from ours'.[68] Van Gogh's life experience until this point was based on being born in and then brought up in small rural towns, and he still considered himself of rural stock. He had lived from 1869 to 1873 in The Hague, which was not a metropolis but had a sizeable population with a bourgeois component. He eventually came to a negative view of city life, expressed in 1888 in his justification for leaving Paris: 'It seems to me almost impossible to be able to work in Paris, unless you have a refuge in which to recover and regain your peace of mind and self-composure. Without that, you'd be bound to get utterly numbed'.[69] Soon after, he reinforced the benefit of a change of scene from the overbearing city to the idyllic countryside, writing: 'At times it seems to me that my blood is more or less ready to start circulating again, which wasn't the case lately in Paris, I really couldn't stand it any more'.[70] Months later, in May 1888, van Gogh recommended to Theo 'one year of living in the country and close to nature' as a remedy for his ill-health.[71]

68 LT 15, volume 1, 40.

69 LT 577, volume 4, 12.

70 LT 578, volume 4, 13.

71 LT 611, volume 4, 90.

Further evidence of van Gogh's view of the difference between city and country can be seen in his work, best illustrated in a comparison of his choice of subject matter for drawings while living in The Hague with his choice for works executed during his brief stay in Drenthe, a rural province in the north east of the Netherlands. In 1882 when his Uncle Cor commissioned him to produce a series of drawings of The Hague, van Gogh decided to concentrate on everyday scenes of the city and its changing face. His illustrations depicted people in the Jewish quarter, shoppers at the front of a bakery, workers, laundry hanging in rear yards, and gas tanks and factories on the city's outskirts. His sought to convey a sense of life in a city like The Hague. By contrast, the intention and approach that shaped his work in Drenthe was quite different. A year before he traveled to the region, he told van Rappard what he expected to see: 'I imagine it as being like North Brabant *when I was young*, about 20 years ago'.[72] He lamented changes that had affected so many small rural settings, but expressed the hope that Drenthe remained pure and old-worldly:

> The part of Brabant I know well has since changed enormously through land reclamation and industry. It isn't without a certain nostalgia that I now see a new tavern with a red tiled roof at many places where I remember seeing a wattle-and-daub hut with a moss-covered, thatched roof.
>
> Since then have come sugar-beet factories, railways, heath reclamations, &c., which are much less picturesque.
>
> Well, what will remain in me is something of the austere poetry of the true heathland. And it seems that the true heath still exists in Drenthe just as it used to in Brabant.[73]

His thoughts a year before he went to Drenthe clearly suggest what it was that he was looking for – the unspoilt and yet to be corrupted – sentiments further reinforced when he tells Theo his reasons for making the trip: 'I need it to make progress. Drenthe, Katwijk, Brabant, I don't mind. To stay for a time with a farmer or someone, far, far away in the country, far enough away for nature there to be real'.[74] When he finally arrived in Drenthe, van Gogh compared his surroundings with English prints: 'Well, it's very beautiful

72 LT 256, volume 2, 133.

73 LT 256, volume 2, 133.

74 LT 380, volume 2, 414.

inside these huts, dark as a cave. Drawings by certain English artists who have worked on the moors in Ireland most realistically convey what I observe'.[75]

Perceptions of the city and the country as two opposing worlds is at the heart of van Gogh's print collection. It clearly defined the kind of prints that entered his collection and underpins one of its key thematic aspects. The view of the country as a morally superior environment and the city as a place of corruption was, and continues to be, widely held. The illustrated newspapers espoused it, shaping van Gogh's attitude as much as his personal experience. *The Graphic*'s passages of text accompanying two images, *London Sketches – A Country Visitor* and *Heads of the People – "The Agricultural Labourer", Sunday* (Figure 37), are cases in point.[76] Of the first, *The Graphic* wrote:

> An imaginative person may construct a complete novelette from this picture. Here, we may suppose, is Polly Hedgerow, who has passed her entire existence hitherto "in the shires," "all among the barley." But at last she has been drawn up by the power of that mighty magnet called London. Perhaps her father is dead; perhaps he has been ruined by the perpetual rains; at any rate she has come up to town to seek employment, and she is being escorted through the streets by her town-bred cousin, Miss Minnie Diaper. Observe the contrast between Polly's serviceable shoes, stuff gown, plain cloak, and uncompromising bonnet, and Minnie's natty Balmoral boots, smart petticoat, extensive chignon, and "Brighton cloud" round her neck… Such simple lasses as Polly Hedgerow in our picture are rather exceptional, but we do not say they are non-existent; and wherever they are they deserve to prosper, because they have an element of contentment and stability in their characters which preserves them from the hollow excitements and frivolous pleasures which too often prove the ruin of the young maidens in great cities.[77]

In the description of the second, country inhabitants were spoken of in religious terms:

> No more worthy men are to be found in the world than some of our labourers. They spend lives of unceasing toil, and often contrive, by dint of self-denial and frugality, to bring up large families decently on

75 LT 386, volume 3, 13.

76 G. Pinwell, *London Sketches – A Country Visitor* (*The Graphic*, 22 February 1873) and H. Herkomer, *Heads of The People – "The Agricultural Labourer Sunday"* (*The Graphic*, 23 October 1875).

77 *The Graphic*, 22 February 1873, 167–70.

> means which to the well-to-do seem fabulously small. In the widest sense of the term, they are by no means uneducated men, for spending most part of their lives out of doors, they acquire a vast fund of practical knowledge concerning animals, plants and the weather, besides which, their occupations are far more varied than those of many so called "intelligent" artisans. With books, it may be admitted, the old generation of rural poor are but scantily acquainted. If however, such a patriarch as is here represented can read, we may be pretty sure that he spends some of his well-earned leisure over the well-worn pages of his family Bible, and that, poor and humble as his lot may be, he derives thence lessons of cheerfulness and contentment, as well as a foretaste of the happy future which awaits him in the next state of being.[78]

The picture painted by *The Graphic* of the rural population is one of wide-eyed conservatism, dignity in poverty, sacrifice, resourcefulness and simple piety. Worthy, even admirable, the rural population are, nonetheless, perceived as intellectually inferior in the context of the modern world, but they are in touch with nature. In contrast, the city population are better-off financially, but wasteful, their occupational experience is limited but more focused, their choice of reading is greater, favouring literature more than the Bible. Ultimately, however, for all the positives, city-dwellers were viewed as more likely to be insincere and to indulge in vices and be tempted by corrupt pleasures, in comparison to their rural counterparts.

Van Gogh's understanding of the nature of cities and the way they were depicted can be traced back to as early as 1877, when he wrote to Theo about Gustave Doré's images from the publication *London, a Pilgrimage*.[79] He suggested that both he and Theo subscribe to the weekly Dutch publication *Katholieke Illustratie*, as it contained 'Doré's prints of London – the wharves on the Thames, Westminster, Whitechapel, the Underground railways'.[80] Years later, at the height of his collecting, he discussed these important illustrations again, this time with van Rappard: 'the other day I saw the whole of Doré's works on London – I say, that's splendidly beautiful and noble in sentiment – for example in the room in the night refuge for beggars, which you have, I believe, and otherwise can still get'.[81] Doré depicted various aspects of London life as experienced by a foreigner, similar to van Gogh's experience.

---

78 *The Graphic*, 9 October 1875, 350.

79 Blanchard Jerrold & Gustave Doré, *London, a Pilgrimage* (London, 1872).

80 LT 101. volume 1, 138.

81 LT 267, volume 2, 160.

There were illustrations of life on the docks and the River Thames, factory life and industries, the lives of both the poor and the middle class, horse races, boat races, the opera, places of worship and places of drinking. Doré was criticised at the time for concentrating on the darker sides of London life, as noted by the *Westminster Review* critic: 'Doré gives us sketches in which the commonest, the vulgarest external features are set down'.[82] While a significant number of his images conveyed London's bleaker side, Doré did present a broad view of the city, which appealed to van Gogh's sensibilities and is reflected in the choices he made for his collection of prints. There are images of the wealth and opportunity that moving to the city afforded – of the rich taking leisurely strolls through parks or at the seaside; of people in their comfortable homes or enjoying leisure time in dining halls, reading rooms and salons; of ladies at leisure; of people playing musical instruments in domestic settings; of theatre and music hall audiences; and of cultural pursuits like visiting art galleries and zoos.[83] But van Gogh also collected images of the darker side of city life – of lodging houses, foundling hospitals and philanthropic organisations, soup kitchens, the lost and homeless, beggars, and street scenes of the poor.[84]

The Graphic series 'Sketches in London' matched Doré's illustrations from *London, a Pilgrimage* by offering an overview of this diversity of city life. Eighteen prints from this series can be identified in van Gogh's collection.[85] Illustrations of popular recreational activities enjoyed by the wealthy are plentiful. James Linton's *London Sketches – At a Music Hall* depicts well-dressed couples mingling and enjoying the social delights of a music-filled gallery.[86] In *London Sketches – A Waxwork Exhibition*, a young boy listens attentively to

---

82 Doré, Gustave, *Doré's London: All 180 Illustrations from* London, a Pilgrimage (London: Dover, 2004).Publisher's note.

83 Examples include: F. Holl, *Wintering at Hastings: A Sketch on the Esplanade* (*The Graphic*, 15 March 1873); J.E. Millais, *Christmas Story Telling* (*The Illustrated London News*, 20 December 1862); G. du Maurier, *Battledoor and Shuttlecock* (*The Graphic*, 13 May 1871); G. du Maurier, *A Musical Rehearsal* (*The Graphic*, 14 September 1872); J.D. Linton, *London Sketches – At a Music Hall* (*The Graphic*, 5 April 1873); C. Green, *Holiday Folks at the National Gallery* (*The Graphic*, 3 August 1872).

84 Examples include: T. Green, *Sunday at the Foundling Hospital* (*The Illustrated London News*, 7 December 1872); L. Fildes, *Houseless and Hungry* (*The Graphic*, 4 December 1869); G.H. Garraway, *Beggars in Brittany* (*The Graphic*, 3 March 1872); E. Buckman, *People Waiting for Ration Tickets in Paris* (*The Graphic*, 19 November 1870).

85 Some can be found in the extant collection and some mentioned in van Gogh's letters. A number of double-page illustrations have not been identified but could well have been part of van Gogh's collection.

86 J.D. Linton, *London Sketches – At a Music Hall* (*The Graphic*, 5 April 1873).

his father, while a lady and her daughter stand at the rear enjoying the exhibition.[87] There are also scenes of London street life, such as James Macbeth's *London Sketches – A Horse Down*, showing a horse fallen on a treacherous road in front of an astonished crowd, while *London Sketches – The Battle of the Pavements* shows workers laying the newly invented asphalt wood paving along London's main thoroughfares.[88] Holl's *Sketches in London – A Flower Girl* illustrates one of many types of street sellers benefiting from the city's burgeoning population.[89] Vices that tempted city-dwellers were also illustrated bringing contrast to the positive and homely images of London life. *Sketches in London – Before the Bar* shows a worker enjoying his 'supper beer', which ultimately led to drunkenness.[90] Complementary images included those of urban poverty. Holl's *London Sketches – The Foundling* depicts a police officer cradling a homeless baby, while a crowd watches on.[91] In the background the mother leans against the river barricade, deciding against jumping to her death as her motherly instincts takeover. Young, homeless and poor, she has no other option but to desert the child in the hope that it will be found, adopted and cared for. The text accompanying the images intones, 'this picture represents one of the scenes in a tragic drama which is being perpetually performed by a continuous succession of hapless actors'.[92] Undoubtedly this image would have connected with van Gogh's Evangelical outlook; he would

87 M.G. Stone, *London Sketches – A Waxwork Exhibition* (*The Graphic*, 14 December 1872).

88 J. Macbeth, *London Sketches – A Horse Down*, *The Graphic* (21 December 1872); E.F. Brewtnall, *London Sketches – The Battle of the Pavements* (*The Graphic*, 24 February 1877).

89 F. Holl, *Sketches in London – A Flower Girl* (*The Graphic*, 22 June 1872). For *The Graphic*, the flower girl symbolised the opportunities of industrialisation: 'Flowers, we know, existed long before railways, but to the dwellers in great cities railways have multiplied flowers fifty fold, because the swiftness of our present means of communication has so immensely extended the area of production'. The flower girl crossed class lines and represented for many a rite of passage: 'There are flower girls of various grades. There are well-dressed young ladies, who abide in trim shops, and who fasten yellow roses into the coats of young dandies at two shillings apiece, and there are ragged, miserable children who merely use the flowers which they carry as an excuse for beggary. The flower girl in our picture belongs to neither of these extremes. She is a decent, honest girl, tidily though humbly clad, who really wishes to sell her sweet-scented wares. Most likely she belongs to the Irish persuasion, and when she gets older, unless she marries a man who is both self-denying and prosperous, she will probably abandon the flower business to younger competitors, and come out with a matronly basket of apples and oranges' (*The Graphic*, 22 June 1872, p. 574).

90 A. Boyd Houghton, *Sketches in London – Before the Bar* (*The Graphic*, 11 May 1872).

91 F. Holl, *London Sketches – The Foundling* (*The Graphic*, 26 April 1873).

92 *The Graphic*, 26 April 1873, p. 385.

not have passed judgement on this mother, but would have felt empathy and dedication to help. Furthermore, this image, which he listed with others in the context of 'various sketches of poor neighbourhoods' reminded him of his time in London.[93] 'For me', he wrote to van Rappard, 'looking through them brought back all the memories of London 10 years ago',[94]

Many of the illustrations from this series juxtaposed the wealthy with the poor, further reinforcing the complexities of city life. Although there was a class system, it could not separate people in the hurly-burly of the streets. *London Sketches – Curds and Whey in St James's Park* (Figure 2) shows a myriad of people coming together to enjoy a mug of fresh milk supplied by farmers from the country. Following a tradition spanning two centuries, the image contrasts rural simplicity with the wealth and magnificence of London. It also brings together the different residents of London to enjoy the farmers' offerings – the wealthy, invalids, workers, children, both homeless and otherwise, and those who would rather have a ginger beer than a mug of milk. This egalitarianism appealed to van Gogh.

Throughout van Gogh's collection prints that concentrated on the various aspects of city life are to be found. Van Gogh was not only interested in the city's darker side of the city; he also collected images that portrayed city life as he knew and experienced it. He identified readily with these works. Moreover, for an artist who wished to build a career portraying scenes of everyday life, the subjects of his chosen prints were broad. They informed his choice of subject matter when he began his own career and helped him decide how to tackle those subjects.

Although industrial and mining centres like Sheffield and Manchester were not metropolises like London, they represented much that was new in the world. They were incarnations of the gains made by industrial society. Furthermore, they produced objects and materials that were often purchased and used by growing cities. The illustrated newspapers published hundreds of images depicting the industrial progress of these cities. Like the images of the rural country and associated farmers they published, they were often presented with empathy and in a context of wonder and pride. The industries and associated technological advances achieved in the regions fascinated the population at large, and van Gogh was no exception. As he had a deep empathy for the workers in extractive and manufacturing industries, it is of no surprise to find a large set of images of miners and associated industries

93 LT 303, volume 2, 241.

94 LT 301, volume 2, 241.

in van Gogh's print collection, which reflect his personal experience of the Borinage where he had lived and worked amongst the miners and witnessed first-hand their tiring and dangerous work.[95] There are images of accidents, of life underground, of the factory floor and of wondrous industrial achievements, which are integral to van Gogh's collection, because they illustrated the good and bad of modernity. They complemented images of the city in his collections and counterposed those of the country.

The prints in van Gogh's collection that depicted the country were rarely as multi-faceted as the images of the city and industry. Almost exclusively, they promoted a view of farmers, peasants and rural people living a pleasant life, close to nature and as the worthiest of citizens.[96] Where hardship was depicted, as in the many images of the Irish peasants still extant in van Gogh's collection, it was depicted with empathy and reverence bordering on religious. Gordon Thompson's *The Good Shepherd* (Figure 6) represents both the positive view and religious sentiment of the country and its population.

A shepherd on a lush hillside watches a flock of sheep. The animals and their human companion seem at one with nature, contented and healthy. The sky is clear, the space uncluttered, and a lightness dominates the composition. This lightness is in direct contrast to images of city life, which were often dark and foreboding, as, for example, in Walker's *The Harbour of Refuge* (Figure 20) whose background landscape is dark to the point of minimising detail.

The religious sentiment of the shepherd in Thompson's work, reinforced by the inclusion of a crucifix amongst the roaming sheep, would not have been lost on the viewer, especially someone like van Gogh. Other prints, while not so overtly religious, promoted a positive view of the country, including *An English Ploughing Match* by one of van Gogh's favourite artists, William Small.[97] Small captured the essence of the hard-working farmer in his illustration and depicted the country landscape as bounteous and clean. The fields roll into the distance, empty of any signs of industrial progress. The farmers follow their horse-drawn ploughs, which hark back to pre-industrial times and suggest an admiration of manual labour. On their own, these rural images

95 For instance, van Gogh wrote to his family about the mining disaster at the Agrappe colliery in Frameries on 17 April 1879 (LT 151, fn 3). For van Gogh's experience of the Belgian Borinage mining districts, see Sjraar van Heugten (ed.), *Van Gogh: The Birth of an Artist* (Brussels: Mercatorfonds, 2015), particularly Pierre Tilly and Pierre-Olivier Laloux 'Vincent van Gogh in the Borinage'.

96 The simplicity and purity of rural life was captured in Flora Thompson's autobiographical trilogy, *Lark Rise to Candleford* (London: Oxford University Press, 1945).

97 W. Small, *An English Ploughing Match* (*The Graphic*, 13 March 1875).

seem not to have much in common with those of the city, but in the context of van Gogh's print collection they are closely intertwined. In order to view the city as exciting and corrupt in equal parts, van Gogh needed the idyllic and pious representation of the country.

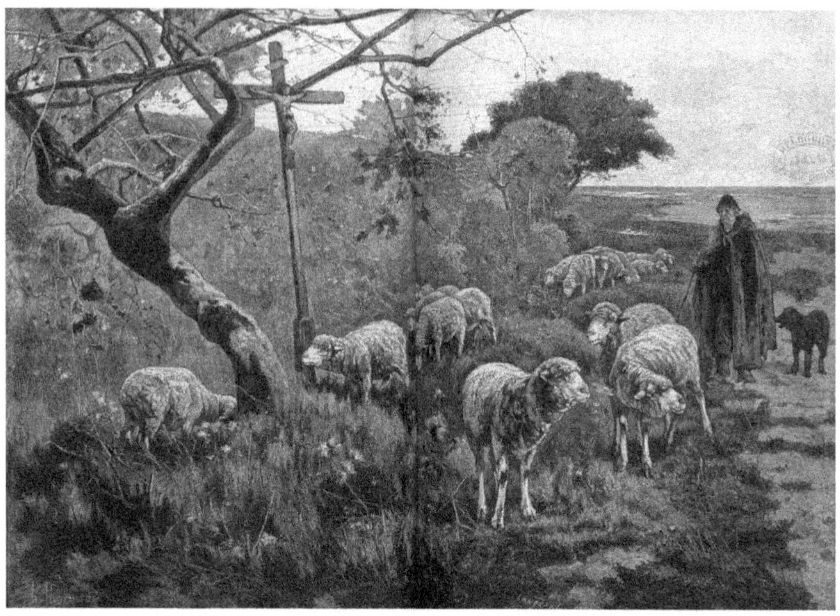

Figure 6. Gordon Thompson, *The Good Shepherd* (*The Illustrated London News*, 9 August 1884).

Throughout his life van Gogh experienced both city and rural lifestyles. He considered himself to have morals and ideals similar to those of country people, but was at the same time very much a cosmopolitan with contemporary views. He longed to live in the country, sourcing its subjects for his work, but realised the importance of the city, where most of his professional peers lived and thrived. His choice of prints reflected the complexity of his situation. Van Gogh was fully aware of the contrasts between those living in the cities and those living on the land and this awareness of difference informed his choice of prints and the way he categorised his collection. There are as many images of the city in his print collection as there are of rural life, in spite of the fact that van Gogh is viewed principally as a painter of landscapes that presented rolling country populated by the peasantry. He did, however, spend considerable time in several cities and was influenced by what he saw and experienced there.

The many illustrations of the diversity of city life parallel and celebrate van Gogh the cosmopolitan. Although he returned in later life to the countryside in France, becoming thoroughly reacquainted and enamoured with it, as a young city-dweller van Gogh embraced city living. In England as a young art dealer he revelled in the hum of the world's greatest metropolis. He wore his top hat and enjoyed the public parks with the middle class for whose leisure they had been laid out. He revelled in the delights of Paris, visiting its cafés, brothels, art galleries, theatre, ballet and cabarets. He enthusiastically joined his bohemian peers of Montmartre. As a budding artist, he ensured he was well versed in what the newspapers demanded from their illustrators, at the same time remaining true to what he believed were worthy subjects. From these experiences emerged the strong thematic structure in his collection and ultimately his own work – a structure that celebrated the dichotomy between the city and the countryside.

The second defining theme of the collection reflects van Gogh's moral ideals, shaped initially by institutional religion and later by his idiosyncratic empathy with the lower and working classes and the ills they faced in a changing world. Van Gogh collected works that addressed his views and sentiments overtly and others that he interpreted within his moralistic and idealistic parameters.

The van Gogh family had a long tradition of involvement in the church, which had a lasting impression on the artist. Generations of van Goghs – Vincent's father, uncle and grandfather – were pastors in the Dutch Reformed Church; his father was one of the first graduates of the Groningen School of Theology, a modernising and moderate Calvinist group within the Reformed Church. The central premise of this school of thought was the life led, rather than doctrine.[98] Following the example set by Jesus was of greater importance than the texts prescribed by the Church. Van Gogh's father was a shining example of this creed. The grocer whose store was opposite the parsonage occupied by the van Goghs recalled that Theodorus van Gogh would give money for food to be distributed to the poor Catholic families. Marc Tralbaut wrote that his research repeatedly turned up descriptions of Theodorus van Gogh as 'the image of goodness'.[99]

The young Vincent remained devout after he had left the family home at the age of sixteen to take up his apprenticeship as an art dealer. He attended

98 One tenet of the group was 'not the doctrine but the life' (James Hutton Mackay, *Religious Thought in Holland during the Nineteenth Century* (London: Hodder and Stoughton, 1911), 50).

99 Marc Edo Tralbaut, *Vincent van Gogh* (London: Macmillan, 1969), 20.

church regularly and surrounded himself with religious images. His religious commitment grew over time and by the age of 23 he had left the world of art for a new vocation as a man of the church, following in the footsteps of his father and grandfather. That he never fully realised this vocation is well documented. Van Gogh's religious zeal went far beyond the standards accepted by the church, even of those of evangelical persuasion or as progressive as the Groningen School of the Dutch Reformed Church. The years that he devoted to becoming a preacher and to the study of how to lead an exemplary Christian life of sacrifice and support for one's fellow man were to have a lasting impact on him. They shaped his view of the world, his humanity and his faith, and eventually his print collection and artistic practice.

Although van Gogh grew up in the household of a Dutch Reform pastor and studied its traditions in order to join its preaching fraternity, the religious views he held as an adult had more in common with the writings of John Bunyan and Thomas à Kempis. He was an avid reader of Bunyan's *The Pilgrim's Progress* and Thomas à Kempis' *The Imitation of Christ*, a foundational text of the Groningen School. He told Theo that *The Pilgrim's Progress* was 'very worthwhile reading' and that he loved it 'with heart and soul'.[100] Of Thomas à Kempis he wrote:

> there are words so deep and serious that one cannot read them without emotion and almost fear, at least if one reads them with a sincere desire for light and truth, that language is indeed the eloquence that wins hearts because it comes from the heart.[101]

Both of these authors preach that one must endure pain and suffering in order to reach the afterlife, and both encourage leading a life that closely parallels the example set by Christ of self-denial, sorrow, pain, helping others, forgiveness, humility and remaining on a continuous journey to God and the afterlife. While the theology of van Gogh's father's church was framed in similar ideas, it was overlaid by the constant caveat that one should aim to be a respectable gentleman and not descend to a level of hardship and struggle that might have beset others in one's congregation. It was in this context that van Gogh's religious sensibilities moved away from those of his father and became increasingly aligned with a literal, even didactic, reading of the teachings of Bunyan. Van Gogh admired Bunyan's focus on helping the poor and the humble worker, on his disdain for material wealth, and his view of God

100 LT 99, volume 1, 133.

101 LT 129, volume 1, 190.

as a source of love, rather than as a deity to be feared. Over time, he adopted strict observance of these ideas as his modus operandi as a preacher.[102]

Although van Gogh abandoned organised religion after he failed to get a permanent position as a clergyman, he did not renounce his spirituality and firm beliefs. The morals and idealism he had derived from his upbringing, experience, and reading of Bunyan and Thomas à Kempis stayed with him throughout his life. As Kathleen Erickson noted 'his break was not a theological but a deeply personal one, rooted in a fundamental mistrust of the clergy'[103] – mistrust that led him to refer to the clergy as *le rayon noir* (the black ray), which he felt his father represented.[104] For van Gogh the clergymen's God was 'as dead as a doornail'.[105]

Religion and art were the two constants in van Gogh's life, to the extent that his artistic career can, in many ways, be seen as an attempt to preach from the easel. Remembering van Gogh years after his death, M.B. Mendes da Costa, van Gogh's Latin and Greek teacher in 1877, noted that van Gogh always had art close by:

> As I was not so busy in those days, he often stayed talking for a while after the lesson, and naturally we often discussed his former profession, the art dealing business. He had kept quite a number of the prints which he had collected in those days, little lithographs after paintings, etc. He brought them to show me repeatedly, but they were always completely spoiled: the white borders were literally covered with quotations from Thomas à Kempis or the Bible, more or less connected with the subject, which he had scribbled all over them.[106]

---

102 Deborah Silverman argues that Bunyan attached salvation specifically to the poor and the lower classes: 'Material deprivation gave the lower social orders a natural spiritual advantage in this theology of self-denial, humility and worldly renunciation' (Silverman, 'Pilgrim's Progress and Vincent van Gogh's Metier', in Martin Bailey, *Van Gogh: Portrait of the Artist as a Young Man in England* (London: Barbican Art Gallery, 1992), 97). Van Gogh's application of this in his own life was most evident in his work as an evangelist in the Borinage and, years later, as an artist.

103 Kathleen Powers Erickson, *At Eternity's Gate: The Spiritual Vision of Vincent van Gogh* (Grand Rapids, MI: W.B. Eerdmans Publishing, 1998) 61.

104 'If prejudices, which Pa has carried with him throughout his life with as assiduousness worthy of a better cause, stand in his way – to me he's a black ray. The only criticism I have of Pa is: why isn't he a white ray?' (LT 403, volume 3, 60).

105 LT 193, volume 1, 340.

106 Letter from Mendes da Costa to *Het Algemeen Handelsblad*, Amsterdam, 2 December 1910, in *Van Gogh's letters*, at http://webexhibits.org/vangogh/letter/6/etc-122a.htm, accessed 16 August 2019.

Van Gogh's tendency seems to have been to naturalise religion, by depicting God and religious sentiment not didactically but by turning to the natural world. During the sermon he delivered at the Wesleyan Methodist Church in Richmond in October 1876, he referenced George Boughton's 1874 painting *God Speed!* and its depiction of a golden-lit landscape. Years later, entrenched as an artist, he was still able to bring together nature, art and religion to articulate his views on how best to compose modern-day spiritual paintings. Writing to his sister Wil about Émile Bernard's forays into painting 'bizarre Biblical subjects', he argued that the naturalist symbolism employed by the English pre-Raphaelites resulted in artworks that were more serious and conscientious.[107]

This deep spirituality is reflected in the prints van Gogh collected. At times he imbued images with a religious sentiment, while on other occasions he admired and collected illustrations because of their innate sympathy, empathy and humility – qualities he found admirable and reflective of his religious beliefs. For van Gogh the black-and-white illustrators surpassed what the church represented and had given him:

> What I value in Herkomer, in Fildes, in Holl and the other founders of The Graphic, why I find and will continue to find them even more sympathetic than Gavarni and Daumier, is that, while the latter seem to view society more with mockery, the former, like such men as Millet, Breton, De Groux, Israëls, chose subjects which are – while as *true* as those of Gav. or Daum. – have something noble and in which there's a more serious sentiment. That, above all, must remain, it seems to me. An artist need not be a minister or a collector in church, but he must have a warm heart for people, and I find it a noble thing that, for example, no winter passed without The Graphic doing something to keep alive the sympathy for the poor.[108]

This sense of empathy for the underprivileged – 'a warm heart for people' as van Gogh put it – is a key element throughout his print collection. The underprivileged ranged from peasants and workers of the land to beggars and the homeless who were a regular part of city life, themes reflected in van Gogh's list of folios. Many prints in the collection depict subjects that conform to van Gogh's view of who was underprivileged and worth commemorating in art. Among them were miners, factory workers, fishermen and farmers, Irish types

107 LT 827, volume 5, 162.

108 LT 278, volume 2, 188.

(that is, displaced people in Ireland), and the poor of London's Whitechapel and Seven Dials districts. Fildes' *Houseless and Hungry* (Figure 7), Buckman's *People Waiting for Ration Tickets in Paris* (Figure 8) and Small's *A Queue in Paris* (Figure 31) all show groups of homeless and destitute people seeking assistance in big cities. Van Gogh described Fildes' illustration, one of the first he was to locate, as 'superb'.[109] He also revered William Small.[110] Of Buckman and his peers, van Gogh wrote, 'one is astonished by that steadiness of the drawing, that personal character, that serious of approach, and that fathoming and presentation of the most everyday figures and subjects found on the street, on the market, in a hospital or orphanage'.[111]

A Christmas drawing reproduced in *The Graphic* reveals the black-and-white artists' respect and sympathy for the underprivileged. *Our Artist's Christmas Entertainment – Arrival of the Visitors* by Arthur Boyd Houghton depicts a procession of men visiting his studio for some Christmas cheer.[112] Van Gogh greatly admired the sentiment of this illustration, describing it to Theo as including street urchins, invalids, a blind man and others.[113] Proud of its artist's reputation for working with and assisting the poor, *The Graphic* published a letter of thanks from the illustration's models, who were inmates of the Islington Workhouse.

> Gentlemen,
>
> We, your Humble Servants wish to return our Greatfull thanks for the kind reception we received from you on Tuesday the third of December, we returned home quite comfortable before five o'clock all safe. We remain your most Humble Servants the Cripple Leading the Blind the Blind Carrying a Cripple and Leading the Blind.
>
> THOMAS WAGER
> JAMES LARGE
> WILLIAM EIKING
> JOHN BAYLISS
> with Three Good Hearty Cheers![114]

109 LT 199, volume 2, 18.

110 LT 304, volume 2, 242–51.

111 LT 358, volume 2, 364.

112 A. Boyd Houghton, *Our Artist's Christmas Entertainment – Arrival of the Visitors* (*The Graphic*, 28 December 1872).

113 LT 305, volume 2, 252.

114 *The Graphic*, 28 December 1872, 599.

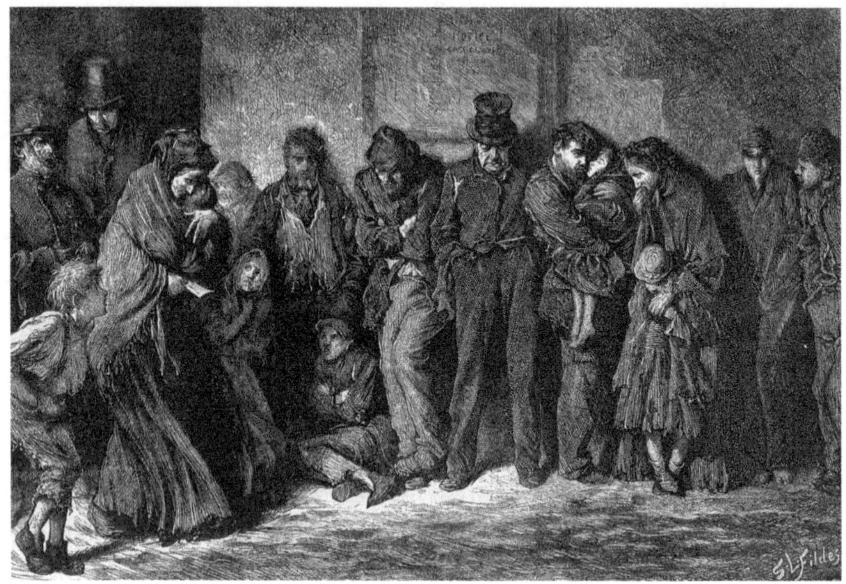

Figure 7. Luke Fildes, *Houseless and Hungry* (*The Graphic*, 4 December 1869).

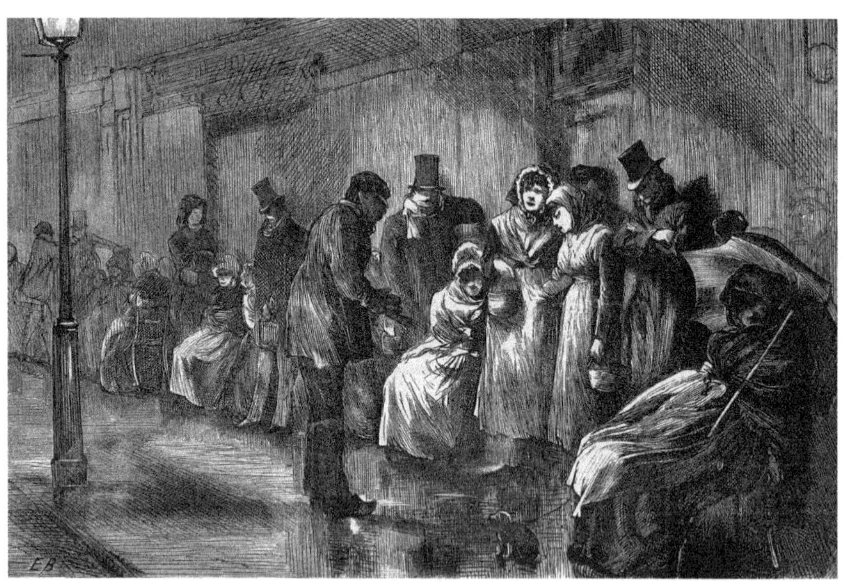

Figure 8. Edward Buckman, *People Waiting for Ration Tickets in Paris* (*The Graphic*, 19 November 1870).

The sentiment of the drawing, the enthusiasm of the models and the generosity of the artist appealed to van Gogh; there was no exploitation in the relationship. Like the message preached by Bunyan and Thomas à Kempis, the illustration was a picture of kindness, of supporting your fellow man, of humility and true nobility. Van Gogh could relate to such an image, as it reinforced his views and morals. Moreover, these types of illustrations were examples that showed it was possible to preach without being a preacher.

Walker's *The Harbour of Refuge* (FIGURE 20), more poignant than Boyd Houghton's illustration, is likewise full of empathy. *The Graphic* described it as having 'a considerable power of exciting sympathy in the spectator'.[115] Mother and daughter walk arm-in-arm in the gardens of an almshouse. Simple in composition, it succinctly captures the poles of life – youth and age. For van Gogh it went further. It was caring and noble, and paralleled his earlier life when he too had aimed to help the old and the disenfranchised. Moreover, it depicted the state of the poor and the need to look after them; van Gogh could not 'imagine anything more beautiful'.[116]

The question of how best to care for the poor and the homeless in the mid-nineteenth century was a key concern for policy-makers, institutions such as the church and the Salvation Army, and anyone enlightened enough to be concerned about the plight of their fellow citizens in dramatically changing times. Van Gogh had experienced first-hand the negative outcomes of industrialisation and had witnessed efforts to counter the challenges they posed. Workhouses, lodging houses and shelters, and the perpetuation of almshouses had been promoted as solutions, but by van Gogh's time there was widespread criticism of them. At the heart of these initiatives was the Victorian concept of charity and helping the deserving poor. Bound up within this philosophy was the need to change the habits of those being helped. According to Jerry White, such reform had 'manners at its heart', and was supported by developments that included:

> Workhouses visiting, bringing the gospel to paupers; Sunday-night services in theatres, claiming the platform for God; working men's clubs, serving coffee and lemonade but no beer; orphanages and children's homes; gospel halls and meeting rooms; rescue homes for prostitutes; evening and debating classes, hot on elocution; industrial schools for reforming thieves; Christmas dinners for children; thieves' suppers; more hospitals and dispensaries; help to the blind, deaf and

115 *The Graphic*, 7 April 1877, 328.

116 LT 321, volume 2, 283.

> dumb; infant crèches and nurseries; assisted emigration for discharged prisoners, prostitutes and others; penny banks and loan societies; tracts and cheap wholesome literature; homes for the domestic servants between berths; homes for the respected aged poor; shoe-black battalions and street orderlies; temperance societies; the Young Men's Christian Association (1844) and Young Women's Christian Association (1855); societies for persecuting brothels; night refuges for homeless adults and children; missions to costermongers, police courts, common lodging houses, pubs.[117]

White's long list could almost serve as an inventory of van Gogh's print collection, as the subjects of its contents were often set within a context of charity. Furthermore, they were often framed in a religious paradigm, as was Herkomer's *Christmas in a Workhouse*, in which an elderly workhouse resident, aided by a younger woman, receives a small gift.[118] Various religious messages that were heavily rooted in Victorian society are embedded in the image: the benefit of the workhouse and community support; the religious significance of celebrating Christmas as a time for sharing, caring and review; the message of happiness as an outcome of goodwill, seen on the old woman's face; the notion of intergenerational caring represented in the relationship between the two central figures; and, most importantly, the beneficence and responsibility of the middle and upper classes, represented in this image by the well-dressed young donor who represents the Victorian ideals of charity, philanthropy, helping the deserving poor, and changing the habits and nature of the poor. The image evoked empathy, which would have resonated with van Gogh, rather than elitism and disrespect.

The miners and their families were a particular subset of society that fitted the idea of the deserving poor, with whom van Gogh worked and lived during his years in the Borinage. His time there working as a lay preacher and aiming to live a life parallel to that of Jesus, is remembered by Reverend Bonte, a pastor in a neighbouring village:

> He found his lodgings too luxurious; it offended his Christian humility; he could not bear his shelter to be so different from that of the miners. So he left these people who surrounded him with sympathy to go live in a little shack. He lived alone; he had no furniture, and it is said that he slept huddled in a corner of the hearth.

---

117 Jerry White, *London in the 19th Century* (London: Vintage Books, 2007), 429.

118 H. Herkomer, *Christmas in a Workhouse* (*The Graphic*, 25 December 1876).

> Moreover, the clothing he wore outdoors revealed the originality of his aspirations; one saw him dressed to go out in an old soldier's jacket and a shabby cap, and in this attire he roamed the village.
>
> We never again saw the fine clothes with which he had arrived, and he did not buy new ones.
>
> And while his salary was low, it was sufficient to have enabled him to dress more appropriately for his station.
>
> How did this lad come to such a pass?
>
> Confronted with the miseries he encountered on his visits, his pity had been moved to give away nearly all his clothing; his money, too, had gone to the poor; he had kept virtually nothing for himself. His religious beliefs were very ardent, and he desired to obey the teachings of Jesus Christ to the letter.
>
> He felt bound to imitate the early Christians, to sacrifice everything he could do without, and he sought to be even more destitute than most of the miners to whom he preached the Gospel.[119]

Van Gogh's dedication to remaining true to his ideals and morals extended to his work with the miners. He tirelessly assisted those less fortunate than himself. He 'gave no thought to his own well-being' because 'his heart was roused by the needs of others'.[120] He provided food, clothing and warmth and tended the sick and the injured, on one occasion nursing a man left for dead by the authorities back to health.

Miners, often portrayed as poor and among the lowest of the lower classes, were also considered noble workers and living examples of the lessons in *The Pilgrim's Progress*. They experienced a life of drudgery and hardship and were the ideal candidates for redemption before the eyes of Christ, which raised them to the highest levels of reverence for a follower of Bunyan's teachings, like van Gogh. They were for van Gogh 'labourers of the underground, who crawled in the dark recesses of the centre of the earth' and were 'the most receptive and deserving of God's transfiguring light'.[121] It is not surprising

119 Louis Piérard, 'La Vie Tragique de Vincent van Gogh: Among the Miners of the Borinage, 1939', in Susan Alyson Stein (ed.), *Van Gogh: A Retrospective* (Sydney and London: Bay Books, 1986), 46.

120 Piérard, 'La Vie Tragique' 46.

121 Silverman, 'Pilgrim's Progress and Vincent van Gogh's Metier', 103.

that there are many images of miners in van Gogh's collection, many of which express overt religious sentiment, including one of his most treasured prints – Matthew Ridley's *The Miner*, which portrays its subject with reverence rather than scorn and emphasises the view that people from the rural heartland were more pious than city-dwellers (Figure 39). The composition of the image reflects one of the fundamental ideas in *The Pilgrim's Progress* of moving 'from darkness into light'. The miner is depicted underground with his lamp as a guiding light that makes his face seem surrounded by a halo. The religious sentiment is further elicited by the pick slung over the miner's shoulder, calling up ideas of Christ carrying the burden of his cross.

The religious nature of the miners is also seen in the portrayal of accidents, which were familiar occurrences and a subject for many illustrators – a theme clearly present in van Gogh's collection. While these images reinforced the dangerous nature of the occupation, they were not always documentary, often focusing instead on human aspects of the accident, particularly those affected and left behind. It was this aspect that resonated most with van Gogh, who had witnessed the human trauma of such accidents first-hand. Charles Staniland's *The Risca Colliery Explosion – The Two Widows, 1860 and 1880* (Figure 3) reveals the pain and suffering of families who lived in the shadow of the mines. In the foreground of the illustration stand a young and an old woman, both of whom have been widowed, the younger after the latest accident. Surrounding them are grief-stricken women and men offering comfort. In the distance stands the mineshaft, smoke billowing. Van Gogh described this image as 'most beautiful' and expressed the hope that he 'could make studies of them eventually'.[122] It is beautiful, not in composition or technique, but in its honesty, empathy and the depiction of the human spirit. The accident is secondary to the human suffering and the comfort offered by the community. The notion of helping others was central to van Gogh's ideals and moral philosophy and he had applied this notion unreservedly during his days in the Borinage. The black-and-white illustrators reinforced this in their art, and van Gogh wanted to emulate this in his own artistic practice.

The illustrations of farmers, miners, workers, and the disenfranchised are central to van Gogh's collection. They reflect his religious ideals and morals and are evidence of his belief that religious and moral inspiration could be found beyond the institution of the church, in art and especially in the black-and-white illustrations he so loved. These images were also manifestations of the dichotomy between city and rural life, the other defining feature of van

122 LT 263, volume 2, 152.

Gogh's collection. While the cultural and artistic framing of social realism looms large, it is the two ideas expressed above that are the thematic DNA of van Gogh's collection, as van Gogh himself viewed it. For an even greater appreciation and understanding of his collection, its stylistic aspects must also be acknowledged and analysed. Viewed through this additional prism a clearer picture emerges to deepen our understanding of what motivated van Gogh in his collecting.

Stylistic Analysis of the Collection

Illustrations that appeared in the newspapers were generally of two types. The first were quick documentary line drawings, expeditiously produced and accompanying news stories. The second were more complex, being usually stand-alone images, accompanied by a pious text, that could be viewed as works of high art for the masses. It is the second type of print that dominates van Gogh's collection.

When *The Graphic* was launched as a challenger to other illustrated newspapers, in particular *The Illustrated London News*, it differentiated itself by the quality of its illustrations. It commissioned work from respected artists, ensuring that its illustrations were not only of superior quality but also images that could be considered high art, a practice soon followed by most of its competitors. The images were tonal, rather than simple line drawings. Line was important, but it manifested more as a bold outline, defining figures and space. They were often full- or double-page illustrations and were usually framed by a border. Almost always they carried the artist's signature, or at least simply a set of initials. Sometimes they were copies of paintings, especially of popular works that had appeared at institutions like the French Salon and the Royal Academy; sometimes the illustrations became the basis for paintings. What was consistent was that they all carried the weight of high art. The illustrations were considered pieces of art in their own right and it was precisely this stylistic quality that attracted van Gogh. He praised the artists often, particularly those whose works appeared in English publications, arguing that they should be recognised among the works of acknowledged masters. He encouraged van Rappard in their prolonged study 'for they are great artists, these English' and compared them to the authors he so admired:

> For me the English draughtsmen are what Dickens is in the sphere of literature. It's one and the same sentiment, noble and healthy, and something one always comes back to. I would very much like it if sooner

> or later you had an opportunity to quietly look through my whole collection. It's through seeing a lot together that one gets an overall view and it begins to speak for itself, and one sees clearly what a splendid entity this school of draughtsmen forms. Just as one must read Dickens or Balzac or Zola in their entirety to know them separately.[123]

Theo was included in this exchange and was told of the artistic virtues of the black-and-white illustrations. Van Gogh argued that they had the capacity for greater resonance than paintings:

> Anyway, some paintings in their huge frames look very substantial, and later one is surprised when they actually leave behind such an empty and dissatisfied feeling. On the other hand, one overlooks many an unpretentious woodcut or lithograph or etching now and then, but comes back to it and becomes more and more attracted to it with time, and senses something great in it.[124]

Reinforcing this view years later, long after he had ceased collecting prints, he told Theo that large paintings left him bored and that purchasing small black-and-white prints by Lhermitte would be of greater value 'for they are masterpieces that one gets for 50 centimes'. In the same letter, contemplating the greatness of artists such as Fred Walker, of whom he had just read in *The Graphic*, he compared the work of the black-and-white illustrators to that of the revered Hague School and concluded that, like their Dutch peers, the English artists 'restored nature over convention, feeling and impression over academic stuffiness and dullness' and that they 'were the first tonists'.[125]

The tonal characteristic of black-and-white illustrations distinguished the works van Gogh collected from the purely documentary illustrations that also appeared in the newspapers. For van Gogh, and many of the illustrators, the tonal effect achieved through the woodblock process was equal to painting. This partly explains why artists would often translate the illustrations into paintings and why the newspapers felt comfortable reproducing monumental paintings in black-and-white. During his formative years as an artist when he experimented with lithographic crayon in order to replicate this tonal effect, van Gogh wrote to Theo, 'I try to be guided to some extent by the English reproductions'.[126] While this letter predates van Gogh's bulk purchase of *The*

123 LT 267, volume 2, 159–60.

124 LT 290, volume 2, 213.

125 LT 500, volume 3, 237.

126 LT 298, volume 2, 229.

Graphic – a foundational acquisition for his collection – by just over a month, he had already established a substantial body of prints, which was taking shape and driven by this interest in dark, moody tonal works.

The earliest prints known to have been collected by van Gogh had this tonal feature in common. As Pickvance has demonstrated, van Gogh's first comprehensive haul were images from *The Graphic Portfolio*, a publication that brought together the best illustrations this pioneering newspaper had produced.[127] Of this collection, van Gogh singled out Herkomer, Holl, Fildes and Walker as artists of most interest to him, citing works such as Fildes' *Houseless and Hungry* (Figure 7) and Walker's *The Old Gate*, Holl's *"Gone" – Euston Station* (Figure 9) as representative of the quality of illustrations in the *Portfolio*.[128]

"Gone" – Euston Station and *Houseless and Hungry* are classic examples of this tonal style. Both images confirm aesthetically with the high-art concept of chiaroscuro – predominantly dark with clever use of light to focus our attention on key aspects of the composition. The backgrounds of both images are a dark velvety black, carefully punctuated with highlighted areas. This juxtaposition of light and dark adds to the drama of each image and reinforces the trauma and desperation of the subjects it depicts. Fildes sandwiches his frieze-like crowd huddled against a wall between a band of light above their heads and another running across the foreground of the composition. This ensures that the viewer's focus is directed towards the wretched souls who hungrily await admittance into a shelter for the night. The foreground and backgrounds are similarly constructed in Holl's illustration. A lamp high in the top right corner of the composition and a lightened floor in the left foreground that wraps around the group in a horseshoe shape serves to draw attention to the sentimental nature of the drawing. Both use light spilling around the heads of their subjects to give a strong religious tone to the work. Fildes includes a shimmering light on the wall from an unknown light source, creating a halo effect above the huddled mass of street sleepers. A similar effect is created by Holl in his use of a lamp to the right of the figures to cast a halo around the head of the old woman comforting the young mother, of which the religious connotations would not have been lost on someone like van Gogh. This chiaroscuro technique is evident in other key areas of the composition. The young girl's arm in Holl's illustration glows against her black dress, drawing attention to her hand, which holds her mother's dress

127 Pickvance, *English Influences on Vincent van Gogh*, 33.

128 LT 199, volume 2, 17.

tightly, while the comforting hand of the old woman hovering on the back of the anguished central figure is similarly lit, reinforcing her empathy and care for the crying mother. The distressed faces of the three adult females, all central to the story being told, are similarly bathed in light. Fildes' drawing follows similar compositional rules.

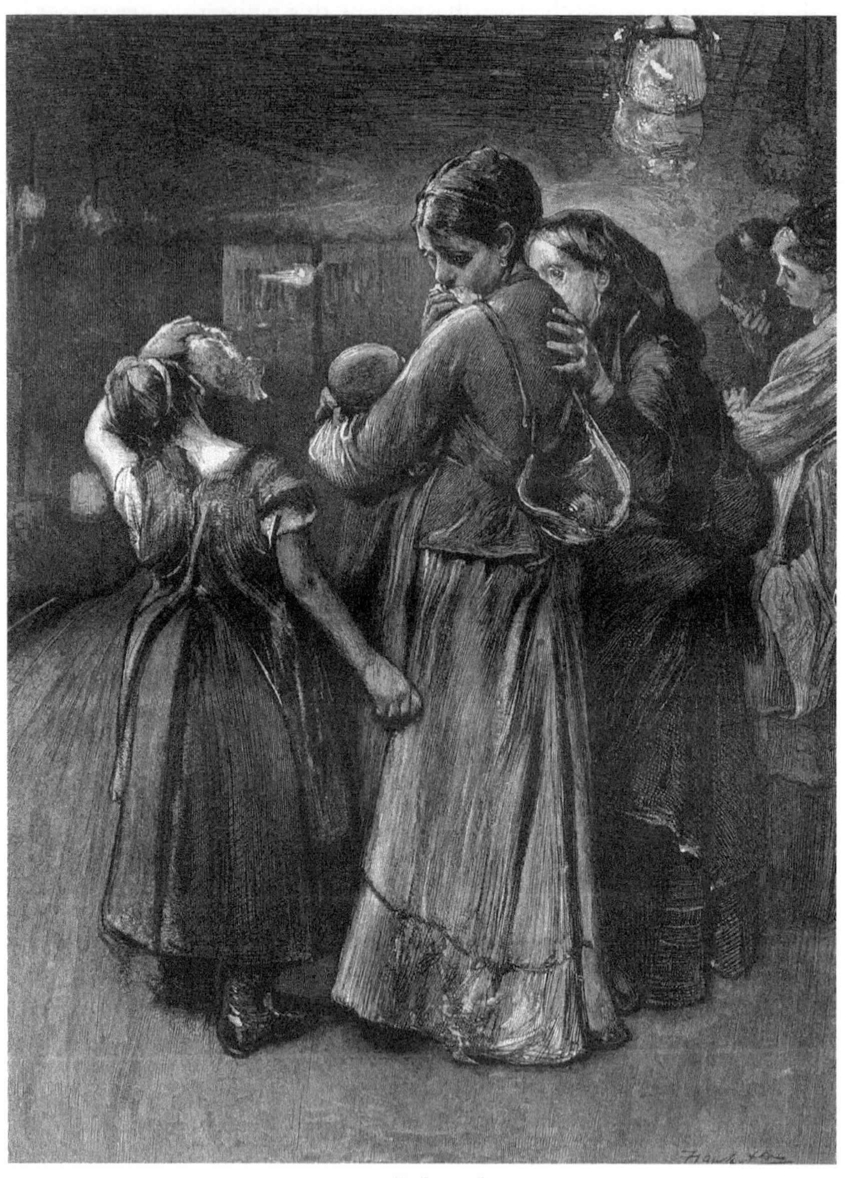

Figure 9. Francis Holl, *"Gone" – Euston Station* (*The Graphic*, 19 February 1876).

Light captures every face in the line of downtrodden people, as the artist aims to identify each, not out of shame, but to illustrate the distress and sorrow they endure in the newly industrialised urban world. The young woman surrounded by her children to the left is washed in light, reinforcing the plight of young families and single parents in particular. The faces of the policemen huddled in the corner also glow in the night light. They look on with concern and empathy, presenting a metaphor for how those struggling in society should be viewed.

The overriding tonal structure dominating these two illustrations ensured their dramatic effect. It reinforced the weighty nature of the subjects depicted, which were representative of important contemporary problems that the viewer would be aware of and should assist in trying to solve. The tonality paralleled the chiaroscuro technique found in the work of past masters and raised these drawings to the realms of high art. It distinguished them from simpler line drawings dispersed throughout the newspaper, appealing to van Gogh, not only because of his sympathy for the content, but also because he believed in bringing a high-art aesthetic to the masses.

Complementing the tonal quality found in most of the prints in van Gogh's collection were their thick bold outlines. Thick line added weight, increased the darkness of the overall composition, and emphasised the nature of the drawing. It was, with the dark tonal quality, the key distinguishing feature of these mass-produced art works. Herkomer was a great exponent of the bold outline, as he reveals in both the key and secondary elements of the composition of *Sunday at Chelsea Hospital* (Figure 10).

The facial features of the two main protagonists are drawn with bold confident lines, as are their hands, which are key indicators of the subject matter, but it is in the incidental objects surrounding the figures that the bold outline comes to the fore. It can be seen surrounding many of the arms, legs and torsos of the seated men. The benches are also defined by clear strong lines, especially their ornately carved feet. The three books stacked in the bottom right corner are composed with bold lines, a technique adopted by van Gogh in his own depiction of books, as in his *Still Life with Bible* (1885) and *Piles of French Novels and a Glass with a Rose* (1888).[129] This quality is

---

129 Vincent van Gogh, *Still Life with Bible*, 1885 (Van Gogh Museum, Amsterdam (Vincent van Gogh Foundation) F0177/JH0946); and *Piles of French Novels and a Glass with a Rose*, 1887 (private collection F0359/JH1332). (F numbers are those given in J.B. De la Faille's *The Works of Vincent van Gogh: His Paintings and Drawings* (Amsterdam: Meulenhoff International, 1970); JH numbers are those in Jan Hulsker's *The New Complete van Gogh: Paintings, Drawings, Sketches: Revised and Enlarged ed.* (Amsterdam: J.M. Meulenhoff: Philadelphia: John Benjamins, 1996).

a dominant feature in other prints in van Gogh's collection. Strong black lines demarcate the main figures and box in the foreground of Herkomer's *Christmas in a Workhouse*,[130] and the figures in William Murray's *Canal Life: Tea-Time on a "Monkey Boat"* (FIGURE 34) and Fitzgerald's *A Pawn Office at Merthyr-Tydfil* (FIGURE 32).

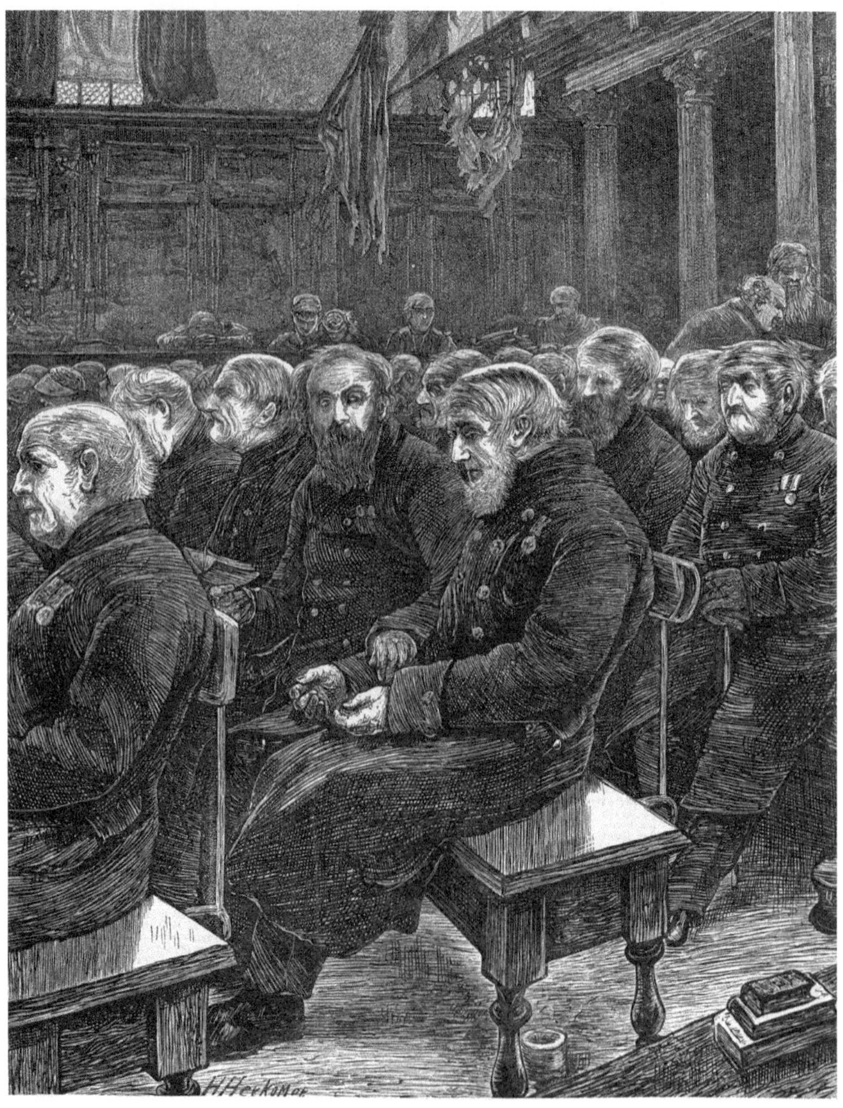

Figure 10. Hubert Herkomer, *Sunday at Chelsea Hospital* (*The Graphic*, 18 February 1871).

130 H. Herkomer, *Christmas in a Workhouse* (*The Graphic*, Christmas number 1876).

In Félix Régamey's *American Sketches: Prison Life in Blackwell's Island: No 1 Returning from Work*, line defines and dominates the whole composition, taking over the usual dominant tonal nature of such drawings.[131] In the same issue of *The Illustrated London News*, E. Frère's *Snowballing* is completely composed of strong dark outlines.[132] It relies on the strength and conviction of its line and, while it is an oddity in van Gogh's collection because it lacks tonal quality, he was no doubt seduced by the confidence of the simple mark-making in achieving a scene of great joy.

Black-and-white popular illustrations produced in the context of art for the masses were also reliant on scale. Most of the images were printed as single- or double-page illustrations. Of the hundreds of references to black-and-white illustrations in van Gogh's letters, ninety are to double-page illustrations and most of the rest refer to single-page works. An analysis of the extant collection gives a similar picture, with most being single-page works. While none of the double-page illustrations still exist in the collection, we know of their importance to van Gogh because he created a separate folio for them in his collection. Van Gogh's praise for these types of illustrations can be found in numerous letters to van Rappard, in which he described them as superb, full of character, splendid, serious, deeply moving and remarkable.[133] Writing of the double-page version of Holl's *At a Railway Station* he had just acquired, he declared it 'infinitely finer' than the small version he had previously sent to van Rappard.[134] His highest praise for one of his most admired illustrators, Small, was directed at two double-page illustrations: *The Caxton Celebrations – William Caxton Showing Specimens of His Printing to King Edward IV and His Queen* and *An English Ploughing Match*:[135] 'Of course there are many beautiful things by Small, but this [*The Caxton Celebrations*] and the ploughing match are the finest by him that I know'.[136] Likewise, the prints that van Gogh considered of most importance for a new collection, for both van Rappard and his newly found artist friend Herman Johannes van der Weele, were all single or double-page prints. For van der Weele he identified Herkomer's

131 F.E. Régamey, *American Sketches: Prison Life in Blackwell's Island: No 1 Returning from Work* (*The Illustrated London News*, 19 February 1876).

132 E. Frére, *Snowballing* (*The Illustrated London News*, 19 February 1876).

133 For example, see letters 275, 303, 304, 329, 359, 431.

134 LT 304, volume 2, 242.

135 W. Small, *The Caxton Celebrations – William Caxton Showing Specimens of His Printing to King Edward IV and His Queen* (*The Graphic*, 30 June 1877), and *An English Ploughing Match* (*The Graphic*, 13 March 1875).

136 LT 304, volume 2, 244.

At Death's Door (double-page), Adolf Menzel's *The Siesta* (single-page) and Frère's *Snowballing* (double-page) as important.[137] For van Rappard he singled out six works he wished to send, all double-page, describing them as 'some of the very finest' produced by *The Graphic* and stressing that they 'are the *core* of a woodcut collection'.[138]

The single- and double-page illustrations that constituted the bulk of van Gogh's collection demonstrated other characteristics of the high-art aesthetic. Like the major paintings that hung in museums, the Royal Academy, or the French Salon, many of the prints van Gogh admired and collected contained a frame, which emphasised the possibility of pinning these works to a wall, as one would hang a painting. Many of these works also contained the signature of the artist, although it was often merely a monogram, which van Gogh spent a significant amount of time deciphering. Sharing this knowledge with van Rappard, he wrote:

> When I began collecting wood engravings, I often regretted that I didn't know who they were by if I couldn't make head or tail of the monograms, which many English draughtsmen use. Even now I don't know everything, but do know a few, and a list of these may be of some use to you, although you may know them all.[139]

The identification of an artist by their monogram was important to van Gogh. It identified artists as individual masters rather than as mere contributors to a newspaper and elevated them and their illustrations to a higher level.

High art was referenced in the illustrated prints not only by the characteristics outlined above. Many of the works in van Gogh's collection were either after significant paintings – usually those shown in contemporary exhibitions – or were later used as the basis for major salon-style canvases. Fred Walker, one of the most admired and influential Victorian artists, started his career working for magazines such as *Good Words*, *Once a Week* and *The Cornhill*. Van Gogh was a great admirer of his work, describing him as one of the 'true masters as "draughtsmen", over and above their qualities in other directions', a reference to Walker's talent and his other career as a painter.[140] The first

137 H. Herkomer, *At Death's Door* (*The Graphic*, 26 August 1876); A. Menzel, *The Siesta* (*The Graphic*, 9 September 1876); and E. Frère, *Snowballing* (*The Illustrated London News*, 19 February 1876).

138 LT 307, volume 2, 257.

139 LT 272, volume 2, 173. Van Gogh listed the monograms and names of 29 artists in this letter.

140 LT 164, volume 1, 265.

work by Walker to appear in *The Graphic* was *Lost Path*, which van Gogh did not own. It appeared in the newspaper's fourth issue on a double-page spread and established the practice of reproducing fine paintings as black-and-white illustrations for the masses to enjoy.[141]

Fildes' *Houseless and Hungry* (Figure 7), one of the prints van Gogh discussed the most, would become one of the great Victorian paintings, which Anne Helmreich describes as exemplifying 'the social realist genre' of the period.[142] Retitled *Applicants for Admission to a Casual Ward*, 1874, the painting was completed five years after the illustration appeared in *The Graphic* and took almost two years to finish. It varies from the original illustration; the scene is extended on both the right and left borders to add more figures, including the less desirable such as a professional beggar. Detail added to the background included two posters offering a £2 reward for a missing child and a £20 reward for a missing dog. The two policemen in the original have been replaced by a single officer conversing with a homeless adventurer, and the main female figure is posed so that she looks away from the crowd huddled against the wall. In spite of these amendments, the overall aim and sentiment of the work remained the same; it was, as the *Art Journal* claimed at the time, 'the most notable piece of realism we have met with for a long time'.[143]

Walker and other artists van Gogh frequently mentioned in his letters, such as Herkomer, Holl, and Fildes, were acknowledged as master painters and also great illustrators. Van Gogh firmly believed that what they produced as illustrators were significant, genuine works of art; furthermore, he believed that mastering illustration was essential for becoming a great painter, a view reinforced by Herkomer in 1882.[144] Herkomer advocated a non-academic approach to the teaching of art, pointing to Walker, who had developed from copyist, to illustrator, to master water-colourist, to recognised and respected painter, as an example. 'In his most perfect work', wrote Herkomer, 'the wood

141 F. Walker, *Lost Path* (*The Graphic*, 25 December 1869).

142 Malcolm Warner, *The Victorians: British Painting 1837–1901* (Washington: National Gallery of Art, 1996), 148.

143 *The Art Journal*, July 1874, 201, quoted in Warner, *The Victorians*, 148.

144 Herkomer argued that a career as a black-and-white illustrator was a good precursor to an artist's career: 'Good Art work in a weekly newspaper of high quality is far more advantageous to the artist – opening out, as it does, more possibilities to the development of his art – than either the Greek line in clay, or the Gothic line in colour (of stained glass), ever could have done' (H. Herkomer, 'Drawing and Engraving on Wood', *The Art Journal*, 1882, 133).

draughtsman was ever visible'.[145] Although such training was not always perfect, Herkomer believed it had peculiar triumphs:

> In this art there is a sensitiveness of drawing and a delicacy of gradation of tone seen in no other art in that particular guise. It was this school that first thought of painting a figure subject under the effect of a grey day, showing us how beautiful grey days really were.[146]

Van Gogh embraced such comments and his own career development can be viewed through a similar frame. However, Herkomer's approach was not only a path for van Gogh's artistic development; it was also important in his print collecting. It validated black-and-white illustrations, van Gogh's admiration for them, and the collection's continued growth. Moreover, it shaped the collection stylistically: almost all of the items in van Gogh's collection fell within the context of high art. The images were majestic and their elements paralleled those of fine art painting: size (single- and double-page images); signatures; borders; bold outlines; heavy tonal qualities; and a connection to academic painting. When van Gogh's collecting is viewed in this context, his need for such a collection becomes apparent. In the first instance, the collection was a repository of a valid art form. Secondly, and more importantly for van Gogh at the time, it was both a teaching aid that helped him with issues of composition and structure as well as with subject matter. It provided focus as he strove to become an accomplished draftsman and, ultimately, it shaped his 'hand' and helped him find his unique artistic voice.

145 Herkomer, 'Drawing and Engraving on Wood', 134.

146 Herkomer, 'Drawing and Engraving on Wood', 135.

Chapter 4

VAN GOGH THE DRAUGHTSMAN

'Best-kept Secret'

When van Gogh set out on his artistic career, he intended to find a career in which he could be financially independent and could meet his family's middle-class standards. He took up his pencil, not wanting to be a painter or an artist in the traditional sense, but hoping to become an illustrator of magazines and newspapers. Van Gogh believed such a job would bring in 100 French francs per month, which would allow him to live with no further financial assistance from his family, particularly from his younger brother Theo. According to Albert Boime, 'the best-kept secret in van Gogh scholarship is the critical significance of the painter's initial overriding ambition to become a reportorial illustrator and cartoonist' to meet family and economic expectations.[1] However, when many think about van Gogh they are instantly drawn towards the mythology surrounding his personal life rather than to the craftsmanship and dedication with which he worked diligently in his early years, always with an eye on financial independence and familial acceptance. His early aspirations, 'the best-kept secret' that Boime refers to, have been forgotten.

An integral part of the van Gogh mythology has been the documenting of his perceived failures: as a young art dealer, teacher, and missionary; as a tortured genius living a lonely life without friends and not selling any work during his lifetime; as a madman who cut off his ear and committed suicide. Unfortunately, truth has been distorted in order to maintain the drama of van Gogh's life, ensuring that the myth of the struggling artist and misunderstood genius is perpetuated. So, in light of the documentation of his failures,

1 Albert Boime, 'Van Gogh, Thomas Nast and the Social Role of the Artist', in Joseph Masheck (ed.), *Van Gogh 100* (Westport, CT: Greenwood Press, 1996), 71–2.

was van Gogh's attempt to become a draughtsman yet another one of these failures? The question is raised with no intention of adding to the mythology, but to demonstrate gross misunderstandings of periods of the artist's life. Furthermore, it is intended to lead towards the view that he was able to build upon most things he turned his hand to, whether he succeeded in them or not, to develop a unique outlook on life and create a unique personal artistic style. This chapter addresses the 'best-kept secret' of which Boime writes – van Gogh's early years as an artist mastering his craft, not through academic channels but rather through design manuals and his growing collection of black-and-white popular prints. It assesses the nature of van Gogh's first commission of drawings, as well as his early attempts to create a series of lithographs to further his persistent aim to become a draughtsman for illustrated magazines and newspapers.

In June 1880, two months before van Gogh embarked on this artistic path, he wrote to his brother Theo to thank him for the 50 francs he had sent – part of a financial exchange that would continue until the artist's death in 1890. In this letter van Gogh pleaded his case against his family's accusations that he was idle and rebellious. The brothers had not corresponded for over a year, during which time van Gogh had left the theology faculty in Amsterdam and had failed to get a posting as a missionary in the Borinage mining districts of Belgium. This prompted his family, especially his father, to criticise him for his appearance and unwillingness to conform, pointing to these traits as reasons for his failure to obtain employment. Van Gogh argued otherwise and hoped that he would be able to repair his relationship with Theo and with their father and re-establish 'entente cordiale'.[2] This important letter marks the point at which van Gogh relinquished his aim of joining the clergy and began working towards being an artist. It was an honest statement of his moral outlook and ideals, outlining attributes that would influence all facets of his life. Throughout the letter van Gogh drew parallels between his situation and beliefs and those of artists and writers such as Rembrandt and Shakespeare. He continued to counter Theo's claims that he had 'impossible ideas on religion and childish scruples of conscience':

> If I have any that are impossible or childish, may I be freed from them; I'd like nothing better. But here's where I am on this subject, more or less. You'll find in Souvestre's Le philosophe sous les toits how a man of the people, a simple workman, very wretched, if you will, imagined

2 LT 155, volume 1, 246.

> his mother country, 'Perhaps you have never thought about what your mother country is, he continued, putting a hand on my shoulder; it's everything that surrounds you, everything that raised and nourished you, everything you have loved. This countryside that you see, these houses, these trees, these young girls, laughing as they pass by over there, that's your mother country! The laws that protect you, the bread that is the reward of your labour, the words that you exchange, the joy and sadness that come to you from the men and the things among which you live, that's your mother country! The little room where you once used to see your mother, the memories she left you, the earth in which she rests, that's your mother country! You see it, you breathe it everywhere! Just think, your rights and your duties, your attachments and your needs, your memories and your gratitude, put all that together under a single name, and that name will be your mother country.
>
> Now likewise, everything in men and in their works that is truly good, and beautiful with an inner moral, spiritual and sublime beauty, I think that that comes from God, and that everything that is bad and wicked in the works of men and in men, that's not from God, and God doesn't find it good, either. But without intending it, I'm always inclined to believe that the best way of knowing God is to love a great deal. Love that friend, that person, that thing, whatever you like, you'll be on the right path to knowing more thoroughly, afterwards; that's what I say to myself. But you must love with a high, serious intimate sympathy, with a will, with intelligence, and you must always seek to know more thoroughly, better, and more. That leads to God, that leads to unshakeable faith.[3]

It was a remarkable testament. Van Gogh continued citing examples of his admiration for Rembrandt and knowledge of the French Revolution as evidence for raising everyday thoughts to a higher plane, which he believed that he himself had achieved. He confessed that he had suffered from periods of absent-mindedness, which he had overcome:

> Now, afterwards, we may well at times be a little absent-minded, a little dreamy; there are those who become a little too absent-minded, a little too dreamy; that happens to me, perhaps, but it's my own fault. And after all, who knows, wasn't there some cause; it was for this or that reason that I was absorbed, preoccupied, anxious, but you get over that.

3 LT 155, volume 1, 248.

> The dreamer sometimes falls into a pit, but they say that afterwards he comes up out of it again.
>
> And the absent-minded man, at times he too has his presence of mind, as if in compensation. He's sometimes a character who has his *raison d'être* for one reason or another which one doesn't always see right away, or which one forgets through being absent-minded, mostly unintentionally.[4]

Van Gogh insisted that he would ultimately reach his goal:

> One who has been rolling along for ages as if tossed on a stormy sea arrives at his destination at last; one who has seemed good for nothing and incapable of filling any position, any role, finds one in the end, and, active and capable of action, shows himself entirely different from what he had seemed at first sight.[5]

Significantly van Gogh does not mention anywhere in the letter his real secret – that he was becoming an artist. He certainly discusses art with Theo, but limits the discussion to parallels between his life and ideals and those of the great masters and their works. The letter indicated a clear break from his preceding radical years of striving to join the clergy by living a life of poverty. Its tone was no longer one of 'extreme religiosity', as van Heugten puts it, but one of 'a more adult tone'.[6] This letter also intimated that van Gogh was ready to make sure that he did not descend into the lower classes, which would have appalled his middle-class family. In his next letter to Theo, on 20 August 1880, van Gogh asked him to send etchings by Millet and mentioned that he had been trying to sketch large drawings after him.[7] He was ready to begin a new phase of his life, as a draughtsman.

It seems that van Gogh's sudden enthusiasm for drawing had been prompted by Theo, a year earlier in October 1879.[8] In a letter in April 1882 van Gogh

---

4 LT 155, volume 1, 248–9.

5 LT 155, volume 1, 249.

6 Sjraar van Heugten (ed.), *Van Gogh: The Birth of an Artist* (Brussels: Mercatorfonds, 2015), 17.

7 'You should know that I'm sketching large drawings after Millet, and that I've done The four times of the day, as well as The Sower' (LT 156, volume 1, 250).

8 Van Heugten draws attention to this: 'Although this change of course has always been presented as van Gogh's own idea, it was in fact Theo's' (Sjraar van Heugten, *Vincent van Gogh Drawings*, vol. 1: *The Early Years 1880–1883* (Amsterdam: Van Gogh Museum, 1996), 14).

recalled his initial reaction to Theo's suggestion that he begin work as an artist or draughtsman:

> I remember very well that when you spoke to me back then about my becoming a painter, I thought it very inappropriate and wouldn't hear of it.
>
> What made me stop doubting is that I read a clearly written book on perspective, Cassagne, Guide de l'Abc du dessin, and a week later drew an interior of a little kitchen, with stove, chair and table and window in their place and on their legs, whereas it used to seem to me downright witchcraft or coincidence that one had *depth* and proper perspective in a drawing.[9]

Chris Stolwijk argues Theo's suggestion was most likely to ensure van Gogh 'would not slip any further down the social ladder', rather than acknowledgement of any artistic ability.[10] Theo might have been prompted by van Gogh's situation at the time, as he was living in terrible conditions, neglecting his appearance, and in a strained relationship with the rest of the family. Although van Gogh was desperate, his decision to accept Theo's advice was not immediate, as he recalled that at the time he 'wouldn't hear of it'.[11]

Van Gogh's letters from previous years reveal a pattern of constant drawing, which meant that his new ambition was not without foundation and familiarity. In April 1876, just before he left for England, van Gogh drew the parsonage and church of Etten, to which his parents had moved in 1875. The drawing was a present for his sister Wil, as a note on the back in van Gogh's handwriting indicates.[12] Soon after arriving in England he sent two drawings back to the Netherlands showing locations and landmarks from his travels – one to Theo and the other to his parents.[13] In November

---

9 LT 214, volume 2, 46.

10 Chris Stolwijk & Richard Thomson, *Theo van Gogh: Art Dealer, Collector and Brother of Vincent* (Zwolle: Waanders, 1999), 33.

11 LT 214, volume 2, 46.

12 van Heugten, *Vincent van Gogh Drawings* vol. 1, 57.

13 Vincent van Gogh, *View of Royal Road, Ramsgate*, 1876 (Van Gogh Museum, Amsterdam (Vincent van Gogh Foundation) Juv. XXVII), and *View of Royal Road, Ramsgate*, 1876 (Van Gogh Museum, Amsterdam (Vincent van Gogh Foundation) Juv. XXVI). The first drawing has been confidently dated at May 1876 and was sent to Theo (LT 67). The second drawing is a little more problematic and has been dated at April–May 1876. Van Heugten suggests that it was sent with a letter to van Gogh's parents, as there is no mention of it in the letter sent to Theo (see van Heugten, *Vincent van Gogh Drawings* vol. 1, 61 and Martin Bailey (ed.), *Van Gogh in England: Portrait of the Artist as a Young Man* (London: Barbican Art Gallery, 1992), 121 (cat. 11)).

1876, after moving on from Ramsgate, a sketch of two small churches, one at Petersham and the other at Turnham Green, appeared in a letter sent to Theo. A further drawing, *Au Charbonnage Café*, was included in a letter of November 1878, a humble record of van Gogh's travels to Belgium.[14] As with the previous drawings, it does not express any serious artistic intent; it was merely a memento, a record of a place he had visited. Van Gogh wrote that he would like to continue making rough sketches of the many things he encountered, but that it would be best if he didn't start as it would keep him from his real work.[15] His 'real work' was of course as an evangelist among the miners of the Borinage, a post he held until he was expelled in July 1879.[16]

During the years van Gogh sought to realise a life as a clergyman, especially while he was in the Borinage, he continued to produce small sketches of his immediate surroundings. Although we cannot be certain of van Gogh's activities during these years, Marije Vellekoop argues that he was certainly drawing, mostly figure drawings and 'types from here'.[17] Interviewed in 1939 about van Gogh's time in the Borinage, the Reverend Bonte remembered him drawing as he worked around the mines:

> He used to squat on the slag heaps and make portraits of the women gathering coal there, or leaving, burdened with sacks. We noticed that he did not reproduce things of splendour, to which we attribute beauty. He did a few portraits of old women. Besides, we didn't attach any importance to what we considered his hobby.[18]

Another acquaintance from the Borinage, M.G. Delsaut recalled van Gogh drawing:

---

14 Vincent van Gogh, *Au Charbonnage Café*, 1878 (Van Gogh Museum, Amsterdam (Vincent van Gogh Foundation) Juv. XXXI).

15 'I hereby enclose that scratch, 'The Au Charbonnage café'. I should really rather like to start making rough sketches of some of the many things one meets along the way, but considering I wouldn't actually do it very well and it would most likely keep me from my real work, it's better I don't begin' (LT 148, volume 1, 233).

16 Preaching was still van Gogh's priority in late 1878, as he indicated to Theo: 'As soon as I got home I began working on a sermon on "the barren fig tree", Luke XIII:6–9' (LT 148, volume 1, 233).

17 van Heugten, *Van Gogh: The Birth of an Artist*, 53.

18 Louis Piérard, 'La Vie Tragique de Vincent van Gogh: Among the Miners of the Borinage, 1939', in Susan Alyson Stein (ed.), *Van Gogh: A Retrospective* (Sydney and London: Bay Books, 1986), 47.

> While eating, he made drawings in his lap, or read. All his time was given to drawing. He often went to the Ghlin woods, to the Mons cemetery, and often into the countryside.
>
> He drew mostly landscapes, castles, a shepherd with his flock, cows at pasture.
>
> The most striking picture, the one that has stayed in the memory of my sister-in-law, with whom he lodged, is the drawing that shows the family harvesting potatoes, some are digging, the others (the women) are gathering up the potatoes.[19]

Although the two accounts were recorded almost fifty years after van Gogh's death and may have been affected by the artist's subsequent fame, they correspond with van Gogh's letters, which confirm that he was drawing actively as a side pursuit to his work as a preacher. His drawings, those that still exist or are known of from his letters, as well as those described by acquaintances such as Delsaut and Bonte, are best described as depicting van Gogh's surroundings and as such can be classed as scenes for his remembrance and information for relatives and friends. Although his output at the time was very small and amateur in execution, that he was drawing regularly may have helped van Gogh in his decision to follow an artistic career later in life.

In addition to drawing, van Gogh was also happy to talk about art after his time as an art dealer. In March 1879 he wrote to Theo from the Borinage recounting a recent visit from their father and telling him of their visits to several ministers, attendance at Bible readings and a trip to an active mine site. Although his father's visit was at the front of his mind, he reminded Theo that he was still interested in news of artists and paintings: 'write a few words soon, and remember that if you tell me something about the painters, I still understand something of it, even though it's been a long time since I've seen many paintings'.[20] Van Gogh often recalled paintings he had seen, and the art world, within which Theo continued to work, remained an area of mutual interest and understanding between the two brothers. Through 1878 and into 1879, as the likelihood of his becoming a lay preacher diminished, their exchanges about paintings had changed in tone. Two weeks after reminding Theo of his continuing knowledge and interest in art, van Gogh described a trip he had taken down a mineshaft, noting that it would make

19 Piérard, 'La Vie Tragique', 47.

20 LT 150, volume 1, 238.

a great series of paintings, which would be 'something new and something unheard-of or rather never-before-seen' – confirming Delsaut's and Bonte's recollections long after his death.[21] Four months later, in early August, he asked Theo to visit on his way to Paris, as he had some drawings of 'types from here' that he wanted to share with him.[22] They depicted local families milking cows, digging and picking potatoes, making soup and grinding coffee, as well as mines and miners.[23] Van Gogh also wrote of a sketch of a miner he had given Reverend Pieterzen, an amateur artist who had asked for it after seeing many of his drawings. He also casually confirmed that he was drawing every day and told Theo he had received a box of paints and a sketchbook from his former employer, Mr. Tersteeg, and that the sketchbook was 'already half full'.[24]

Van Gogh's next letter, written two weeks later, after Theo's visit, was downcast and desperate, probably because Theo challenged him with accusations of being idle and having no career path. Their time together and Theo's honest assessment and advice were clearly at the front of his mind:

> As I think back on your visit with thankfulness, our talks naturally come to mind. I've heard such talks before, many, in fact, and often. Plans for improvement and change and raising the spirits – and yet, don't let it anger you, I'm a little afraid of them – also because I sometimes acted upon them and ended up rather disappointed. How much has been well thought out that is, however, impracticable.[25]

The 'plans for improvement' may have included the possibility of van Gogh becoming an artist or something similar. Although there is no mention of him becoming a painter, there is a reference to becoming 'a lithographer of invoice headings and visiting cards'.[26] Van Gogh did not wish to pursue such a path, as he still hoped to be accepted as an evangelist, but he finished the letter with the news that he had just finished drawing a portrait. A year later he told Theo that, after his visit and his subsequent desperate letter to Theo, he had travelled to Courrières in France, mainly to find work but also

---

21 LT 151, volume 1, 239.

22 LT 153, volume 1, 243.

23 LT 153, volume 1, 243, note 1.

24 LT 153, volume 1, 243. There is no mention in earlier letters of any request for these materials. It was in a letter to Theo nearly three years later that he mentioned that Terseeg had sent the paints in exchange for some drawings (LT 221, volume 2, 60).

25 LT 154, volume 1, 244.

26 LT 154, volume 1, 245.

hoping to meet the artist Jules Breton.[27] He had stood outside Breton's studio, but did not have the confidence to enter, so he had wandered the streets of Courrières hoping to find a trace of the artist. While the main purpose of his travel was to find some sort of employment, he had in his suitcase some drawings, which he exchanged along the way for food.[28] There is no doubt that he took these samples of his drawings with him to show Breton or any other artist who might be interested, While he failed to make contact with any artist on the trip, his disappointment did not deter him. In that moment of intense disappointment and desperation, he resolved to become an artist:

> Well, and notwithstanding, it was in this extreme poverty that I felt my energy return and that I said to myself, in any event I'll recover from it, I'll pick up my pencil that I put down in my great discouragement and I'll get back to drawing, and from then on, it seems to me, everything has changed for me, and now I'm on my way and my pencil has become somewhat obedient and seems to become more so day by day.[29]

Van Gogh practised drawing over a long period of time, but it was always secondary to his religious calling. Viewed in the context of Theo's visit, the sudden decision to change his career path can be seen as a logical step in van Gogh's aim to do 'something useful'.

Early in his development as an artist van Gogh was well supported by Theo, who must have felt obliged to do so. Theo offered encouragement and continuously indulged van Gogh's many requests for materials. Writing on 20 August 1880, after van Gogh revealed that he was busy sketching large drawings after Millet, he asked Theo for a number of prints to copy, including Millet's *Les Travaux des Champs* series and prints by Breton, Feyen-Perrin, Brion, Frère and van Ruisdael.[30] Theo fulfilled all his brother's requests rapidly. A few weeks later, van Gogh thanked him for the prints, acknowledging 'you did me a great service by sending them' and commending Theo's foresight in sending additional prints: 'you well understood my thinking when you added Hébert's Malaria to our collection'.[31] Theo continued to send prints and, more importantly, commented favourably on his brother's development. Van Gogh expressed his gratitude: 'your letter did me good; I thank you for writing to

27 LT 158, volume 1, 255–6.

28 'I earned a few crusts of bread en route here and there in exchange for some drawings that I had in my suitcase' (LT 158, volume 1, 256).

29 LT 158, volume 1, 256.

30 LT 156, volume 1, 250.

31 LT 157, volume 1, 252.

me like that'.[32] Theo also suggested van Gogh travel to Paris, presumably so that he would be exposed to other artists and draftsmen, but van Gogh had reservations:

> Now, about coming to Paris. If we found an opportunity to get in touch with some decent, valiant artist, it would be extremely advantageous for me, but, to go there just like that, it would only be a repetition on a large scale of my trip to Courrières, where I'd hoped perhaps to meet some living being of the Artist species, but where I didn't find one.[33]

Nevertheless, van Gogh kept open the possibility of travelling to Paris or to Barbizon and soon wrote to Theo telling him that he was in Brussels.[34] His main reasons for moving there were to find a better studio and to meet other artists. Although Theo did not approve of this sudden move, he continued to provide assistance, suggesting that van Gogh visit the young artist Anthon van Rappard, whom he had met in Paris; van Gogh did so soon after, as a letter of 1 November 1880 confirmed.[35]

Theo not only introduced the two artists, but also corresponded with both of them. At times the three engaged in discussions about all facets of art, which made available to van Gogh advice from someone who was working as an artist. Their exchanges included discussion of artists unknown to van Gogh, such as Norwegian painter Hans Heyerdahl, who was then working at Léon Bonnat's studio in Paris, a popular school for Scandinavian artists. In introducing van Gogh and van Rappard, Theo ignited the two artists' passion for black-and-white prints and their correspondence and friendship encouraged them both to establish extensive collections, as well as adding fuel to van Gogh's ideas of finding employment as an illustrator.

While working in Brussels, van Gogh sent Theo sketches that he thought showed his improvement and reflected the illustrations he had begun to collect: 'I've just finished at least a dozen drawings, or rather, pencil and pen croquis, which are, it seems to me, already a little better. They vaguely resemble certain drawings by Lançon, or certain English wood engravings, but even clumsier, more awkward'. With further progress he felt confident in succeeding 'in becoming more or less capable of working in magazine or

32 LT 158, volume 1, 255.

33 LT 158, volume 1, 256.

34 LT 159, volume 1, 258.

35 Jaap Brouwer, L. Siesling and J. Vis, *Anthon van Rappard: Companion and Correspondent of Vincent van Gogh, His Life and All His Works* (Amsterdam: Van Gogh Museum, 1974), 211.

book illustration'.[36] Two of these clumsy and awkward sketches clearly show van Gogh struggling with perspective and three-dimensionality. The figure in *En Route* appears frozen in time, and the figure in the second drawing, *Devant les tisons*, seems to be neither standing nor sitting.[37] Van Gogh was well aware of these inadequacies and hence only referred to them as sketches, which he used throughout his career for works he considered to be studies. Furthermore, both drawings were captioned in French, whereas van Gogh preferred to use English for the captions of images he thought might be accepted by the English newspapers.[38] These two small sketches were intended primarily to give Theo an idea of his development, but they also indicated the kind of motifs van Gogh was interested in when he spoke frequently with Theo of presentable and saleable drawings. As he made clear in his letters, van Gogh was aware of the standard required for him to approach the editors of newspapers such as *The Illustrated London News*, *The Graphic* and *L'Illustration* with confidence, either about employment or about selling his works. While working in Brussels in February 1881, he wrote to his parents:

> Only if I pursue drawing this thoroughly and seriously, always seeking to portray reality, shall I succeed, and then, despite the inevitable expenses, a living can be made out of it. Because a good draughtsman can certainly find work nowadays, and there's a great demand for such individuals and there are positions to be had that pay very well. So the thing is to try and become as good at it as possible.[39]

During this period his thoughts about becoming a draughtsman intensified, and by 1881 he was referring to himself as one: 'I'm learning a handicraft, and although I'll certainly not grow rich by it, at least I'll earn the 100 francs a month necessary to support myself once I'm surer of myself as a draughtsman and find steady work'.[40] Within a month van Gogh's confidence had increased to the extent that he asked Theo to keep an eye out for any employment opportunities: 'think of me if you happen to hear of a position for a draughtsman

36 LT 162, volume 1, 262.

37 Vincent van Gogh, *En route*, 1881 (Van Gogh Museum, Amsterdam (Vincent van Gogh Foundation)); *Devant les tisons*, 1881 (Van Gogh Museum, Amsterdam (Vincent van Gogh Foundation)).

38 Bailey notes that all of van Gogh's surviving titled drawings and watercolours from April 1881 to the end of 1882 were given English titles, including *The Bearers of the Burden*, *The Lampbearers*, *Winter Tale*, *Shadows Passing*, *Worn Out*, *The Dustman*, *The Great Lady*, *Sorrow* and *Eternity's Gate* (see Bailey, *Van Gogh in England*, 75–6).

39 LT 163, volume 1, 264.

40 LT 164, volume 1, 265.

somewhere or other'.[41] A few months later he again made it clear he thought of himself as a draughtsman in explaining to Theo the problems he had encountered with models dressing in their Sunday best: 'truly, this is one of the petty vexations in the life of a draughtsman'.[42] By September of that year he was writing: 'these days I really feel: "I have a draughtsman's fist"'.[43] Although some of his drawings were still clumsy and stiff, others such as *Peasant Sitting by the Fireplace (Worn Out)* (Plate 1) show how far his skill had developed, earning van Heugten's description as ambitious and 'laden with meaningful inventions'.[44] Van Gogh was now giving his works English titles, revealing his intentions of sending drawings to the editors of the English illustrated newspapers.

In December 1881, after an angry row with his father, van Gogh moved from the family home in Etten, where he had been since April of that year, to The Hague. He stayed in The Hague until September 1883 and intensified his attempts to become a draughtsman. He developed considerably as an illustrator and subsequently as a painter and it was during this time that he accumulated most of his black-and-white print collection, which further inspired his thoughts of joining his artistic heroes out on the streets depicting scenes of everyday life. Within his first month in The Hague van Gogh had purchased a copy of *The Graphic Portfolio*, a collection of fifty of the newspaper's finest prints. He was delighted with his new purchase and referred to drawings in it that would inspire his own work, such as Luke Fildes' *Houseless and Hungry* (Figure 7). The subject matter of such works appealed to van Gogh and gave him ideas for his own drawings, as is evident when he wrote to Theo: 'I quite often go to sketch in the soup kitchen or in the 3rd-class waiting room, or such places'.[45] Van Gogh's work continued in this direction and in February 1882 he again asked Theo questions about illustrators and what magazines required of them: 'If you can find out about it, you must tell me what kind of drawings one might be able to sell to the illustrated magazines. It seems to me they could use pen drawings of types of the people, and I'd like so much to start working on them, in order to make something suitable for reproduction'.[46]

41 LT 166, volume 1, 272.

42 LT 170, volume 1, 277.

43 LT 182, volume 1, 308.

44 van Heugten, *Van Gogh: The Birth of an Artist*, 20.

45 LT 200, volume 2, 20.

46 LT 204, volume 2, 28.

Theo did not come up with any opportunities with the illustrated publications, but van Gogh soon found an alternative outlet for his drawings, not with a magazine, but with his art dealer uncle, Cornelius Marinus van Gogh. In a letter to Theo of March 1882 van Gogh wrote excitedly in a postscript:

> Theo, it is almost miraculous!!!
>
> First of all, a message arrives that I must go and fetch your letter. Secondly, C.M. comes, orders 12 small pen drawings from me, views of The Hague, having seen a few that were finished (Paddemoes. The Geest district – Vleersteeg were finished) for a *rijksdaalder* apiece, the price set by me. With the promise that if I make them to his liking he'll order 12 more, but for which he'll fix the price higher than I do.[47]

This commission was the first of two and it gave van Gogh hope for the future. Although he had not long before sold a drawing to Tersteeg, this was the first and only time he was commissioned to produce a series of drawings for payment.[48]

For the first commission van Gogh sent twelve drawings of scenes from the streets of The Hague, ten of which still exist. Describing the encounter with his Uncle Cor to Theo in greater detail, he hinted at the kind of drawings he planned to execute:

> As a diversion I got out my portfolio with smaller studies and sketches. At first he said nothing – until we came to a little drawing that I'd sketched once with Breitner, parading around at midnight – namely Paddemoes (that Jewish quarter near the Nieuwe Kerk), seen from Turfmarkt. I'd set to work on it again the next morning with the pen....
>
> Could you make more of those townscapes for me? said C.M. Certainly, because I amuse myself with them sometimes when I've worked myself to the bone with the model – here's Vleersteeg– the Geest district – Vischmarkt. Make 12 of those for me. Certainly, I said, but that means we're doing a bit of business, so let's talk straightaway about the price.

---

47 LT 210, volume 2, 39.

48 For a comprehensive review of the drawings sent in both commissions, see Jan Hulsker, 'Van Gogh's First and Only Commission as an Artist', *Vincent: Bulletin of the Rijksmuseum Vincent van Gogh*, 4 no. 4 (1976), 5–19; for an update on the list of drawings commissioned, see Jan Hulsker, *The New Complete van Gogh: Paintings, Drawings, Sketches: Revised and Enlarged ed.* (Amsterdam: J.M. Meulenhoff: Philadelphia: John Benjamins, 1996), 38 and 44–8.

> My price for a drawing of that size, whether with pencil or pen, I've fixed for myself at a *rijksdaalder* – does that seem unreasonable to you?
>
> No – he simply says – if they turn out well I'll ask for another 12 of Amsterdam, provided you let me fix the price, then you'll earn a bit more.[49]

Van Gogh's enthusiasm for the project was obvious, as he completed the twelve drawings within two weeks.[50]

Van Gogh received thirty guilders for the first twelve drawings and was expecting more for the second commission, but was disappointed to receive only twenty. He aired his grievance to van Rappard:

> I've had a reply to my drawings, but received even less for them than I expected, although my expectation was no more than 30 guilders for 7 items. I received 20 guilders with a sort of reprimand to boot: 'did I imagine that such drawings had the least commercial value?[51]

He insisted he would continue to produce work with artistic value rather than commercial value, which his Uncle Cor wanted. Most importantly, though, he defended the role of the artist in withstanding the demands of merchants and art dealers, highlighting what artists had to endure to produce works that people like Uncle Cor felt were worthless:

> My dear friend Rappard, I really don't know whether to laugh or weep at this sort of thing. I find it so typical. Of course, the rich dealers are the good, honest, genuine, loyal, sensitive characters, and we poor devils who sit there drawing, whether out of doors, on the street, or in the studio, sometimes in the early morning, sometimes deep at night, sometimes in the heat of the sun, sometimes in the snow, we're the people without sensitivity, with no understanding of practical matters, without 'manners' above all. Fine by me![52]

Persevering, van Gogh sent more drawings to his uncle. In June 1883, he posted sketches of two compositions in the hope that a third series, of images

49 LT 211, volume 2, 40.

50 Hulsker (*The New Complete van Gogh*, 38) notes that the original discussion between Uncle Cor and van Gogh had taken place on 11 March 1882. By 24 March, van Gogh had told Theo that the commission was complete: 'First, the small drawings for C.M. They're finished, and have been sent to him' (LT 213, volume 2, 45).

51 LT 236, volume 2, 91.

52 LT 236, volume 2, 91.

around the Scheveningen sand dunes, would be commissioned.[53] But the relationship between van Gogh and his uncle remained far from amicable and a third commission never eventuated. The drawings that were sent for the first two commissions are, however, evidence of van Gogh's developing skill and draughtsman-like style. They also indicate the influence of the black-and-white prints and van Gogh's aim to produce work worthy of the genre.[54]

Uncle Cor's first request was for scenes of the city. Rather than depicting significant monuments and buildings in The Hague, van Gogh chose to illustrate everyday scenes, in which 'he was really interested'.[55] Van Gogh's illustrations conveyed the ordinary life of the townsfolk – pedestrians in the Jewish quarter, shoppers outside a bakery and workers in the sand dunes. Other drawings portrayed industrial progress, such as images of the gas tanks on the rural southwestern edge of the city and a factory with billowing smoke stacks. These drawings were a kind of 'Sketches from The Hague' and were influenced, as Luijten argues, by items in van Gogh's print collection.[56] They are line drawings, have a strong horizontal picture plane, candidly show figures in action, and pay homage to the ordinary. Some of the drawings demonstrate van Gogh's greater understanding and grasp of perspective. In *View of The Hague (Paddemoes)* (Figure 11) the perspective line leads the viewer from the right foreground, where a woman walks away through the picture, to the left middle ground, where another figure walks right, leading the viewer back towards the centre.

The trees and buildings in the background lead the eye across the picture towards another perspective point in the upper right-hand side. *Gasworks* (1882) has a single-point perspective and reveals van Gogh's attention to detail; the gas tanks are rendered accurately, as van Heugten has shown by comparing the image with technical design drawings.[57] The same attention

---

53 LT 350, volume 2, 347.

54 Van Gogh sent approximately fifty drawings to Uncle Cor, as confirmed in September 1883: 'I've NEVER SAID that he *must* do something, nor do I now. I count what he did or might do as a favour, and as such something for which I've always thanked him, and for my part have also given him studies, certainly 50 altogether, with the right to swap them later' (LT 388, volume 3, 17).

55 Johannes van der Wolk, Ronald Pickvance and E.B.F. Pey, *Vincent van Gogh: Drawings* (Otterlo: Kröller-Müller Museum, 1990), 62–3.

56 Hans Luijten, 'Rummaging Among My Woodcuts – Van Gogh and the Graphic Arts', in Chris Stolwijk, Sjraar van Heugten, Leo Jansen and Andreas Blühm (eds), *Vincent's Choice: The Musée Imaginaire of van Gogh* (Amsterdam: Van Gogh Museum, 2003), 104.

57 Vincent van Gogh, *Gasworks*, 1882 (Van Gogh Museum, Amsterdam (Vincent van Gogh Foundation). F0924/JH0118); van Heugten, *Vincent van Gogh Drawings* vol. 1, 113–4.

to detail is evident in *Factory* (1882) where the two large cylindrical tanks dividing the foreground and the factory in the background are meticulously drawn, complete with protruding ribbing and bolts, while the circular window on the central building has its internal patterned frame precisely drawn and each pane drawn exactly the same size.[58]

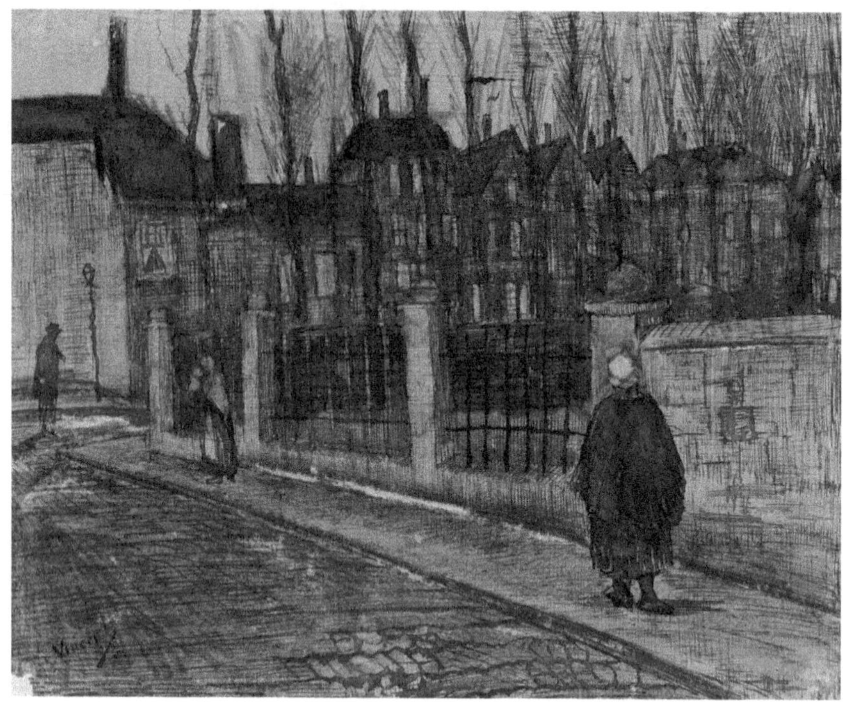

Figure 11. Vincent van Gogh, *View of The Hague (Paddemoes)*, 1882 (Kröller-Müller Museum, Otterlo).

Writing to Theo at the beginning of April 1882, van Gogh confirmed the new commission: 'C.M. paid me, and a new order, but difficult enough, 6 detailed, specific, townscapes. I'll see that I make them in any case, because if I understand correctly I'll get for these 6 as much as for the first 12'.[59] Unlike the first twelve drawings, which he completed within a fortnight, the second

58 Vincent van Gogh, *Factory*, 1882 (Staatliche Kuntsthalle, Karlsruhe. F0925/ JH0117).

59 LT 214, volume 2, 50. Although the original commission was for six drawings, there were actually seven (Hulsker, 'Van Gogh's First and Only Commission as an Artist', 9–14).

commission was fraught with difficulties and took almost two months to complete. Hulsker has described them as 'some of the best landscape drawings of The Hague period'.[60] The new drawings were more complex and of a higher quality than the first series. As in the first, van Gogh depicted scenes of interest to him, reflecting his belief in what draughtsmen should illustrate. Of the seven drawings, five are of work environments, such as a nursery, a fish-drying barn and a carpenter's yard, while the other two are views of the back of the house of the mother of Sien, the woman he lived with for some of his time in The Hague. All of these drawings are very detailed and complex in perspective, as van Gogh told Theo: 'The perspective is rather more complicated than in the Laan van Meerdervoort I sent you, and I've laboured long and hard on it'. He went on to tell Theo of how he would start work on these images as early as four o'clock in the morning, as it was 'the best time to see the broad outlines while things still have tone'.[61] He did not render these drawings simply in line, but combined pen, pencil and white highlights to replicate nature's tonal range, and used strong bold outlines to define key features. In this sense they aesthetically reflected the black-and-white illustrations that appeared in magazines and newspapers. In *Carpenter's Yard and Laundry* (Plate 2) the buildings on the left and the fences throughout the scene are defined by the use of strong bold lines, strengthened by the application of white highlights on a number of posts.

In some instances, as with the central fence, the white highlight becomes a line, assisting with perspective and with dividing the image. The figures are also outlined to add emphasis; the figure closest to the picture plane has a curved stroke above her head to separate her from the clothes-line, while the woman sitting in the barn behind the window is drawn with a few simple but strong lines. Use of parallel lines is a fundamental engraving technique and was used liberally here by van Gogh. The ditch on the right-hand side in *Carpenter's Yard and Laundry* is made up of closely drawn parallel lines, as are the trees receding into the distance. This technique is more pronounced in *Fish-Drying Barn, Seen from a Height* (1882).[62] Parallel lines are used in the earth in the central area of the drawing to indicate direction and varying heights, while the walls of the buildings are rendered in a way that is used in black-and-white prints. Even the fish baskets have closely drawn parallel lines to depict their woven texture accurately. The drawings from van Gogh's

60 Hulsker, *The New Complete van Gogh*, 48.

61 LT 231, volume 2, 79.

62 Vincent van Gogh, *Fish-Drying Barn, Seen from a Height*, 1882 (Kröller-Müller Museum, Otterlo. F0938/JH0152).

second commission reveal that he was gradually becoming more confident, engaging with difficult perspectives and replicating techniques he had seen in his collection of prints, which also influenced the subjects of the drawings. Although these images were destined for Uncle Cor, van Gogh's real clientele were the working class who could relate to the scenes and maybe afford his cheap illustrations. These drawings, therefore, can be seen as an indication of van Gogh's persistent aim to work within the context of a draughtsman employed to produce images of the everyday for mass production in illustrated newspapers and magazines.

While he worked on the drawings for Uncle Cor for several months, van Gogh remained committed to drawing directly from the figure. His study of the figure included drawing both individuals and groups; individual figures were drawn with the intention of using them as models when he composed images, while his depictions of groups tended to be of people in street scenes, such as road workers and customers outside shops. Most of his models, however, were found in places such as soup kitchens and third-class waiting rooms. When people criticised him for associating with such types, who were of a lower social standing to that of him and his family, he justified his practice by comparing himself to the artists of *The Graphic*. In a lengthy tirade to Theo he wrote:

> Do I lower myself by living with the people I draw, do I lower myself by frequenting the houses of workers and poor people or by receiving them in my studio? It seems to me that my profession involves that, and only those who understand nothing of painting or drawing are entitled to find fault with it.
>
> I ask this: where do the draughtsmen for The Graphic, Punch &c. get their models? Do they or don't they go themselves to round them up in the poorest alleyways of London? And the knowledge they have of the people, is it innate – or did they acquire it later in life by living among the people and by paying attention to things that most people walk right past, by remembering what many forget?[63]

He stressed that he had acquired the relevant skills to work as a draughtsman:

> It's precisely because I have a draughtsman's fist that I can't keep myself from drawing and, I ask you, have I ever doubted or hesitated or wavered since the day I began to draw? I think you know very well

63 LT 220, volume 2, 59.

> that I've hacked my way through and am obviously ever more keen to do battle.[64]

Van Gogh's enthusiasm for attaining a position as a draughtsman was not stifled by the criticism and consequent difficulties. Six months later he wrote: 'I would be really pleased if sooner or later, after even more or even less effort, I could supply drawings for illustrated magazines. One might follow from the other. The point is to keep on working'.[65] Of the kind of work he believed the magazines would accept he wrote:

> You'll see from this little scratch that I've begun doing what I spoke about in my last letter, namely trying to make notes regularly, either drawn or painted, of the scenes of workmen or fishermen that strike me, and these are precisely the things that could serve for illustrated magazines, I believe.[66]

His perception of the relevance of subject matter for the magazines was based on the prints he had collected – scenes of labourers and the working class – and is apparent in the scenes he chose for Uncle Cor. The newspapers and magazines were not socialist broadsheets, but reported comprehensively on current events, but van Gogh's interest was focused on the lower classes and their daily struggles.

In October 1882, van Rappard sent van Gogh an article that reinforced his belief in the direction he had embarked on and was a further catalyst in his endeavour in finding employment as a draughtsman. It was Hubert Herkomer's 'Drawing and Engraving on Wood' from *The Art Journal* of 1882. One of the original contributors to *The Graphic*, Herkomer had become a highly respected and renowned painter after successfully showing at the Royal Academy in 1875 a large oil painting *The Last Muster*, which first appeared as an illustration in *The Graphic* on 15 May 1875. Van Gogh owned a copy of the print and spoke highly of it, declaring on one occasion 'what virility'.[67] Herkomer was undoubtedly van Gogh's favourite illustrator; he was mentioned in his letters more often than any other illustrator and was well represented in his print collection.[68] This article had a profound effect on van Gogh, who embraced

64 LT 220, volume 1, 57.

65 LT 264, volume 2, 154.

66 LT 265, volume 2, 156.

67 LT 387, volume 3, 16.

68 For further information on the artistic relationship between van Gogh and Herkomer, see L.M. Edwards, *Herkomer: A Victorian Artist* (Aldershot: Ashgate, 1999), 133–6.

its contents in shaping his artistic practice. It analysed aspects of the black-and-white illustrations appearing in Victorian magazines and newspapers such as *The Illustrated London News* and *The Graphic.*

On 1 November 1882 van Gogh wrote to van Rappard and to Theo about Herkomer's article, opening each letter with sentences that suggest the impact it had on him. To van Rappard he wrote: 'The article by Herkomer is extremely interesting, for which many thanks. I've been completely absorbed by it since its arrival, and I hope that I'll make good use of what he says'.[69] To Theo he began: 'For several days I have been completely taken up by something that may also be of interest to you and I think it well worth writing to you about it especially'.[70] Van Gogh went on to give Theo more detail about the article, quoting some of its content and devoting the letter to ideas he had gained from its pages. He made no reference to his own work other than to observe that, when he was overcome with melancholy after reviewing one hundred of his recent drawings, Herkomer's energetic words comforted him and gave him strength to continue.

The letter to van Rappard was also filled with thoughts and responses to Herkomer's article, although van Gogh neither quoted from it nor summarised it, as van Rappard was already aware of its contents. Instead he discussed Herkomer's views, constantly referring to illustrations by numerous artists and proposed the direction that he and van Rappard should take their own art: 'I believe we'll do well to keep our attention fixed on the work and on the men of the past, namely 20, 30 years ago, if we don't want it to be rightly said of us later: and Rappard and Vincent, too, can be counted among the decadent fellows'.[71] Van Gogh's use of the phrase 'decadent fellows' was undoubtedly a reference to Herkomer's argument that the quality of illustrations in the illustrated press had declined significantly. Herkomer was especially critical of *The Graphic*, the magazine that published most of his work:

> I have spoken so highly of the Graphic, that it is necessary for me to say, I cannot feel the pleasure in their present issues that we all used to feel formerly. The managers declare that the public require the representation of a public event, and are satisfied if it is correct and entertaining, caring nothing for the artistic qualities of the drawing. I do not believe this. The Graphic might be the most artistic periodical, and the most correct, for it is extremely rich. Therefore do not take meekly (without at least

69 LT 279, volume 2, 190.

70 LT 278, volume 2, 189.

71 LT 279, volume 2, 191.

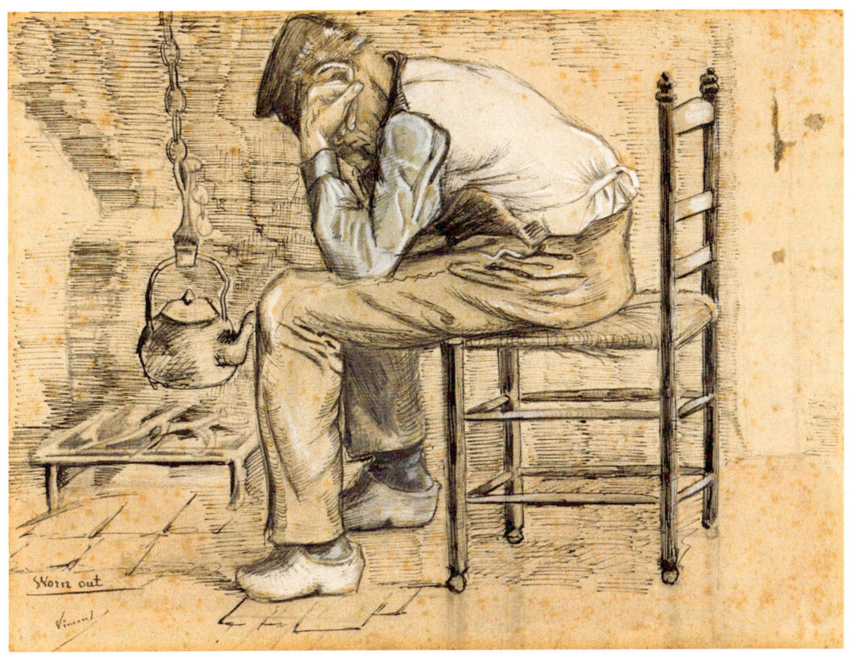

Plate 1. Vincent van Gogh, *Peasant Sitting by the Fireplace (Worn Out)*, 1881 (P. and N. de Boer Foundation, Amsterdam).

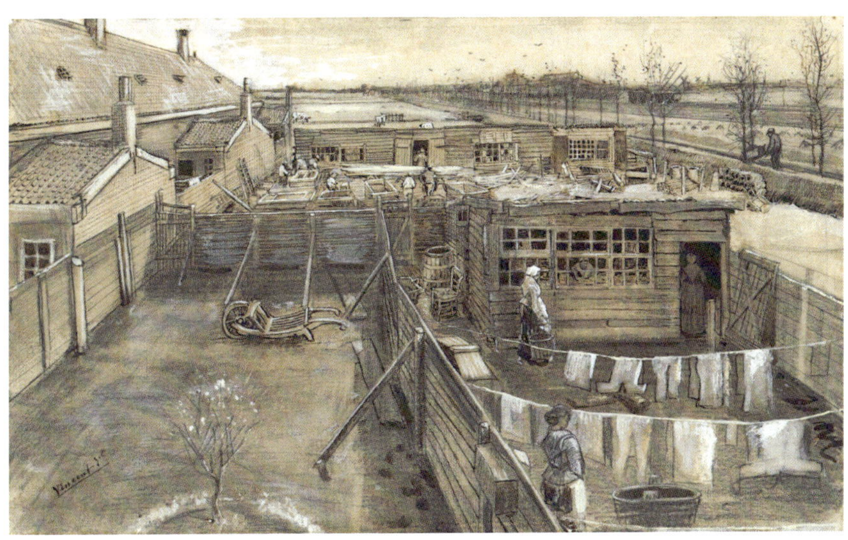

Plate 2. Vincent van Gogh, *Carpenter's Yard and Laundry*, 1882 (Collection Kröller-Müller Museum, Otterlo).

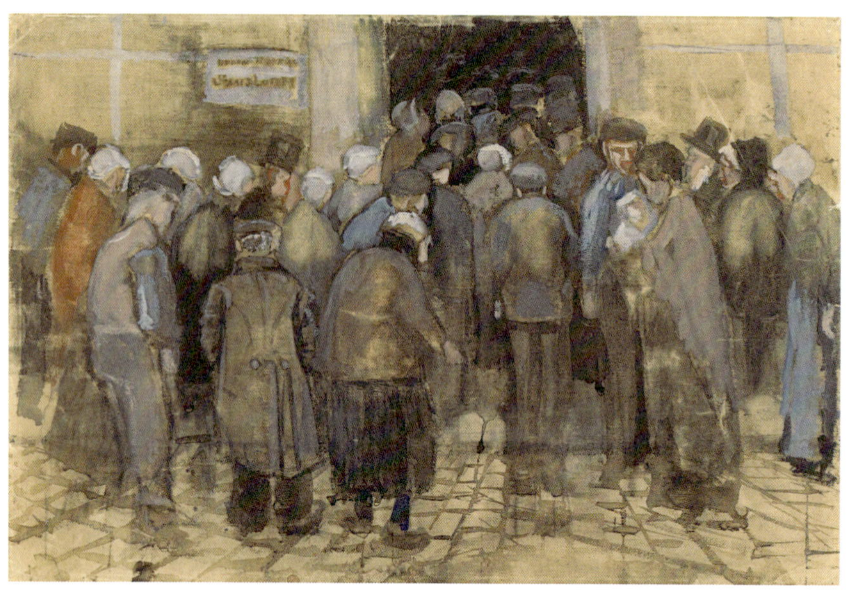

Plate 3. Vincent van Gogh, *The Poor and Money*, 1882
(Van Gogh Museum, Amsterdam (Vincent van Gogh Foundation)).

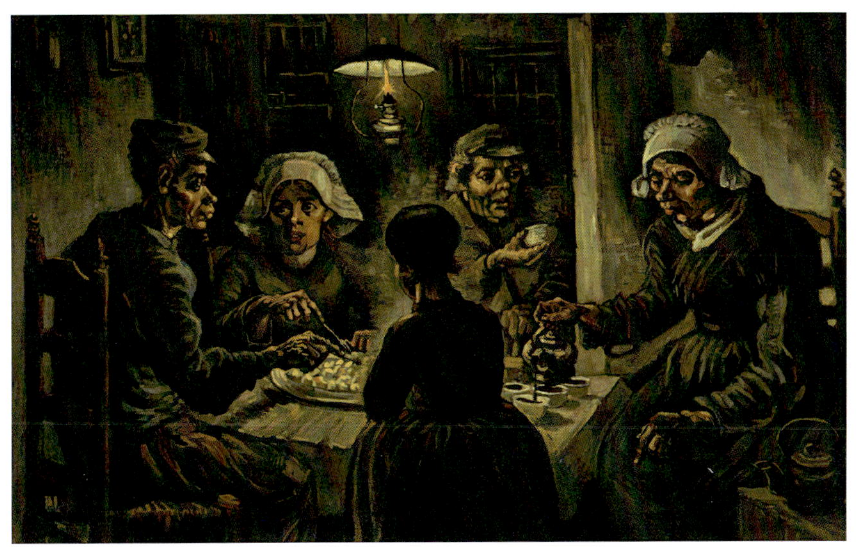

Plate 4. Vincent van Gogh, *The Potato Eaters*, 1885
(Van Gogh Museum, Amsterdam (Vincent van Gogh Foundation)).

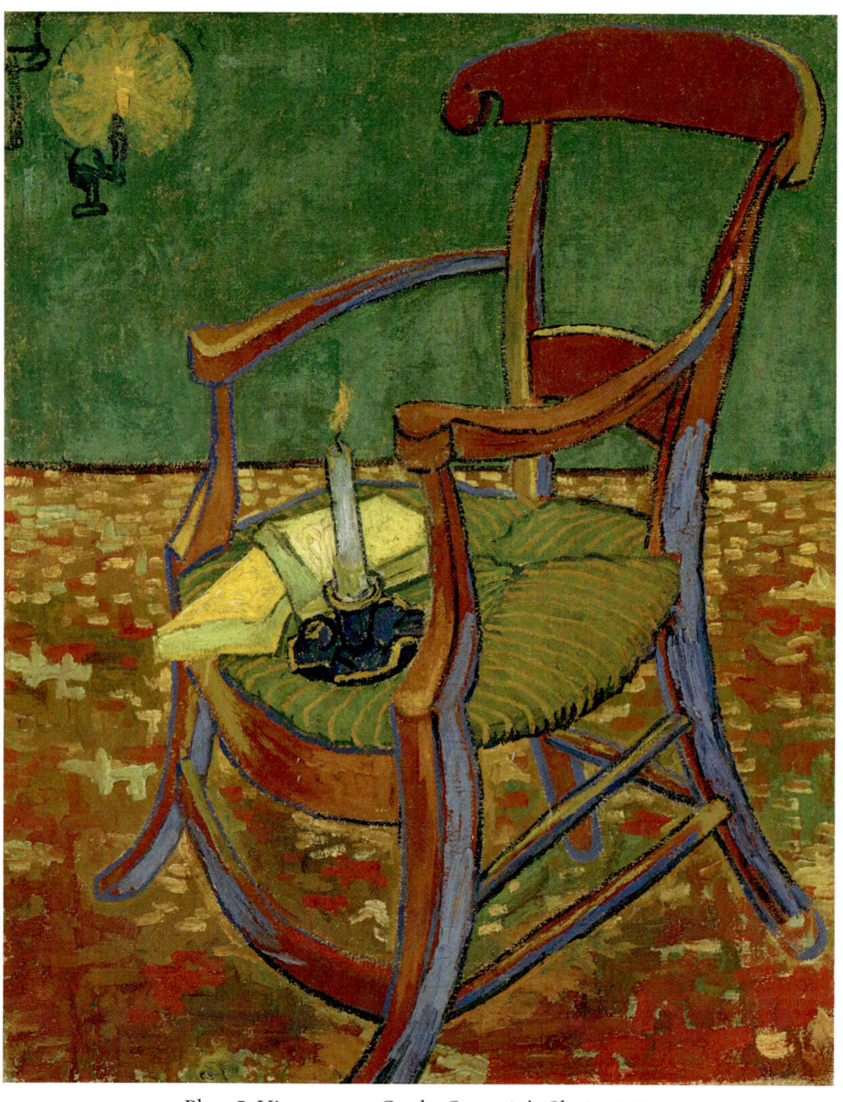

Plate 5. Vincent van Gogh, *Gauguin's Chair*, 1888
(Van Gogh Museum, Amsterdam (Vincent van Gogh Foundation)).

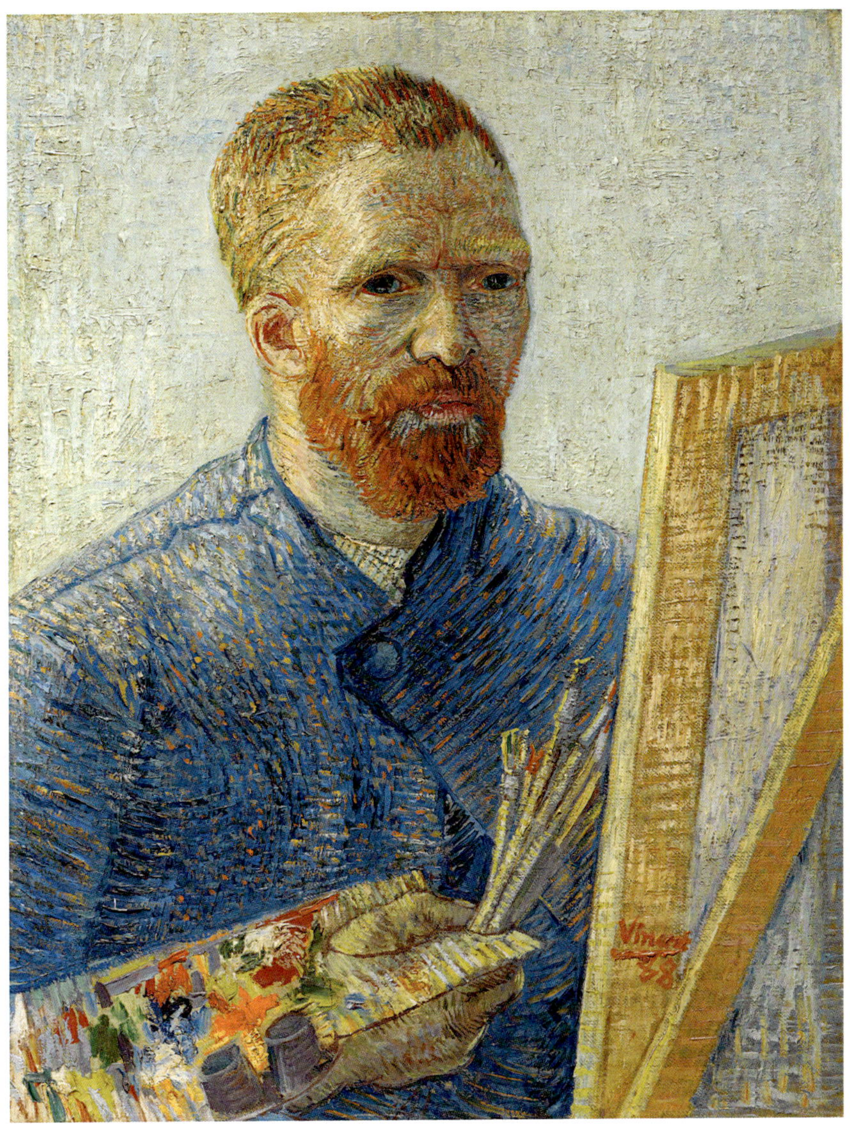

Plate 6. Vincent van Gogh, *Self-Portrait as a Painter*, 1887–88 (Van Gogh Museum, Amsterdam (Vincent van Gogh Foundation)).

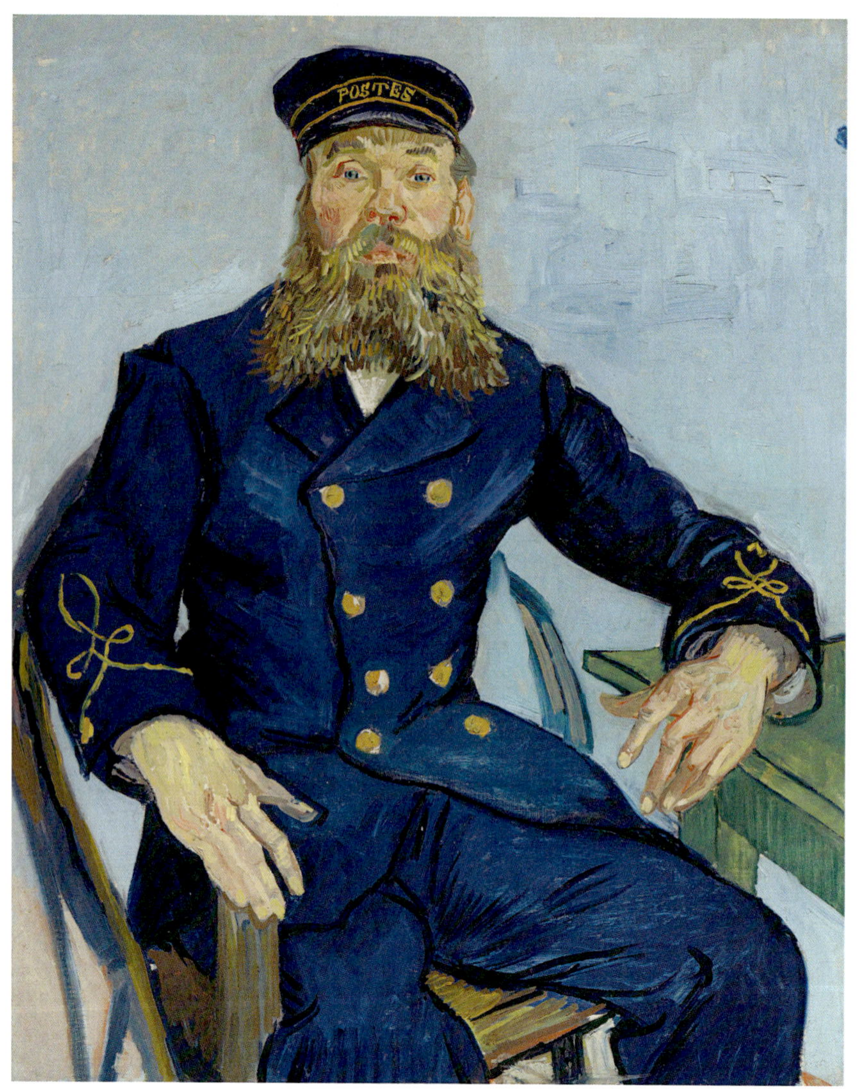

Plate 7. Vincent van Gogh, *Postman Joseph Roulin*, 1888
(Museum of Fine Arts, Boston).

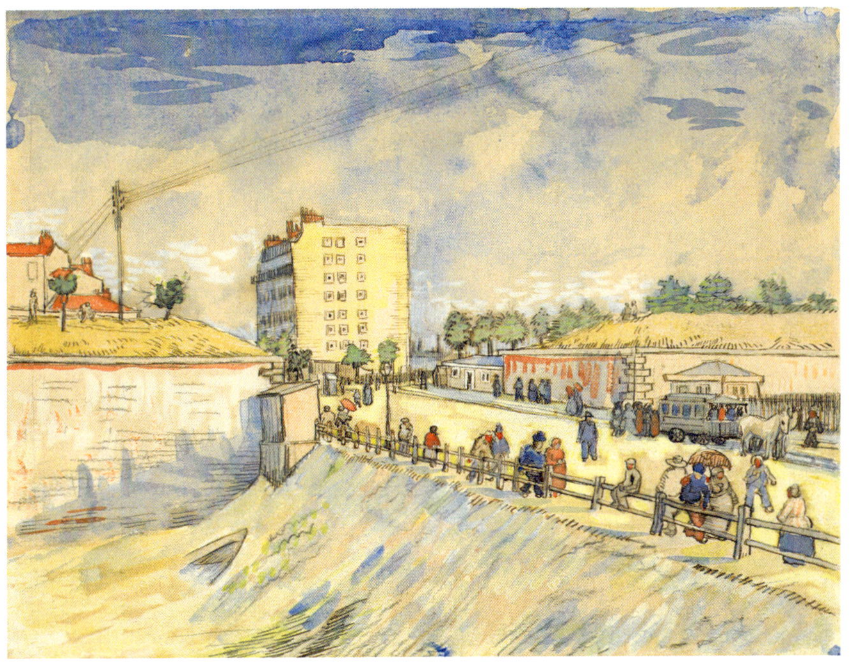

Plate 8. Vincent van Gogh, *Gate in the Paris Ramparts*, 1887 (Van Gogh Museum, Amsterdam (Vincent van Gogh Foundation)).

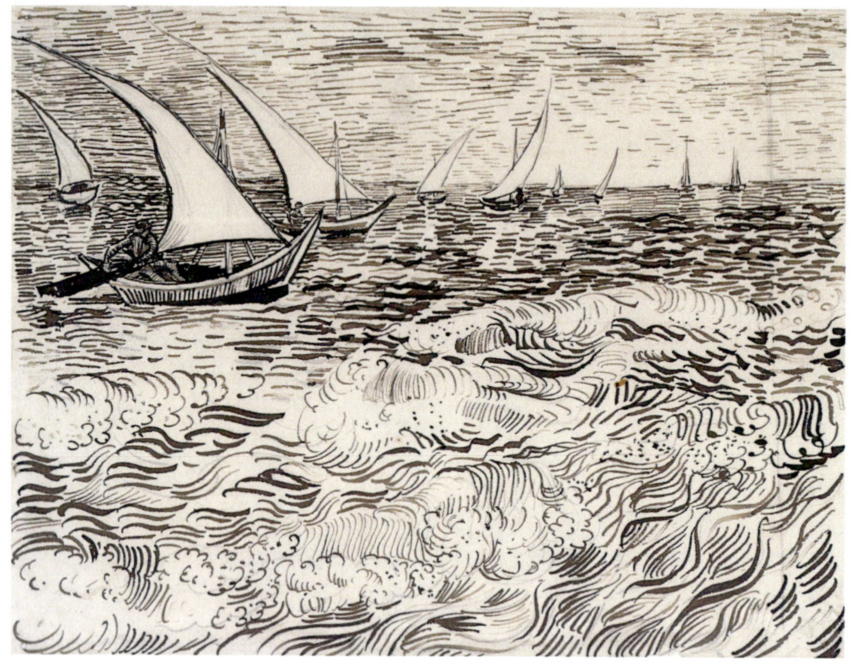

Plate 9. Vincent van Gogh, *Fishing Boats at Sea*, 1888
(Kupferstichkabinett, Staatliche Museen zu Berlin).

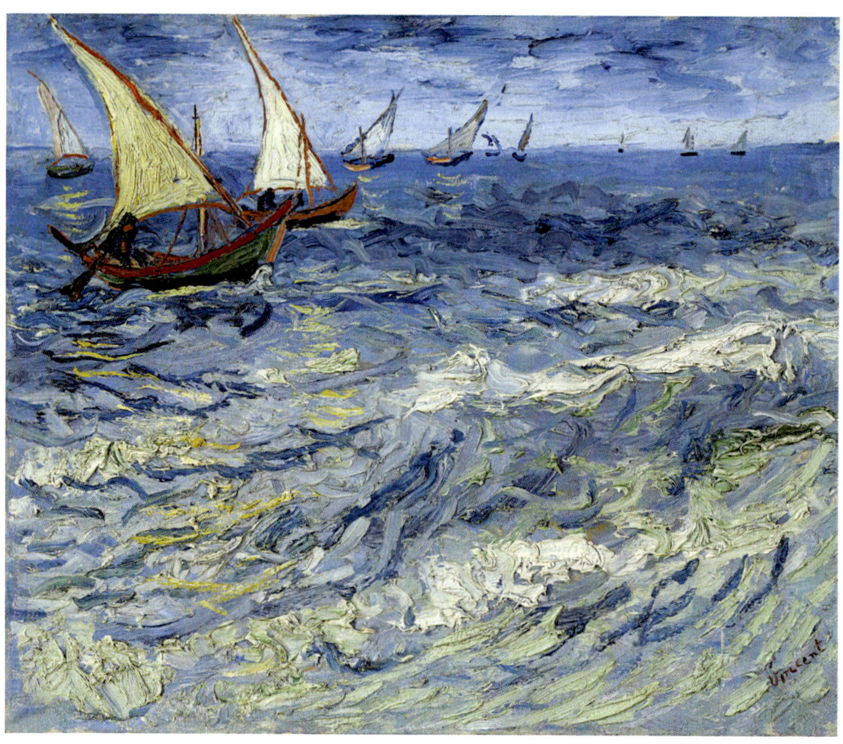

Plate 10. Vincent van Gogh, *Fishing Boats at Sea*, 1888
(Pushkin Museum, Moscow).

> some resistance) what they offer of inartistic work. The only excuse you may accept is dearth of good draftsmen.[72]

Herkomer's comments echoed van Gogh's belief about the relationship required between artist and subject. Artists needed to be noble, sympathetic and capable of portraying their subjects with sober sentiment. Furthermore, an artist required a warm heart and an understanding of his fellow man. As he told Theo, 'An artist need not be a minister or a collector in the church, but he must have a warm heart for people'.[73] Van Gogh believed artists had followed this creed in earlier issues of *The Graphic* but, as Herkomer had stated, their work had declined in more recent issues. Nevertheless, van Gogh still hoped he could gain employment to produce work that paralleled that in *The Graphic*'s earlier issues. He thought it essential that he provide the editors of illustrated newspapers and magazines a portfolio of studies from the model, rather than single sheets, which he believed would show his skill and his commitment to the salt-of-the-earth sentiments that were so highly regarded when the first issues of *The Graphic* were produced. Moreover, he was convinced that he would be able to fill the void Herkomer identified as a 'dearth of good draftsmen'.

Herkomer argued that black-and-white illustrations were not as heralded as they should be, a view that van Gogh consistently expressed. He wrote admiringly of a group of drawings exhibited by the proprietors of *The Graphic* at the Paris International Exhibition of 1878, describing the exhibit as,

> A collection of drawings such as I venture to say was never before seen – a collection that every Englishman ought to have been as proud of, as every foreigner was charmed by it. I go further, and say there was as much of the truest and most complete Art realised in that collection of drawings as in the whole of the pictures that hung on the endless walls belonging to the different nations.[74]

Van Gogh agreed wholeheartedly. Of the low value the public attributed to the art form he wrote to Theo, 'it's a terrible pity that here there's no enthusiasm, so to speak, for the art that's most suitable for the common people'. In regards to the higher quality of drawings in earlier issues of *The Graphic*, he argued that if works were produced for the public rather than for the academies,

72 Herkomer, 'Drawing and Engraving on Wood', 168.

73 LT 278, volume 2, 189.

74 Herkomer, 'Drawing and Engraving on Wood', 135–6.

artists could in fact 'produce the same results as were produced in the first years of *The Graphic*'.[75]

Not long after he had received Herkomer's article, van Gogh shared the idea that Theo, van Rappard and himself launch their own publication. Van Gogh believed that together they had the financial and artistic resources to produce their own collection of prints to make available to working-class people, resurrecting Herkomer's views of the early *Graphic*. The project would parallel *The Graphic Portfolio* in content and structure. Before fully disclosing the details of this new idea, van Gogh produced his first lithograph, *Orphan Man with a Stick* (1882).[76] Measuring 61 x 39.5cm, it was almost the size of a full-page illustration in one of the illustrated newspapers and magazines. An image of an orphan man standing as a single figure against a blank background, it depicts a type rather than an individual in an identifiable scene.[77] The lithograph was an experiment to 'learn about the process and the strengths of black and white' and was sent to Theo as an example of the work possible for the proposed project.[78] In the letter that accompanied the lithograph van Gogh suggested:

> I think it would be bold if, without involving anyone else, we could show a series of some thirty prints – not laboured but *vigorous* – that we'd had printed at our own expense, this would make us more credible to the people we'll have to approach later on, namely the managers of the magazines.[79]

Van Gogh stressed to Theo he was not being profligate by producing lithographs; they would be required when presenting a body of work for employment with one of the magazines, such as the French magazine *La Vie Moderne*, which van Gogh enquired about in a subsequent letter sent to Theo soon after.[80]

The question of whether the new expense was worthwhile was soon answered when Van Gogh achieved instant success with his first lithograph. A few workmen saw the stone and asked the printer for a copy to hang on their wall. For van Gogh this was the ultimate compliment: 'No result of my work

---

75 LT 278, volume 2, 188.

76 Vincent van Gogh, *Orphan Man with a Stick*, 1882 (Van Gogh Museum, Amsterdam (Vincent van Gogh Foundation). F1658/JH0256).

77 This idea of illustrating a 'type' became a focus in subsequent months as van Gogh worked exclusively on his series of heads.

78 LT 282, volume 2, 198.

79 LT 281, volume 2, 196.

80 LT 283, volume 2, 199.

would be more agreeable to me than the ordinary working men should hang such prints in their room or workplace'.[81] He also saw in the request a parallel with Herkomer's views and a connection with the calling of a draughtsman: 'I believe Herkomer speaks the truth when he says *For you – the public – it is really done*. Of course a drawing must have artistic value, but in my view this shouldn't rule out the possibility that ordinary passers-by may see something in it'.[82]

This success added fuel to van Gogh's ideas about the larger publishing project. It gave him confidence in his skill as a draughtsman and increased his hopes of finding employment with an illustrated magazine. By the beginning of December 1882, after further experiments with lithography, he finally gave the details of the publishing venture he had mentioned earlier. The letter to Theo reveals his sense of public duty in the venture. In a flurry of excitement, he proposed:

> Now such an undertaking like making and printing a series of 30 with Working types, say – sower, digger, woodcutter, ploughman, washerwoman, plus on occasion a cradle or orphan man, in short, the whole vast field lies open, there's an abundance of fine material – an enterprise like that – may one undertake it or may one not? It goes even deeper: is it a duty and just, or is it wrong? That is the question …
>
> It must be a matter of charity, not of bookshops.
>
> And as it will be necessary to have some contact with the bookshops, if only as regards printing and so on, I mention it to you now, not to ask you, 'do you think it will succeed?' from the bookshop's point of view, but just with the question *How to do it?* from the point of view that it would be out of love for the cause.[83]

He continued at length, describing what he believed to be the best approach for the project to succeed and showing his passion for the project:

> Given that it's useful and needful for Dutch drawings to be made, printed and circulated, intended for workers' dwellings, farmhouses, in a word, for every working man, several parties undertake to do their utmost, to exert their best efforts for this goal.

81 LT 283, volume 2, 199.

82 LT 283, volume 3, 199.

83 LT 289, volume 2, 209–10.

This association not to be dissolved before the venture is completed, and endeavouring to carry it out as practically and as well as possible.

The price of the prints is not to exceed 10 or at the most 15 cents.

Publication shall begin when a series of 30 has been made and printed, and the costs involved (for stones, printing wages, paper) have been paid. These thirty prints will appear simultaneously, although available separately, together forming a set in linen cover with a short text, not to go with the prints – which speak for themselves – but to explain pithily how and for what purpose they were made &c.

The *raison d'être* of the association is this. If the draughtsmen stand alone they'll have to bear both the effort and the costs – the venture would founder before it was half way – so the burden must be shared so that each gets the part that he can bear and so that the venture can be accomplished.

The amount raised by sales will be used first to reimburse those who advanced money, second to give everyone who has supplied a drawing an amount to be determined later that is the same for each draughtsman.

When these payments have been made, what remains will be used for new publications to carry on the work.

Those who begin this venture regard it as a duty. Self-interest *not* being their aim, neither those who advance money nor draughtsmen nor those who participate in other ways may claim back what they have contributed in the event that the venture yields no profit, so that their contribution is lost; nor may they claim back more than they have put in should the venture be successful beyond expectation.

In the latter case the surplus will be used to carry on the work, in the former case, however, the stones remain the property of the entrepreneurs; *in any event* though, the first 700 impressions from each stone are intended not for the association but for the people. If the association founders, those prints will be distributed free of charge.

Immediately after the publication of the first series of 30 there must be a debate and decision on whether or not to continue, and at that point, but not before, whoever so wishes may withdraw from the association.

> This is the idea that took shape in my mind – now I say to you: How to do it? Will you take part?[84]

While the grand idea was most likely quelled by Theo who may have considered it a logistical and financial nightmare, van Gogh saw the project as a public responsibility and an opportunity for Dutch artists to emulate Herkomer: 'It has always been said: in Holland we can't make magazines for the people. I've never been entirely able to believe this. I see now: it CAN be done'.[85] His reference to having witnessed the possibilities of being able to complete a publication that represented a democratic culture of art for the people undoubtedly arose from two major factors. First, he had been able to produce a lithograph successfully at what he thought was a low cost, that was attractive to his target audience – workers. Second, he was an avid admirer of black-and-white prints and, like Herkomer, thought they were appropriate for distribution to a wider public and had real artistic merit.

Van Gogh produced five more lithographs, all similar to *Orphan Man with a Stick*. Four were intended for the proposed publishing venture and depicted general types of people rather than individuals. Two were images of workers, one digging and the other taking a break, and the other two were of orphan men, one drinking coffee and the other a sorrowful, poverty-stricken man, which was a subject van Gogh had previously tackled and would continue to do so throughout his career. It was entitled *At Eternity's Gate* (Figure 29). The fifth lithograph, although produced at the same time as the others, did not form part of the intended series of thirty or more images. Entitled *Sorrow* (1882), it is now one of van Gogh's most recognised works. It does not depict a worker or an agricultural type, but Sien, the prostitute with whom he lived for a while in The Hague.[86] While the image can be identified from references in van Gogh's letters as Sien, it is also a universal representation of van Gogh's empathy for humanity, an image that, according to Fieke Pabst and Sjraar van Heugten, 'embodies the abstract concept of Sorrow'.[87]

Midway through 1883 van Gogh returned to lithography, but with his focus firmly on producing works for the illustrated magazines. Over several weeks he produced two new lithographs: *Gardener by an Apple Tree* (1883) and *Burning*

84 LT 289, volume 2, 210–11.

85 LT 289, volume 2, 210.

86 Vincent van Gogh, *Sorrow*, 1882 (Van Gogh Museum, Amsterdam (Vincent van Gogh Foundation) F1655/JH0259).

87 Sjraar Van Heugten & Fieke Pabst, *The Graphic Work of Van Gogh* (Zwolle: Waanders, 1995), 39.

Weeds (1883).[88] Both are heavily linear and make use of cross-hatching and parallel lines to create depth and tone. For example, the clouds hovering above the peasant in *Burning Weeds* are constructed with short sharp lines, while the rooftops and thatched fence in the background of *Gardener by an Apple Tree* are defined by a group of parallel lines. The figures in both prints are given form by cross-hatching, as are the main objects – the wheelbarrow in one and the tree in the other. Van Gogh also placed white areas against dark to define objects, a technique used in woodblock printing to ensure a heavily carved area was supported by a less engraved part of the block. Although van Gogh did not compose his drawings with this in mind, as they were transferred to stone and no engraving was required, he aimed to give the drawings the impression of prints from engravings found in his collection. While the two lithographs are experimental in nature, van Gogh maintained an aesthetic that strongly paralleled the effects achieved in woodblock printing.[89] For example, in *Burning Weeds* a wash of ink was applied during the printing process, while in two of the impressions of *Gardener by an Apple Tree* ink was added with a roller, and the figure, tree, foreground and the houses in the background were retouched so they resembled magazine illustrations.[90] Van Gogh also drew a frame around one of the impressions of the weed-burner, a clear indication of his intention for these prints to be made available for publication. Van Heugten and Pabst also argue that the size of the prints was deliberately chosen so that they paralleled an 'illustration croquis' (a rapid sketch for the magazines).[91]

At the end of 1882 a despondent van Gogh asked Theo: 'Will we have more luck in making saleable drawings in the new year, or finding work for an illustrated magazine?'[92] Even though his drawing had progressed, he had still not sold any work, other than the drawings to Uncle Cor, and he had had no success in finding employment as a draughtsman. Van Gogh's proposal for a large series of prints or having any of them published was not realised, and it seemed that his efforts in making his own lithographs were in vain. Nevertheless, the knowledge he gained from his experiments

88 Vincent van Gogh, *Gardener by an Apple Tree*, 1883 (Van Gogh Museum, Amsterdam (Vincent van Gogh Foundation) F1659/JH0379); *Burning Weeds*, 1883 (Van Gogh Museum, Amsterdam (Vincent van Gogh Foundation) F1660/JH0377).

89 For analysis of all the impressions, see van Heugten & Pabst, *The Graphic Work*, 1995.

90 One of the two impressions is in Staatsgalerie, Stuttgart; the other was in Josefowitz Collection (dispersed in 2016) (see Van Heugten, & Pabst, *The Graphic Work*, 1995).

91 Van Heugten & Pabst, *The Graphic Work*, 22.

92 LT 296, volume 2, 226.

with lithography was to surface in a unique form – the use and adaptation of lithographic crayon directly onto drawings, a technique that was, according to van Heugten, 'decidedly unorthodox' and not found in the work of any of his peers.[93] On New Year's Eve 1882 van Gogh informed Theo: 'When I made the lithographs, I was struck by the fact that the lithographic crayon was very pleasant to work with, and I thought of making drawings with it'.[94] Theo's criticism may well have indirectly prompted the introduction of this material into van Gogh's work. In a letter of 3 January 1883, van Gogh discussed his use of lithographic crayon, asking Theo twice whether he viewed the technique as a solution to the objections he had raised about some of the drawings: 'What I'd like to know from you is whether you think that this new way of working would perhaps remove some of the objections you had to pencil'. He returned to the question later: 'Let me know whether you think some of the objections to using pencil alone could be removed somewhat by using crayon as well'.[95] From these questions we can deduce that Theo believed his brother's drawings did not have enough depth and life to show to possible clients and magazine editors. This is reinforced by van Gogh's constant reference in this letter to creating works that would better resemble those found in illustrated magazines and his request for a copy of *La Vie Moderne* so that he could assess their illustrations.

The use of crayon transformed van Gogh's drawings from a predominantly grey scale to an intense and deep black, a process van Gogh described as 'painting in black'.[96] He saw parallels between this newly discovered technique and the work of the black-and-white artists who sought to replicate the lightest and darkest tones with 'a few simple ingredients'.[97] Highlighting the experimental nature of his work and his enthusiasm for the new material, van Gogh detailed his application of the crayon within a drawing context:

> But I had the idea of first doing a drawing in carpenter's pencil and then working in and over it with lithographic crayon, because (owing to the greasiness of the material) it takes on pencil, whereas ordinary crayon does *not*, or only poorly. Having done the sketch in this way, one can confidently work in the lithographic crayon where necessary without

93 Sjraar van Heugten, 'Working in Black-and-White and Colour: Van Gogh's Regard for Tonality and Technique', in Stolwijk, van Heugten, Jansen and Blühm, *Vincent's Choice*, 124.

94 LT 297, volume 2, 226.

95 LT 298, volume 2, 229–30.

96 LT 297, volume 2, 228.

97 LT 297, volume 2, 228.

> having to search or rub out a lot. So I went quite a long way towards finishing my drawings in pencil, as far in fact as I possibly could with it. Then I fixed them and made them matt with milk. And then drew over them again in lithographic crayon, where the greatest strengths were, reinforcing them here and there with a brush or pen with lampblack, and working with white body-colour in the light passages.[98]

Van Gogh intended these drawings for mass production either by the illustrated magazines or in large-scale editions of prints by firms such as Goupil & Cie. Confirming that the technique was ultimately an experiment in preparing drawings suitable for duplication, he stressed that he had 'hopes that the drawings done in this way will be suitable for reproduction using the process you've described to me'. Further, he declared that the deep black he achieved by using the lithographic crayon in his unique style was 'really essential for reproduction, where photogravure and galvanoplasty are involved'.[99] He further confirmed this aim in his next letter to Theo in which he wrote of continuing with his experiments in black-and-white and of wanting to consult a professional to ascertain whether the new drawings could be printed and whether the magazines would take a selection. Van Gogh also made it clear that he was not interested in selling one or two drawings, but wanted to obtain full-time work as an artist: 'You'll see clearly enough from what I've said above that I'm more eager to put together a serious work for reproduction than have the satisfaction of seeing one drawing printed some day'.[100]

An example of van Gogh's experiments with lithographic crayon is a work inspired by *The Graphic*'s 'Heads of the People' series. *Old Man with Top Hat* (Figure 12) reveals the success of his experiments at the time and exemplifies the many techniques he commented on in his letters.

It is a composition essentially in black-and-white, although parts of the drawing now appear to be brown.[101] Van Gogh used numerous materials to achieve a diversity of tone and employed the lithographic crayon to achieve the dark velvety blacks found in printed illustrations. This is most evident in the shadows between both arms and the torso of the sitter, as well as in the many shadows of his clothing and top hat. These areas were modelled after he had applied water, as van Gogh explained:

98 LT 297, volume 2, 227.

99 LT 297, volume 2, 228.

100 LT 298, volume 2, 229.

101 For an analysis of this drawing and comments on the fading of the ink, see van Heugten, *Vincent van Gogh Drawings* Vol. 1, 176–8.

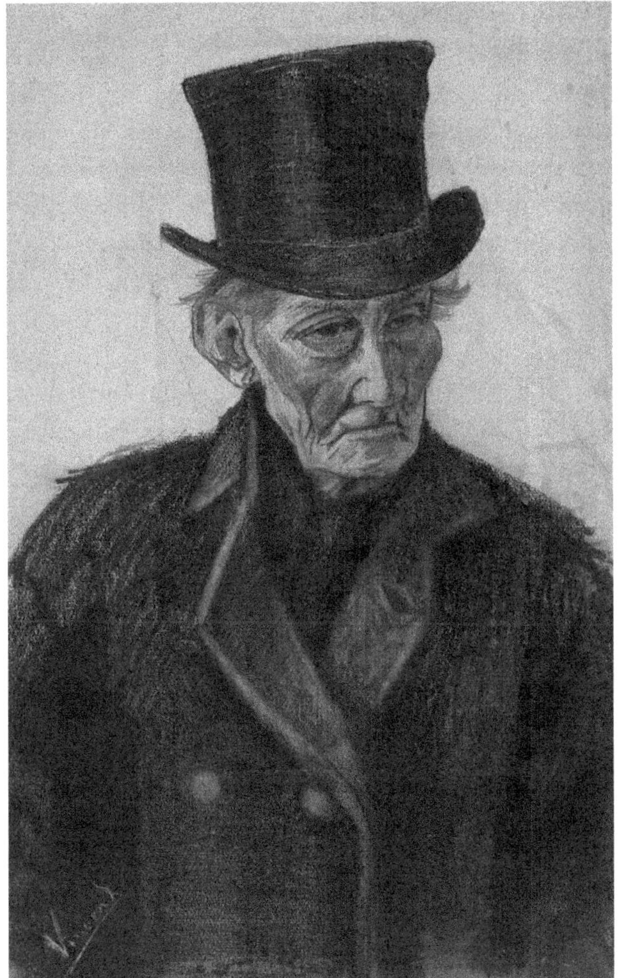

Figure 12. Vincent van Gogh, *Old Man with Top Hat* 1882–83 (Van Gogh Museum, Amsterdam (Vincent van Gogh Foundation)).

It really pleases me that you found the old man's head 'true' – the *model* is wonderfully *true*, I have more drawings of him. Today one that I drew with lithographic crayon. Then I tipped a bucket of water over the drawing and began to model with a brush in the soaking wet. In this way one gets very delicate tones if it works, for it's a dangerous method that can turn out wrong on occasion. But if it works, the result is very 'unburred', delicate tones of black that most resemble an etching.[102]

102 LT 300, volume 2, 232.

A further technique that resembled both etchings and woodblock prints was the scraping of the lithographic surface. Van Gogh used this technique for signing the work and as an artistic device in the drawing. Evidence of scraping is most pronounced on the left lapel and in the top hat. He scraped horizontal lines into the deep black lithographic crayon to give the illusion of a reflection, a technique full of freedom and paralleling that of printed illustrations in its spontaneity and reliance on line to achieve depth and shade. Van Gogh classed this drawing as more than a sketch and must have sent it to Theo for him to sell or to present to editors and managers of magazines. Two elements of the drawing strongly suggest this to be the case. Firstly, the drawing was signed at the bottom left-hand corner, with the signature scratched into the drawing as if in relief and reminiscent of the engraved signatures on the woodblock prints in illustrated magazines. The second element was the border drawn around the image, a feature that appears in many of the illustrated prints that van Gogh had collected, especially in the large single- and double-page illustrations.

Throughout this period of experimentation van Gogh remained focused on relieving Theo of his financial burden. One possibility constantly in his thoughts was of returning to London to find employment. He raised it again during this time of lithographic crayon experimentation, but did so cautiously and pessimistically:

> I begin to feel in myself that if, for example, I went to England and tried right and left, I would indeed have a chance of finding a place. To achieve that was my ideal, was and is, despite everything, still what spurred me on to overcome the enormous initial difficulties. – But my heart becomes heavy at times when I think of what's going on – my pleasure vanishes. I really want to do my best in my drawings, but all those editors and having to present oneself there – bah! I shudder at the thought.[103]

Within six months he was no longer hesitant, writing boldly and confidently in June 1883 about contacting London's two major illustrated magazines:

> Do you know what I often consider? It's to establish relations in England with The Graphic or London News. Now that I'm making progress, I want so very much to carry on working on some larger compositions suitable for an illustrated magazine. Boughton and Abbey are together doing drawings of '*picturesque Holland*' for Harper of New

103 LT 293, volume 2, 220–1.

> York (also the agent for The Graphic). I saw these illustrations (very finished although they're small, definitely done after larger drawings) at Rappard's. Now I think to myself that if The Graphic and Harper send their draughtsmen to Holland, they wouldn't be unwilling to take on a Dutch draughtsman if he could supply them with something good for not too much money. I'd like to work towards being PERMANENTLY employed for a monthly wage rather than selling a drawing now and again for a relatively higher sum. And commit myself to a series of compositions following on, for example, from these two that are on the easel or from others that I'll add.[104]

Van Gogh's bravado continued, as he made clear his preference to travel to London himself in order to approach artists such as Herkomer, Green and Boughton, rather than just the magazines' managers. He also claimed that he could produce a double-page illustration each month along with supplying 'other formats too, the whole page and the half page'. Such was his confidence that he declared, 'I believe that it isn't every day that the managers of illustrated magazines find someone who regards those magazines as his special goal'.[105] Theo supported his brother in his plan to travel to London, as is evident in van Gogh's response to a letter from Theo: 'as for going to London sooner or later for a while, long or short, I too believe that there would be more chance of doing something with my work over there'. He believed that in London he could not only sell drawings, but could also continue working on subjects he enjoyed and for which he felt empathy such as the 'beautiful things to do on the wharves beside the Thames'.[106] In preparation for approaching the magazines he ordered photographs of his drawings, believing that they would help him promote himself.[107] He also saw them as useful for exposing his work to potential clients in Paris.

Organising photographs to assist his employment prospects soon became a priority for van Gogh. Within a week he had ordered reproductions of more of his drawings. He listed enthusiastically for Theo the works he had got photographs of and those he intended to get done:

---

104 LT 348, volume 2, 343.

105 LT 348, volume 2, 343.

106 LT 361, volume 2, 375.

107 'This morning I saw the negatives of the three photos. I'm looking forward to the prints, and have hopes that in this small form they'll be something with which we'll be able to make approaches to the illustrated magazines' (LT 362, volume 2, 379).

> Well, as you see, the photos are Sower – potato grubbers – Peat diggers. I've now done some more, Sand quarry, weed burners, Dung-heap, Potato grubber 1 figure, Coal loaders, and at Scheveningen this week I worked on Mending nets (Scheveningen fishermen's wives).
>
> And two larger compositions of Dune workers (one of which I showed to Tersteeg again) which, although they'll require a lot more labour, are still what I'd most like to complete.
>
> Long rows of diggers – poor fellows set to work by the city – in front of a piece of dune land that's to be dug over. But to do that is terribly difficult.
>
> *Peat diggers* gives you a first idea of it.[108]

Even though Theo had not yet received the photographs, he may have challenged his brother on the expense of such a venture, as it appears that he had written about their financial position, which soon dominated van Gogh's letters.[109] Responding to Theo's concerns, van Gogh assured him he would try his best to 'place something with the illustrated magazines',[110] and later, as the financial strain became more palpable, he suggested that they should perhaps begin to look at alternatives to London for employment and possible sales.[111] He asked for his brother's patience:

> I am as my work is, and you must take this into consideration a little. I don't know whether or not you think it would be better to see someone like Herkomer, Green or Small, for instance, *now* or *to wait* until both the work and I myself have calmed down. I'd be in favour of the latter. Things inside me may clear up soon, but at the moment I'd rather not have to navigate through complicated London affairs.[112]

Van Gogh again aired his confusion and preference not to travel to London in his next letter to Theo, in which he implied that he was not going to pursue that avenue:

---

108 LT 363, volume 2, 382.

109 LT 363, 364 and 365, volume 2.

110 LT 363, volume 2, 382.

111 'I believe it's still always possible that on looking through the work we may decide on another plan for the future – I don't know what as yet – but somewhere there must be work that has to be done and that I can do as well as someone else. If London were a little closer, I for one wouldn't leave it to others' (LT 368,volume 2, 391).

112 LT 375, volume 2, 404.

> I wish to say again that it seems to me more and more that the most practical and direct way to make progress with the work is not to look too far away and to stay down to earth. When I think of London, it's a stimulating thought, I assure you, but the question is: is it practicable now, is now the right moment?[113]

Van Gogh's thoughts turned from London to the northern Dutch province of Drenthe – not as a place where he might find employment or meet the editors of magazines but as a place where he would have access to local workers and peasants as subjects for his work. He also believed the cheaper living expenses would allow him to purchase more expensive materials, such as oil paints. He hoped to become more accomplished as a painter so that he could enter the Hollandsche Teekenmaatschappij (Dutch Drawing Society), an international art society founded in The Hague in 1876, and thereby increase his chances of success in England.[114] The idea of entering the society on the basis of his skills as a painter, and then being able to work as an illustrator, was similar to the view Herkomer had expressed in his *Art Journal* article, in which he had stressed the importance of being a draughtsman first, then a painter, and then combining the two to become a successful and respected artist.[115] It is likely that van Gogh planned his trip to Drenthe on this premise.

Of the works van Gogh produced during this period, a sheet of sketches he sent to Theo shows quite clearly the influence of black-and-white illustration (Figure 13). The collage of drawings is very similar in structure to works made by artists reporting for the newspapers. One comparable example is W.B. Murray's *Market Gardening – A Winter's Journey to Covent Garden* (Figure 14).

113 LT 376, volume 2, 406.

114 LT 381, volume 2, 415.

115 Herkomer, 'Drawing and Engraving on Wood', 168: 'The vital element of the Art power is the pursuit of fact. For the artist's first efforts in this pursuit, wood drawing stands unrivalled. Not only is it mechanically advantageous beyond all other methods, but it offers special advantages to the younger painter, to whom Nature has given the divine spark. It frees him from the bondage of conventionalism. It awakens his subject-seeing faculties. It develops the power of the most delicate draughtsmanship. It trains his powers of composition. It gains for him a livelihood, and he can paint pictures with an independent spirit that is free from the anxiety of sale, so that his first appearance as a painter stamps him once and for all'.

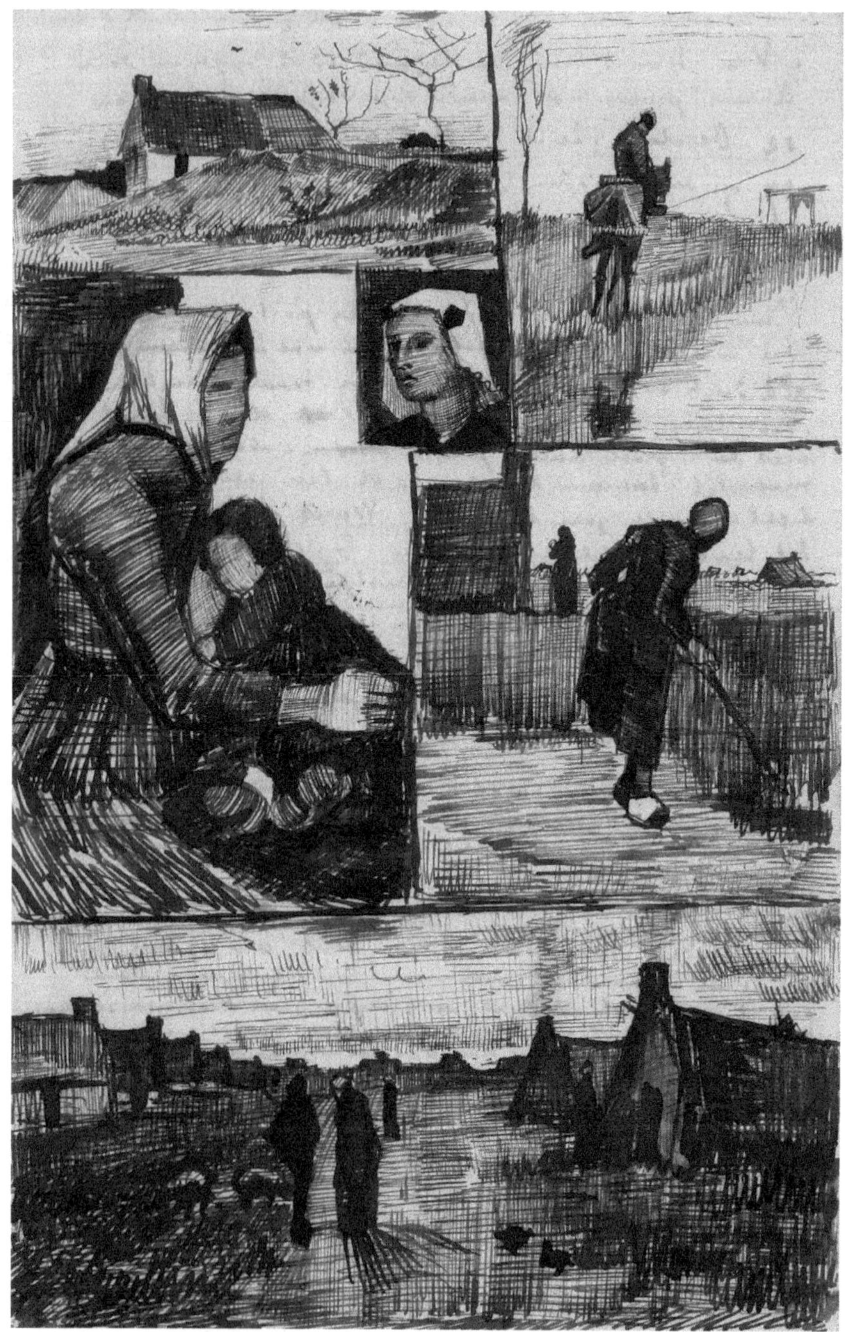

Figure 13. Vincent van Gogh, *Letter from Vincent van Gogh to Theo van Gogh with Sketches of Farm, Rider by a Waterway, Woman and Child, Head of a Woman, Woman Working and Country Road with Cottages (recto)*, 3 October 1883 (Van Gogh Museum, Amsterdam (Vincent van Gogh Foundation)).

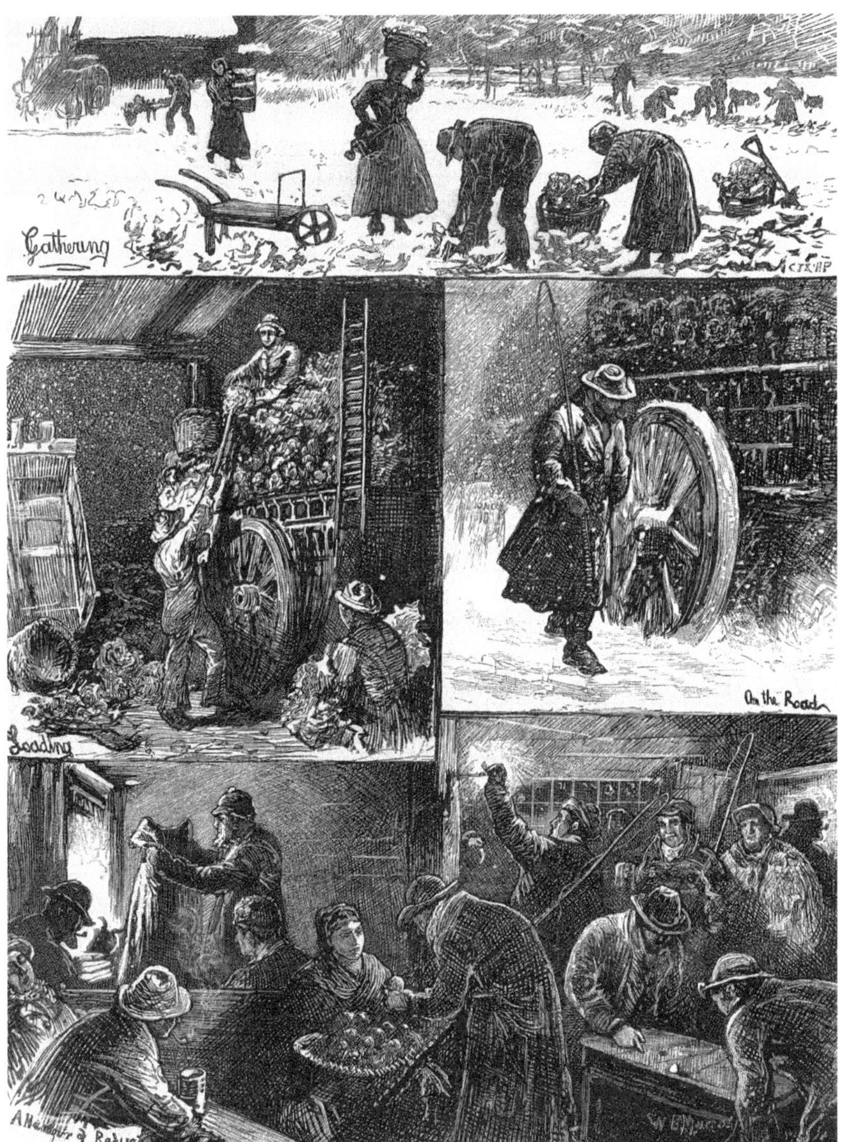

Figure 14. W.B. Murray, *Market Gardening – A Winter's Journey to Covent Garden* (*The Graphic*, 12 February 1876).

In the English print farmers are harvesting their crops, loading a wagon, and then trudging through the snow to find comfort indoors. Van Gogh's sheet is similar. It depicts the lives of local peasants out in the field, at home and walking back from their day of labour in the evening. The format of the two is similar, in that each has a drawing right across the bottom of the page and vertical rectangular framed drawings above. Van Gogh added a small drawing of a peasant's head in the middle of the top third of the page, which has not equivalent image in Murray's drawing. The small drawing is not of an individual, but rather of a type, a motif found in illustrated magazines, as in *The Graphic*'s 'Heads of the People' series, which van Gogh owned and had previously tried to emulate.

Van Gogh's stay in Drenthe was brief; he arrived in September 1883 and had left by December. Unable to cope with the loneliness and the lack of models and materials for him to work with, he returned to the family home in Nuenen, where he later revisited lithography as a medium. Initially his return to lithography was to produce a series, as he told Theo: 'I've been to Eindhoven today to order a small stone, since this is to be the first in a series of lithographs, which I'm planning to start again...I'm thinking of making a series of subjects from peasant life, in short – *the peasants at home*'.[116] His first lithograph, although not as successful as the original painting, was a reproduction after *The Potato Eaters*.[117] Van Gogh agreed with Theo's criticism of the lithograph, explaining why it lacked atmosphere:

> What you say about the lithograph, that the effect is woolly, I think so too, and it isn't my own fault, in so far as the lithographer insisted that it wouldn't print properly because I'd left virtually no white on the stone. On his advice I then bit out light areas. If I had just printed it as the drawing was, it would have been generally darker but wouldn't have lacked cohesion. And there would still have been atmosphere between the planes.[118]

While both brothers considered the lithograph a failure, it was van Gogh's closest emulation of the English prints in technique and, as Maureen Trappeniers argues, in atmosphere.[119] Van Gogh believed *The Potato Eaters* was his first

---

116 LT 493, volume 3, 224.

117 After the lithograph, van Gogh painted the subject again; the second painting is in the Vincent van Gogh Foundation collection in Amsterdam, while the first is in the Kröller-Müller Museum in Otterlo.

118 LT 499, volume 3, 234.

119 Maureen Trappeniers, 'Catalogus', in Evert van Uitert (ed.), *Van Gogh in Brabant* (Zwolle: Waanders, 1987), 175.

great genre painting, and that by producing it as a lithograph he would be able to promote the painting to art dealers and continue his quest of conquering the illustrated magazines. He suggested that Theo show a small sketch of the image to the French magazine *Le Chat Noir*[120] and asked him to send a number of copies to the art dealer Arsène Portier, hoping that he would show his work.[121] He also sent a copy to van Rappard as an illustration of the painting, but van Rappard, who had received copies of all The Hague prints, responded negatively and sarcastically: 'and with such a manner of working you dare to invoke the names of Millet and Breton? Come on! Art is too important, it seems to me, to be treated so cavalierly'.[122] Years later Theo presented copies of the lithograph to Paul Gauguin and to art critic Albert Aurier, thus acknowledging the work's importance in van Gogh's oeuvre and attempting again to spread it to a mass audience.

After his period in Nuenen, van Gogh left for Antwerp, before finally moving to France. The years he spent in Paris were to revolutionise his work, as the dark palette of his Dutch years gave way to the vibrant colours associated with many of his later avant-garde masterpieces. The Paris years also signalled his shift from wanting to be an illustrator to his full commitment to painting. Nevertheless, van Gogh's Dutch period, during which he built his impressive collection of black-and-white illustrations and set about becoming a draughtsman, was of critical importance in the development of his thought and art. Those early years shaped his views, his style and his technique.

Van Gogh's initial desire to seek a career as a draughtsman had more to do with appeasing Theo and their conservative family. He came from the Dutch middle class and his family had an interest in ensuring he did not slide down the social scale. Drawing was not a foreign practice to van Gogh, as it had been a part of his life even before he turned to it as a profession; if he could become an illustrator, he might achieve success within a respectable profession. Although his initial aim to become an illustrator was somewhat humble, especially when viewed in the light of his later years, it is not surprising that his plans quickly became ambitious. Van Gogh was a passionate and spontaneous man, and it was in his nature to be seized by grand plans. The question must be asked then, was his attempt to become a draughtsman a failure? In one respect, we must answer in the affirmative. Van Gogh never returned

120 LT 493, volume 3, 225.

121 LT 495, volume 3, 228.

122 LT 503, volume 3, 244. Van Gogh was so incensed by van Rappard's response that he returned his letter and did not correspond with him for almost two months (see also LT 504 and 514).

to England as he had planned and never earned any money from sales of his work to the illustrated magazines that he so admired. Yet, if we look beyond financial gain as a measure of success, it is clear that van Gogh's aims were worthy and the results of his effort not entirely fruitless. His aspirations and self-training in his early years can be seen as laying the foundations for his education in the art of drawing and for his understanding of the nature of art. He learnt about perspective, tone and composition. Furthermore, he began to concentrate on a structured course of subject matter. His methodology provided opportunities to experiment with both medium and technique. His absorption in drawing in the hope of gaining employment confirmed his belief in the need to master drawing before attempting to paint. Most importantly, his desire to be a draughtsman encouraged him in collecting the black-and-white prints that shaped his views on subject matter, composition, technique and style and moulded his vision on the duty of an illustrator and artist. Like Herkomer, van Gogh believed that making art was a public duty, a notion shared by the founders and custodians of the illustrated newspapers, and one that was an extension of his earlier life as a lay preacher.

Returning to Herkomer's article of 1882, which had a profound impact on van Gogh, we see how his practice achieved what his favourite illustrator professed about the connection between the work of draughtsmen and of painters:

> It frees him from the bondage of conventionalism. It awakens his subject-seeing faculties. It develops the powers of the most delicate draughtsmanship. It trains his powers of composition. It gains for him a reputation before he touches a brush. It obtains for him a livelihood, and he can paint pictures with an independent spirit that is free from the anxiety of sale, so that his first appearance as a painter stamps him once and for all. To you, as the public, it offers infinite pleasure and edification. For you it is really done.[123]

Van Gogh shared these sentiments, and stressed to Theo that Herkomer's views were altogether 'thoroughly sound, firm, honest'.[124] It is a sentiment that he lived by and which would become more evident years later as he mapped his artistic path, always sure of hand when it came to the primary practice and reason for the creation of his art.

---

123 Herkomer, 'Drawing and Engraving on Wood', 168.

124 LT 278, volume 2, 188.

Chapter 5

MAKING A MODUS OPERANDI

The Influence of Black-and-White Illustrations on van Gogh the Artist

Van Gogh's collection of black-and-white illustrations was not only one of the largest he amassed, it was also one of his most important. He collected the prints for their artistic qualities, their bold tonality, their social-realist subject matter, and the democratic aspects of their distribution and appeal. He also collected them because they assisted him in his initial aim of becoming an illustrator. As an artist van Gogh was essentially self-taught, apart from brief attendance at an academy and advice and training he received from his peers, which meant that his collection of prints was central to his education. The prints influenced his work profoundly, from subject matter to style. While their influence has been acknowledged in the past, it has not been acknowledged to the same extent as the influence of the style and technique of Japanese prints, the Impressionists and other avant-garde contemporaries. This is in part because of widespread fascination and admiration for van Gogh's later intensely coloured and boldly expressive masterpieces. The lower level of recognition of the influence of his collection of black-and-white prints also supports the widely accepted narrative of van Gogh as one of the great avant-garde artists of the late nineteenth century. As we have seen, however, van Gogh's work, including his later paintings, is grounded in the lessons he learnt during his years of collecting and studying black-and-white illustrations – lessons that went beyond mere copying. Early in his career, when van Gogh was preoccupied with drawing, his style, direction and ambition closely paralleled the prints in his collection. Later in his career, especially after his time in Paris, the influence of these illustrations persisted. Although no longer so overt, his unique style and approach towards his art were entrenched in the qualities he admired in his beloved black-and-white prints.

This chapter demonstrates the multiple roles of black-and-white prints in van Gogh's artistic practice through three case studies. The first explores how van Gogh copied from his own print collection and referred to it to solve problems of composition, focusing predominantly on his Dutch years, when he had his complete collection at hand. This second study investigates van Gogh's attempts to create a body of work after *The Graphic*'s 'Heads of the People' series. His early experiments and finished works after this series formed the foundation for the way he viewed portraiture, which became central to his artistic practice. It considers his later portraits and self-portraits in the context of *The Graphic* series, arguing that the lessons learnt in his early days shaped the way he conceived portraiture later in his career, both conceptually and stylistically. The third and final case study explores the practice of creating a series of works, that is, a defined cohesive narrative-based group of works, as developed and practised by van Gogh throughout his career. It considers briefly work produced in his early years, especially the series of drawings of weavers, before focusing on the many works he produced in the second half of his career, after he had given up on becoming an illustrator and turned to concentrating on achieving excellence as an artist in the traditional sense. The three case studies reveal how van Gogh's black-and-white prints started out as a way to help him find employment but ultimately became central to his artistic modus operandi. They argue for the importance of a renewed focus on black-and-white illustration in the complex van Gogh narrative.

More than Just for Copying: The Print Collection as Solution for Compositional Problems

When van Gogh first set out to draw he requested from Theo numerous prints after Millet, which he aimed to copy. Following a long-standing artistic tradition of learning one's craft by copying the masters, van Gogh sought to learn about the figure, proportion and perspective. His collection of black-and-white illustrations extended this logic and was fundamental in his development. Luijten has argued that it provided van Gogh 'with information of a formal nature, for example on the power of contour lines or how to set up a composition and create mood'.[1] Van Gogh's first drawing when he embarked on an artistic career was a copy after a print of Millet's *The Sower*

1 Hans Luijten, 'Rummaging Among My Woodcuts – Van Gogh and the Graphic Arts', in Chris Stolwijk, Sjraar van Heugten, Leo Jansen and Andreas Blühm (eds), *Vincent's Choice: The Musée Imaginaire of van Gogh* (Amsterdam: Van Gogh Museum, 2003), 99.

(1850).[2] Upon completing this work he asked Theo to send him more prints after Millet, such as *Les Travaux des Champs*, as well as works after or by Jules Breton and Auguste Feyen-Perrin.[3] Two weeks later he told Theo of his dedicated activity, advising him that he had completed copies after Millet's *Les Travaux des Champs* and had copied other works by Millet and Théodore Rousseau, as well as sixty sheets from Charles Bargue's *Exercices au fusain*. Van Gogh also stressed that he needed to continue copying as a way to learn: 'I believe I do much better for the time being by first copying some good things than by working without that foundation'. He went on to tell Theo of the direction in which he wished to move, hoping 'that after copying Bargue's two other series as well I'll be able to draw more or less a reasonable miner or female thrutcher'.[4]

Throughout the winter of 1880–81 van Gogh continued his education, always working after prints and from artistic manuals, concentrating his efforts on the human figure. In April 1881 he discussed his progress with Theo:

> I'm sending you three scratches that are still awkward, but from which I hope you'll nonetheless see that there's gradual improvement. You must remember that I haven't been drawing for long, even if I did sometimes make little sketches as a boy. And also that this winter the most important thing for me was to make strict anatomical studies and not my own compositions.[5]

This reinforcement of his progress was followed up within a fortnight when van Gogh advised Theo of two drawings which he had completed while visiting van Rappard. With further work, he believed he would soon be in a position to show a number of drawings to the engraving firm Smeeton Tilly or the 'people from L'Illustration or suchlike'.[6] The two drawings that van Gogh had been working on were both scenes of miners, *The Bearers of the Burden* (Figure 15) and a companion work, *The Lamp Bearers* (1881) of which nothing further is known. They highlighted the kind of work van Gogh was most interested in making and developing in order to find a publisher. *The Bearers of the Burden* reveals van Gogh's continuing difficulty with the human figure. The miners appear rigid and static, planted in the earth rather than walking across it. Rather than

2 Vincent van Gogh, *The Sower (after Millet)*, 1881 (Van Gogh Museum, Amsterdam (Vincent van Gogh Foundation) F0830/JH0001).

3 LT 156, volume 1, 250.

4 LT 157, volume 1, 252.

5 LT 164, volume 1, 268.

6 LT 165, volume 1, 269.

being drawn from life, aspects of this composition are most likely based on two prints from *The Illustrated London News*: Paul Gavarni's *Forts de la Halle – Paris* (Figure 16) and Caton Woodville's *The State of Ireland: Women Carrying Home Meal-Sacks from the Relief Committee* (Figure 17), which suggests van Gogh's commitment to learn from these black-and-white models during this period.

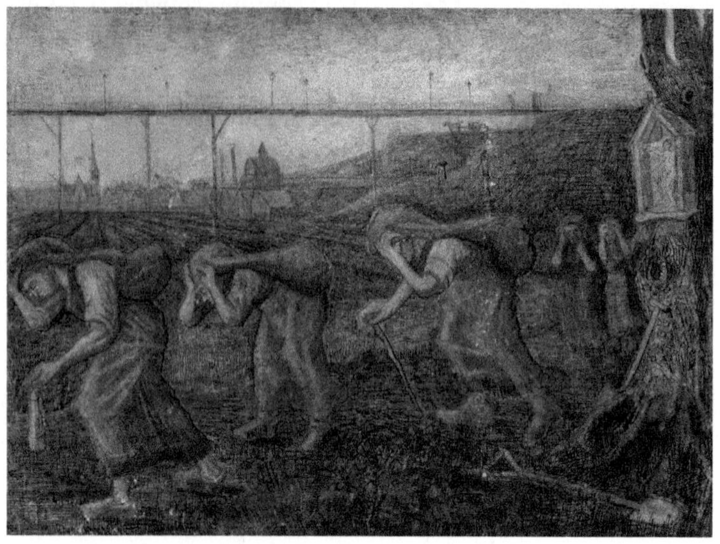

Figure 15. Vincent van Gogh, *The Bearers of the Burden*, 1881 (Kröller-Müller Museum, Otterlo).

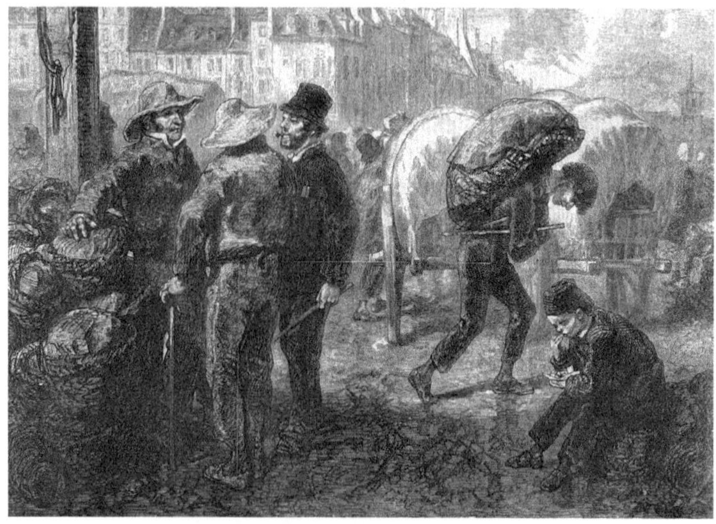

Figure 16. Paul Gavarni, *Forts de la Halle - Paris* (*The Illustrated London News*, 9 June 1855).

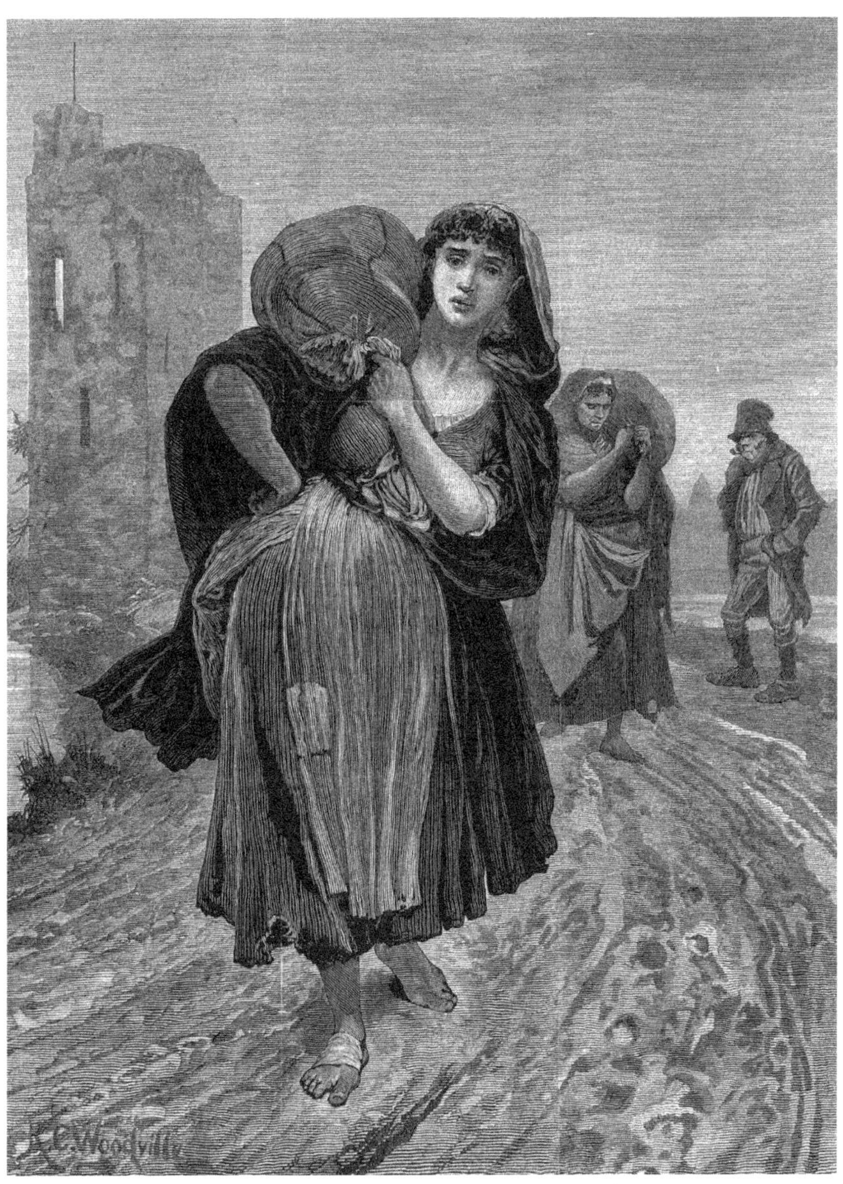

Figure 17. Richard Caton Woodville, *The State of Ireland: Women Carrying Home Meal-Sacks from the Relief Committee* (*The Illustrated London News*, 20 November 1880).

Gavarni's work seems to have informed van Gogh's drawing of figures in profile, while Woodville's assisted with the figures to the far right walking towards the viewer. In Gavarni's drawing a figure, side-on to the picture plane, walks, hunched over under the weight of a sack, similar to van Gogh's three central figures. The positioning of the legs of van Gogh's leading figure is almost identical to Gavarni's figure, whose front knee is bent, taking all the weight, while the trailing leg is ready to move forward. Like van Gogh's figure, Gavarni's is rigid and, surprisingly for such an accomplished artist, seems to be floating above the ground. Woodville's drawing is dominated by a female figure walking towards the viewer carrying a meal sack over her shoulder. Van Gogh's figures in the distance, at the rear of the procession of walkers, are similarly positioned; they have the same angular shape and use of a darkened figure positioned in front of a lighter figure, giving depth and perspective. Although a group scene, *The Bearers of the Burden* can be viewed as single figures repeated, indicating van Gogh's still limited skill and compositional capacity. There is a similarity in all the figures in the drawing, with only slight alterations being made, such as the lamp being substituted by a walking stick in the first and third figures on the left, and the difference in the tonal quality of the almost identical drawings of the two female figures at the rear. At this early stage of his development van Gogh had neither the knowledge nor the extensive library to pose these figures more confidently or distinctively, so he identified models from the illustrations he had as a starting point, and then copied from within his own work to create this first complex group composition. He obviously viewed this effort as beyond his skill level and nothing as ambitious appears again until the following year when he was living in The Hague. However, for all its shortcomings, the work is one of the first to suggest van Gogh's aim of creating work that paralleled that of established draughtsman, and of becoming one himself, and his reliance on the examples in his print collection.

If we view some of van Gogh's single figures, considered sketches and working drawings, we see further evidence of his use of his prints in copying exercises. A sole figure with her head in her hands (Figure 18) is based on a figure from Edward Dalziel's illustration *London Sketches: Sunday Afternoon, 1.00pm: Waiting for the Public House to Open* (Figure 19). In both drawings, the woman holds her head in her hands in a similar way, her skirt falls over her legs in the same manner and her body faces in the same direction.

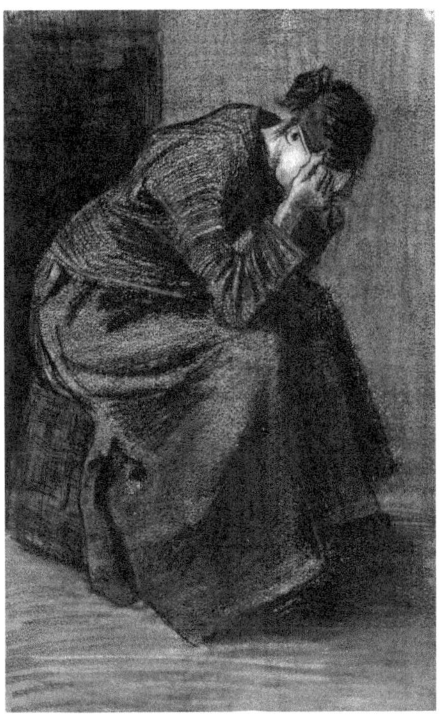

Figure 18. Vincent van Gogh, *Mourning Woman Seated on a Basket*, 1883 (Kröller-Müller Museum, Otterlo).

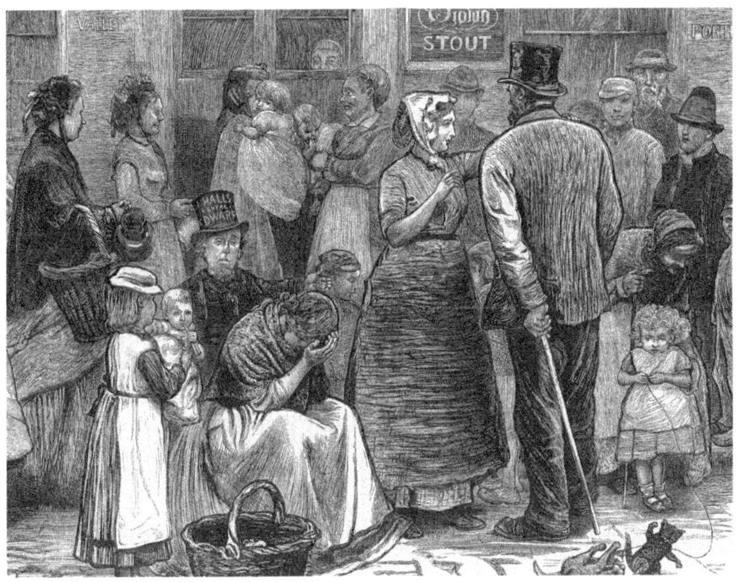

Figure 19. Edward Dalziel, *London Sketches: Sunday Afternoon, 1.00pm: Waiting for the Public House to Open* (*The Graphic*, 10 January 1874).

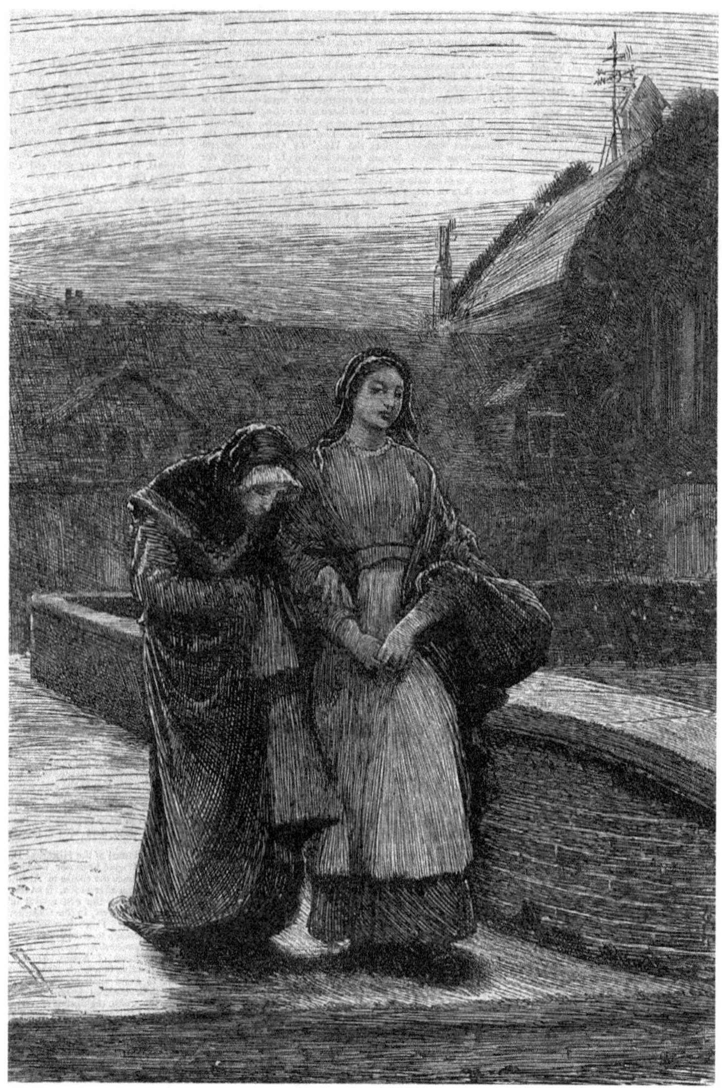

Figure 20. Fred Walker, *The Harbour of Refuge* (*The Graphic*, 7 April 1877).

One of van Gogh's favourite prints, Fred Walker's *The Harbour of Refuge* (Figure 20), of which he wrote, 'I for one can hardly imagine anything more beautiful in woodcut', seems to be the source for a sketch of a sorrowful looking single woman in his *Woman with a Mourning Shawl* (Figure 21).[7] In both images the old woman wears black and has a shawl draped over her head, which she clasps tightly at the front with her hands.

7 LT 321, volume 2, 283.

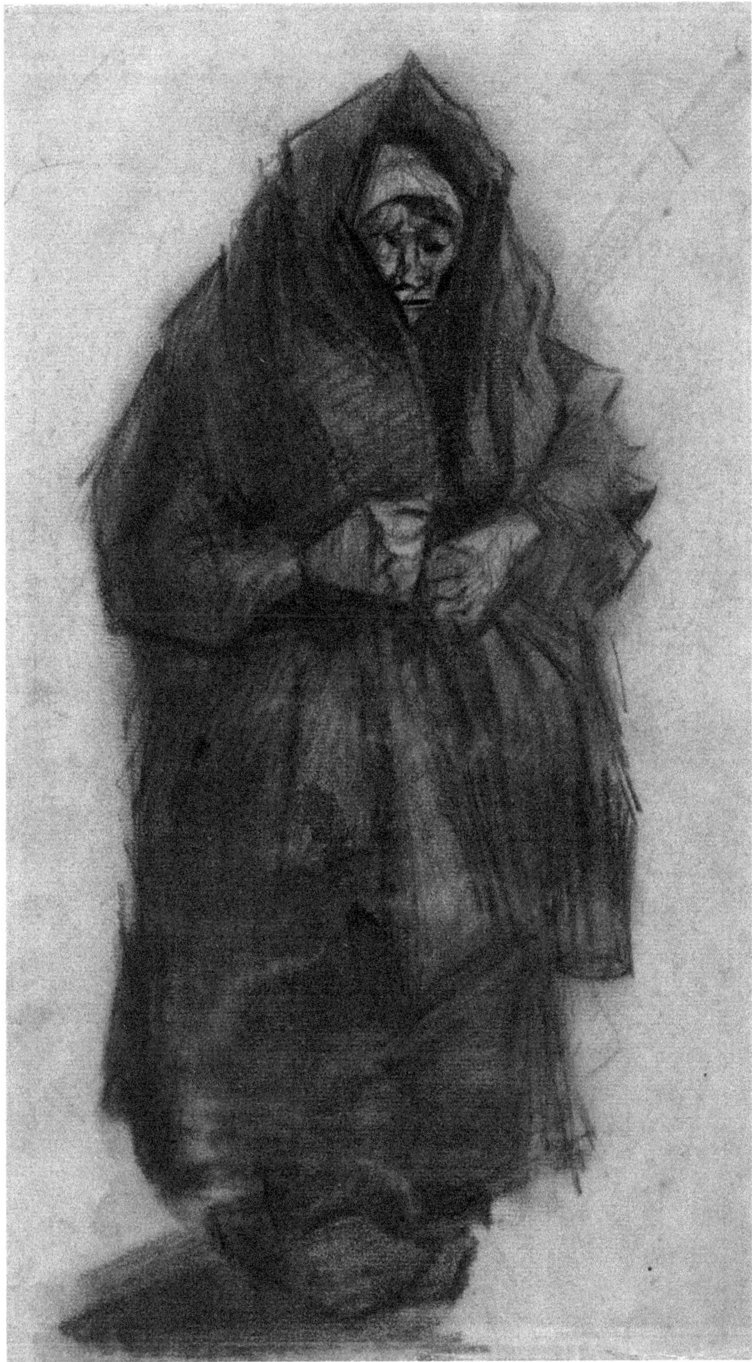

Figure 21. Vincent van Gogh, *Woman with a Mourning Shawl*, 1885 (Van Gogh Museum, Amsterdam (Vincent van Gogh Foundation)).

Van Gogh's drawing is best viewed as a sketch, as the figure is not shown in the context of the landscape through which she walks, and was completed as part of his ongoing education. Leafing through van Gogh's sketchbooks one finds further examples of his sourcing of images from his collection to make quick sketches, continuing his training and developing his artistic hand. Two chalk sketches from his first sketchbook show a remarkable parallel with the head of the woman to the left of the stout sign in the Dalziel illustration that appears above (Figure 19), while another page shows a silhouetted version of a peasant (Figure 22) after Millet's *Le Départ pour les champs* (Leaving for the Fields) (Figure 23), a print with which van Gogh was familiar years before he decided to become an artist.

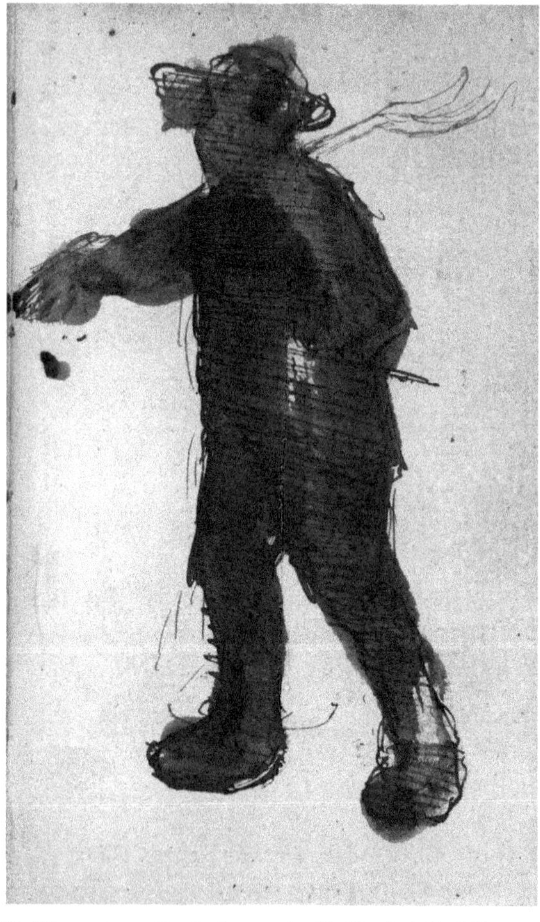

Figure 22. Vincent van Gogh, *Peasant with Hayfork (in Silhouette)*, 1885 (Van Gogh Museum, Amsterdam (Vincent van Gogh Foundation)).

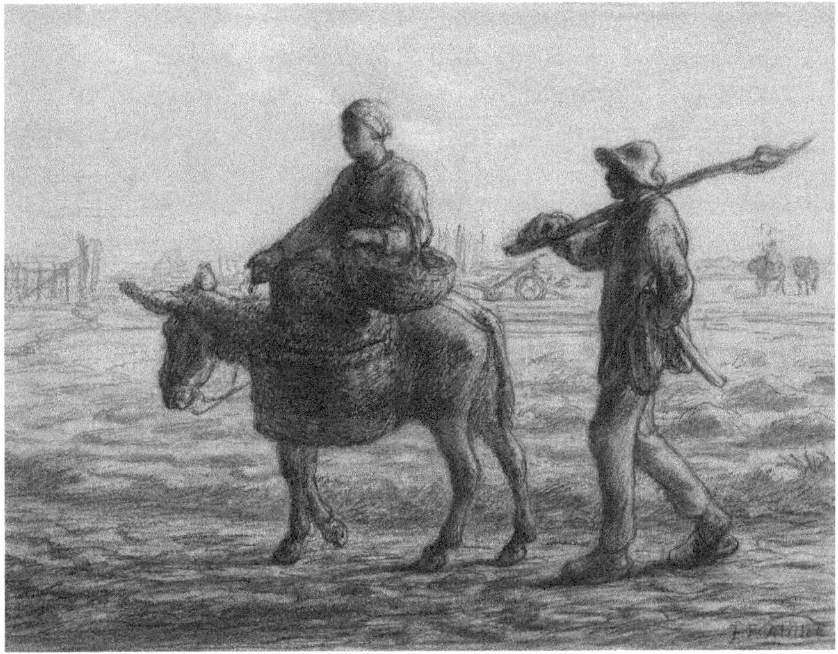

Figure 23. Jean-François Millet, *Le Départ pour les champs* (*L'Illustration*, 19 April 1873).

Although van Gogh relied on his print collection and a select number of academic manuals for study, he was fortunate during his early years to have models with which to work. He was not content, however, to merely draw from life, instead clothing his models in costumes and posing them in positions similar to those held by figures in the prints of his collection. He did this to expand his library of figure studies from which he could eventually compose more complex group scenes. His figures are not direct copies like those he had done in the past, but are examples of him referencing and adapting what he saw in the prints for his own ends. A model from the local old people's hostel, who posed for van Gogh on numerous occasions and was the subject of his first lithographs, is used to replicate figures found in Murray's *On the Retired List*.[8] In Murray's drawing three figures sit on a bench: the first leans forward with his arms resting on his legs; the second sits upright drinking from a mug; the third, legs apart, sits leaning on his walking stick. In the first instance, van Gogh posed his model for two separate drawings of him

8 W.B. Murray, *On the Retired List* (*The Graphic*, 5 June 1875).

drinking coffee, replicating one of the key aspects of Murray's illustration.[9] This was not so much about faithful replication as it was about posing models for van Gogh to construct his own narrative-based drawings. There are, however, compositional and structural similarities. For instance, van Gogh dressed his model in a top hat and overcoat, like one of Murray's figures. There are also similarities with Murray's figures in the positioning of one of van Gogh's figure's arms raised in the act of drinking and in the way a figure leans forward with an arm resting on his slightly opened legs.

Van Gogh used the same model for sketches of a figure with an umbrella seen from various angles – from the front and the rear and square to the picture plane, and also from the front and the rear turned on an angle, which mirror similar moments in different prints.[10] Similar stances are found in Dalziel's *London Sketches: Sunday Afternoon, 1.00pm: Waiting for the Public House to Open* (Figure 19) where a figure with a walking stick is seen from the rear at an angle, in Charles Green's *Holiday Folks at the National Gallery*, which has a gentleman with a walking stick seen from the side while he admires a large-painting, and a distinguished looking gentleman standing front on, without an umbrella or walking stick, in the sheet of sketches, *La Bourse et les Boursiers*, by French artist Charles Paul Renouard.[11]

Van Gogh's drawings of women echo poses found in his prints. A drawing from 1882, *Woman Seated* (Figure 24), showing a woman sitting in thought reflects a number of the prints in van Gogh's collection both in position and sentiment.

In Harry Furniss's *The Distress in Sheffield: Relief Committee at the Institute, Sheffield* (Figure 25), the woman sitting on a bench deep in thought in the far left, leans on her arm in a way that is similar to van Gogh's model. The distribution of weight, especially through the legs, and the use of dark clothes to focus attention on the white face is also similar in both. The isolated female figure in Holl's *At a Railway Station* (Figure 26), although slightly different

9 Vincent van Gogh, *Orphan Man with Top Hat, Drinking Coffee*, 1882 (Collection F. Hagemann, Basel F0996a/JH0264 and Kröller-Müller Museum, Otterlo F0976/JH0265).

10 Vincent van Gogh, *Orphan Man with Top Hat and Umbrella under His Arm*, 1882 (Kröller-Müller Museum, Otterlo. F0972/JH0237); *Orphan Man with Top Hat, Seen from the Back*, 1882 (Guggenheim Museum, New York. F0978a/JH0240); *Orphan Man with Top Hat, Seen from the Back*, 1882 (Van Gogh Museum, Amsterdam (Vincent van Gogh Foundation). F0960 / JH0241); *Orphan Man with Top Hat, Seen from the Front*, 1882 (Van Gogh Museum, Amsterdam (Vincent van Gogh Foundation). F0977/JH0243).

11 C. Green, *Holiday Folks at the National Gallery* (*The Graphic*, 3 August 1872); C.P. Renouard, *La Bourse et les Boursiers* (*L'Illustration*, 18 February 1882).

in pose, still mirrors van Gogh's drawing in sentiment and costume. While Holl's figure faces the viewer directly, whereas van Gogh's is angled away from the picture plane, both figures are sitting quietly on their own in thought and both wear dark dresses that are similar and headwear that focuses the viewer's attention on the face.

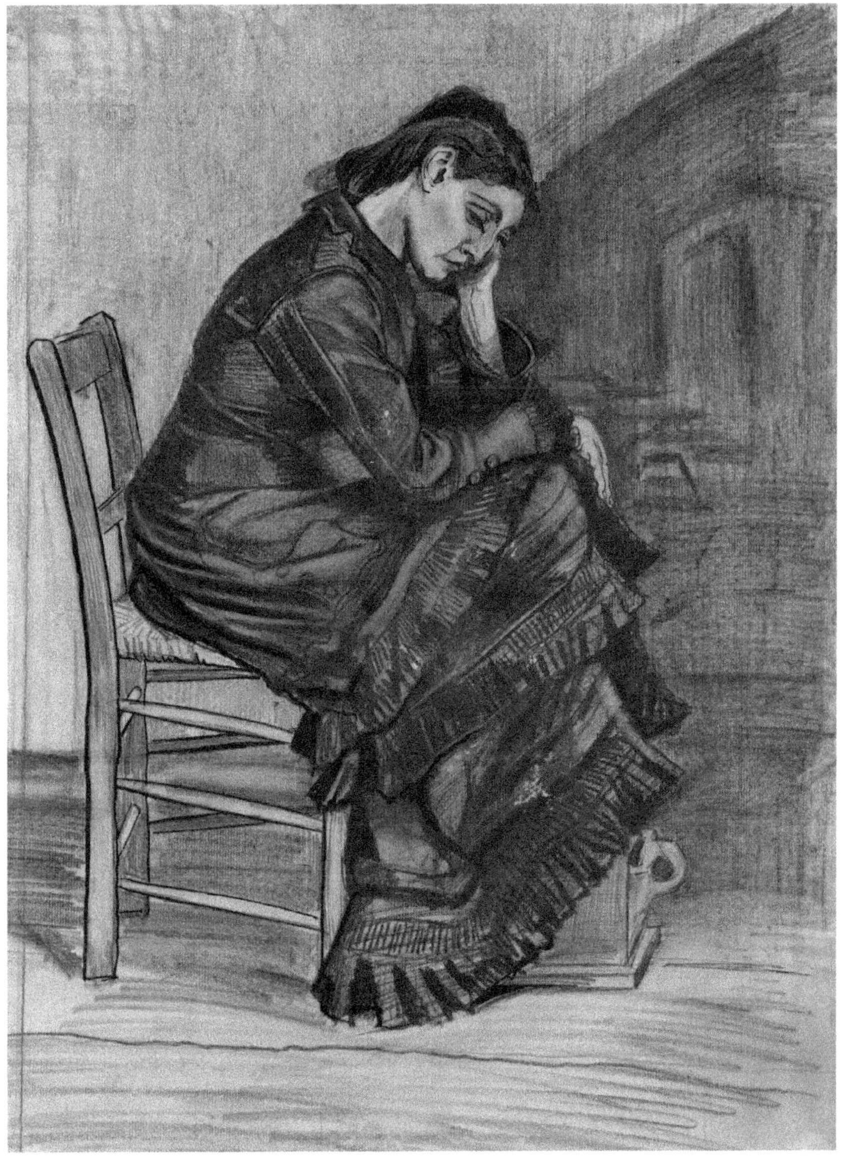

Figure 24. Vincent van Gogh, *Woman Seated*, 1882 (Kröller-Müller Museum, Otterlo).

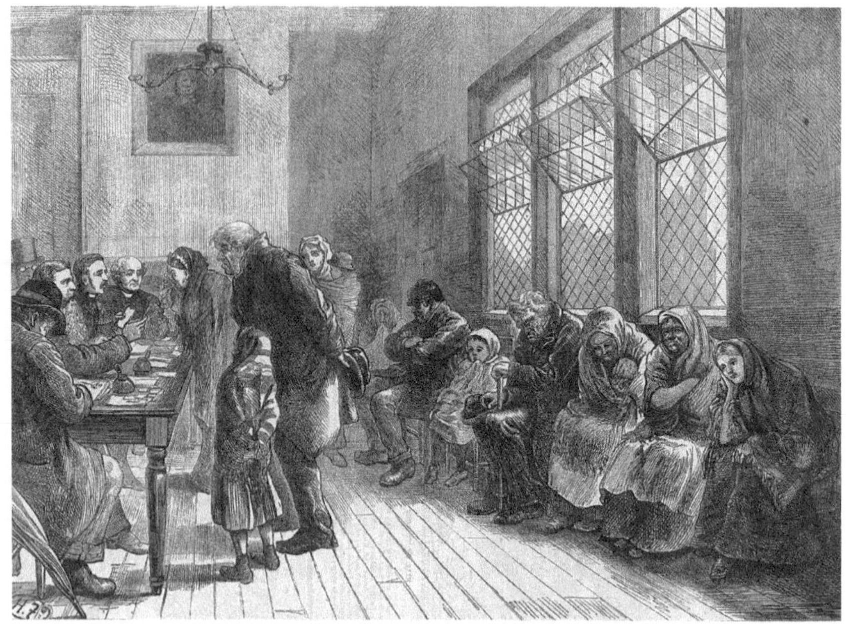

Figure 25. Harry Furniss, *The Distress in Sheffield: Relief Committee at the Institute, Sheffield* (*The Illustrated London News*, 1 February 1879).

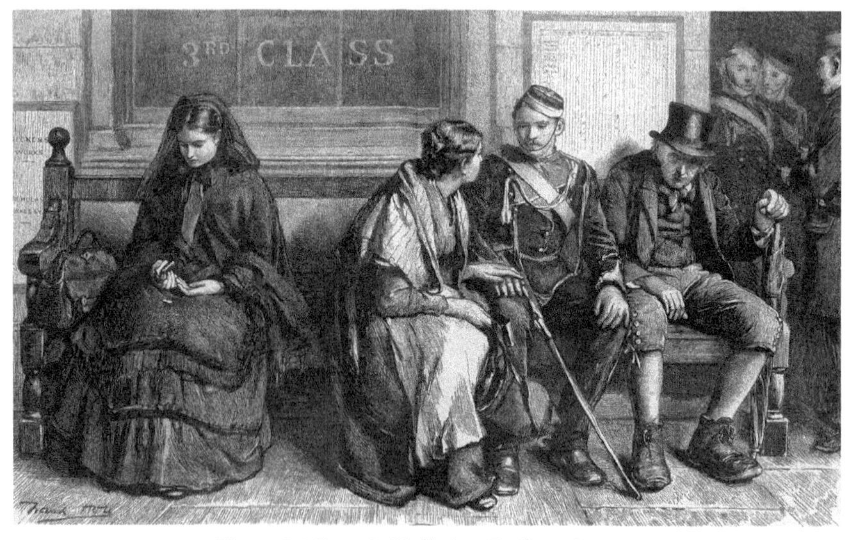

Figure 26. Francis Holl, *At a Railway Station* (*The Graphic*, 10 February 1872).

An important type of figure that van Gogh sought to master and was central to his aspirations of becoming a draughtsman was that of the peasantry in all its manifestations. His admiration for peasants and his belief in their representation as an important subject for contemporary illustration were demonstrated in the many images of peasants in his print collection. Like other subjects he had been trying to master, van Gogh turned to his collection as reference for his own drawings and sketches. For example, a simple drawing of a peasant boy digging (FIGURE 27) is based on a group of figures in W.B. Murray's illustration *Sugarmaking at the Counterslip Refinery, Bristol* (FIGURE 28).

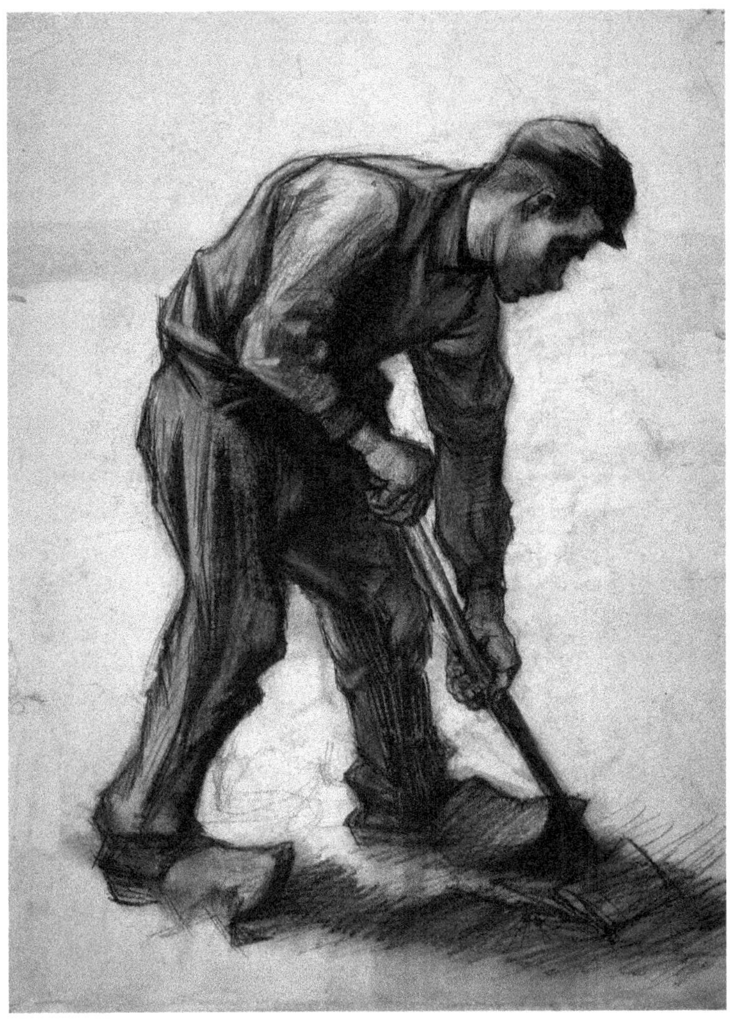

Figure 27. Vincent van Gogh, *Peasant Boy Digging*, 1885 (Nasjonalgalleriet, Oslo).

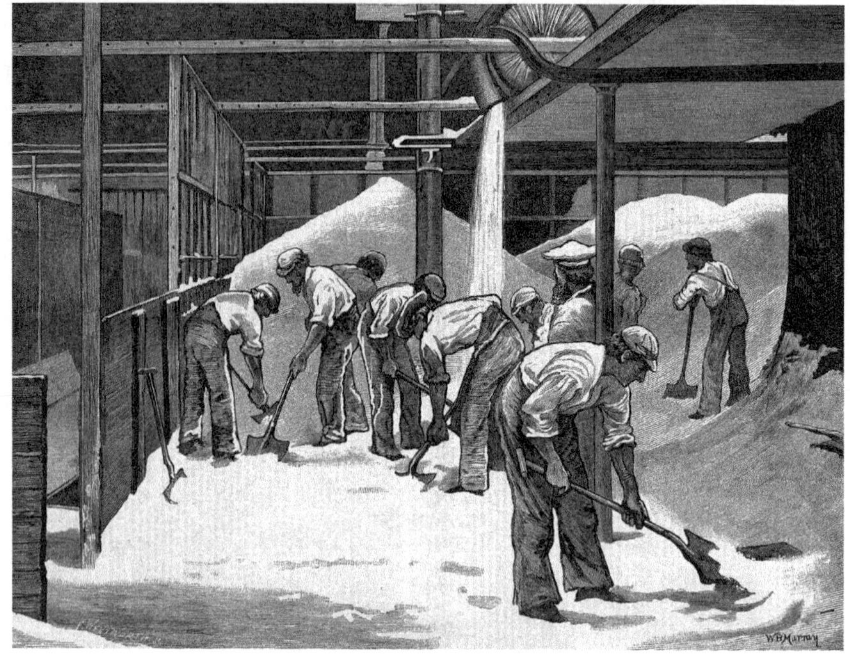

Figure 28. W.B. Murray, *Sugarmaking at the Counterslip Refinery, Bristol* (*The Illustrated London News*, 29 November 1873).

Van Gogh's sketch mostly resembles the figure close to the picture plane of Figure 28 who leans forward in the same manner, ploughing his shovel into the mountain of sugar covering the floor. The placement of the limbs, the curve of the torso and the folds in the clothes are similar, as are their outfits – a worker's hat and loose-fitting shirt and pants.

One of van Gogh's few lithographs presents another agrarian type copied after a print in his collection. In this image, however, the peasant is indoors, resting after a long day in the field. The lithograph, *At Eternity's Gate* (1882) (Figure 29), is undoubtedly inspired by an illustration by Arthur Boyd Houghton (Figure 30) that appeared in an illustrated edition of Charles Dickens' novel *Hard Times*, which van Gogh had read and greatly admired.[12]

12 Others have made this comparison; see particularly Louis van Tilborgh, 'Vincent van Gogh and English Social Realism', in Julian Treuherz (ed.), *Hard Times: Social Realism in Victorian Art* (Manchester: Manchester City Art Galleries, 1987), 122.

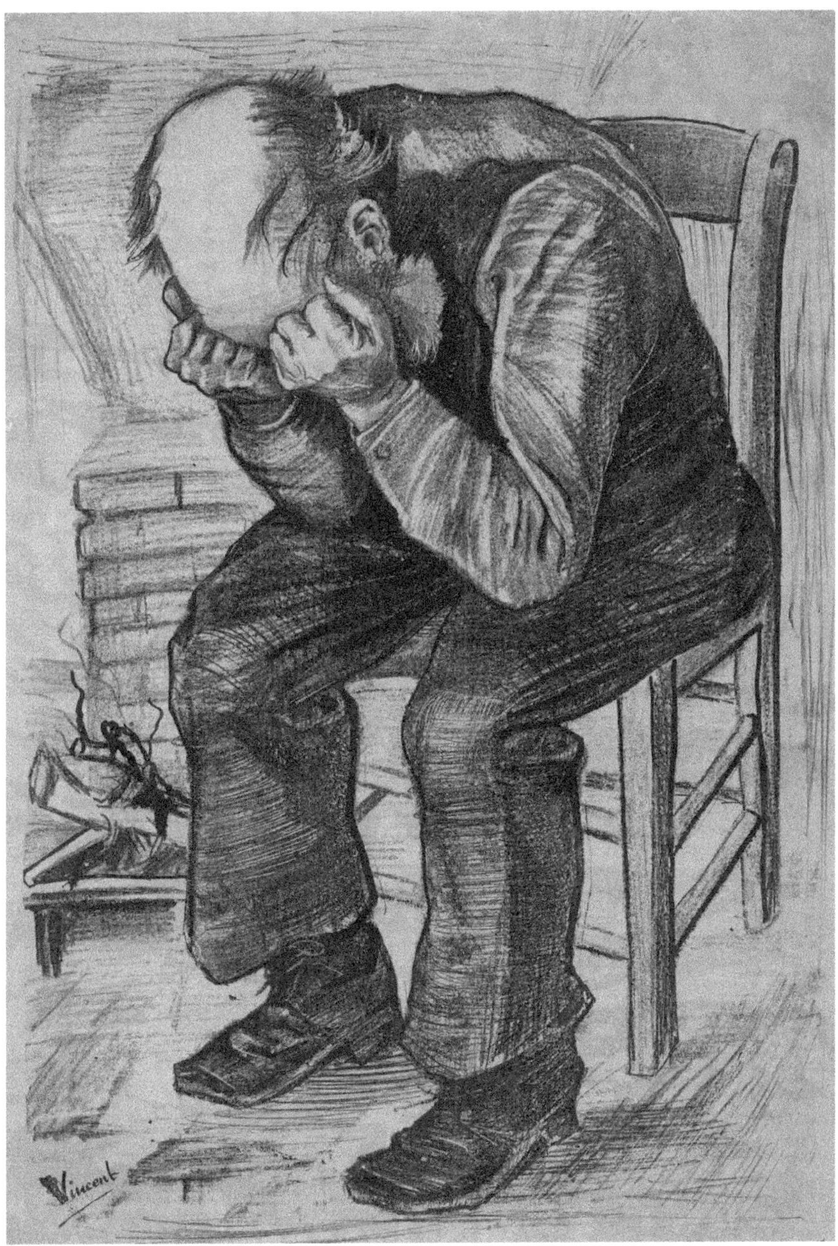

Figure 29. Vincent van Gogh, *At Eternity's Gate*, 1882 (Van Gogh Museum, Amsterdam (Vincent van Gogh Foundation) and other collections).

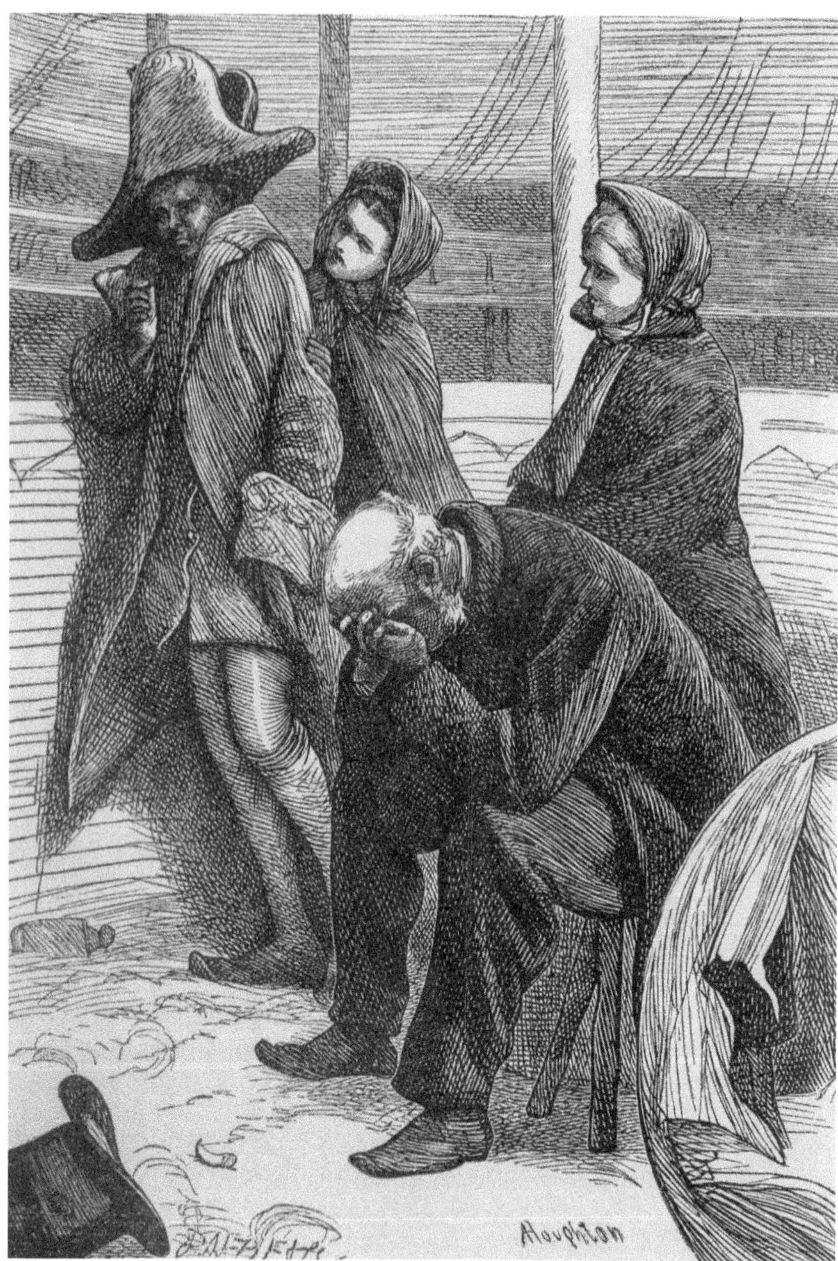

Figure 30. Arthur Boyd Houghton, Frontispiece to Charles Dickens' *Hard Times*, 1866.

The head of the figure in Boyd Houghton's illustration has a crown similar to that in van Gogh's lithograph, their elbows rest on the knees in the same way, and the sitter is positioned almost identically, features van Gogh highlighted in describing the drawing to van Rappard. Van Gogh may have also referred to a secondary print, O.E. Gunther's *The Widower*, whose male figure, kneeling with his head in his hands, is similarly sorrowful and anguished.[13] In van Gogh's lithograph and Gunther's and Houghton's prints the key figure is in a moment of contemplation bordering on despair, revealing how van Gogh sought to copy from his print collection not only technically but also symbolically. Writing to van Rappard about the work, van Gogh declared his aspirations and intentions:

> … a painter has a duty to try to put an idea into his work. I was trying to say this in this print – but I can't say it as beautifully, as strikingly as reality, of which this is only a dim reflection seen in a dark mirror – that it seems to me that one of the strongest pieces of evidence for the existence of 'something on high' in which Millet believed, namely in the existence of a God and an eternity, is the unutterably moving quality that there can be in the expression of an old man like that, without his being aware of it perhaps, as he sits so quietly in the corner of his hearth. At the same time something precious, something noble, that can't be meant for the worms.[14]

Van Gogh gave this lithograph an English title, which suggests he made it in the context of newspaper illustration and intended for it to be shown to the managers and editors of newspapers and magazines, as he declared to Theo: 'prints like the last one I sent you would I believe be suitable for a popular edition'.[15]

While van Gogh used his print collection initially as copying material and instruction for the posing of his models, he also used it as an instruction for complex compositions. Completing such drawings was not only a part of his artistic development, it was necessary if he was going to make drawings for sale, either as stand-alone works or for publication. In September 1882 van Gogh executed a small drawing of people sitting on a park bench, which he

13 O.E. Gunther, *The Widower* (*The Illustrated London News*, 17 April 1875).

14 LT 288, volume 2, 208.

15 LT 289, volume 2, 209.

then reproduced as an almost identical watercolour to send to Theo.[16] In the accompanying letter he wrote:

> As you know, when you were here you said that I should do my best to send you a drawing in the genre known as 'saleable'.... Well, I hope that the small bench, even if not yet saleable, will show you that I have nothing against tackling subjects with something agreeable or pleasant about them, which are thus more likely to find buyers than things with a more sombre sentiment.[17]

Shortly after, van Gogh reworked the image, advising Theo: 'I've come a long way with the large one of the bench' and that he was searching for 'groups of people doing something or other'.[18] This idea of depicting groups in action in particular environments, such as in waiting rooms, soup kitchens, parks and at the beach, was on his mind at the time, as is evident in discussions with van Rappard.[19] They were scenes of interest for his own work, but also in a number of prints that inspired van Gogh to the extent that he confessed they 'made me get up at night to take another look at them, that's how strong an impression they made on me'.[20] A print that may have been in van Gogh's thoughts at the time and which may have assisted in learning about challenging group compositions is William Hennessy's *Sketches in a Norman Cider Orchard*.[21] While van Gogh does not mention this work in particular, in a letter to van Rappard a month later, he includes Hennessy in a group of artists whose works he describes as 'beautiful things'.[22] Hennessy's work appears to be a reference for both the very first drawing and the later, larger watercolour that van Gogh discussed making with Theo. In the first drawing van Gogh framed the top of the work with a tangled mass of branches, as Hennessy had done. His placement of the bench under the shade of the tree and angled away from the picture plane, a feature retained in the watercolour, is also a strong feature of Hennessy's print. In the later watercolour van Gogh made three

16 Vincent van Gogh, *Bench with Four Persons*, 1882 (Kröller-Müller Museum, Otterlo. F0952/JH0194).

17 LT 262, volume 2, 150.

18 Vincent van Gogh, *Bench with Four Persons (and a Baby)*, 1882 (Location unknown. F0951/JH0197), LT 264, volume 2, 154.

19 LT 263, volume 2, 153. Van Gogh included a small sketch after the watercolour at the end of his letter to van Rappard.

20 LT 263, volume 2, 153.

21 W.J. Hennessy, *Sketches in a Norman Cider Orchard I* (*The Graphic*, 19 October 1878).

22 LT 273, volume 2, 173.

significant changes, two of which may have been influenced by Hennessy's work. The first of these was the addition of a figure on the right beyond the tree, an adjustment that balanced the ends of the drawing and created a strong central axis in the composition, paralleling the dominant horizontal structure in the print. The second change was to replace the strolling couple with a mother and child, matching a group of key figures in the centre of Hennessy's print. The final change, which was independent of any influence, was to put a baby in the arms of the first woman on the bench, giving the composition more weight and a light counterpoint in an area dominated by darkly clothed bodies.

Within a few weeks van Gogh attempted an even more complex composition, but once again it seems to have been slightly beyond his capabilities. *The Poor and Money* (Plate 3) depicts a crowd outside a lottery office and is a rumination on the plight of the lower classes, as van Gogh wrote of it at length to Theo:

> You may remember Mooijman's state lottery office at the beginning of Spuistraat. I passed it one rainy morning when a throng of people were standing there waiting to get lottery tickets. For the most part they were old women and the sort of people of whom it's impossible to say what they do or how they live, but who evidently potter along and fret and get on with life. Of course, viewed superficially, a crowd of folk who evidently attach so much importance to 'Draw today' is something that almost makes you and me laugh, because we're not in the least bit interested in the lottery.
>
> But the group of people – and their waiting expression – struck me, and it took on a larger, deeper meaning for me while I was working on it than in the first moment. It becomes more meaningful, I believe, if one thinks of it as the poor and money. That, in fact, applies to nearly all figure groups: one occasionally has to think about them for a while before one understands what one is seeing. The curiosity and delusion about the lottery seem more or less childish to us, but it becomes serious when one thinks about the other side: misery and forlorn attempts by these poor souls to be saved, so they think, by buying a lottery ticket, paid for with pennies saved by going without food.
>
> Be that as it may, I'm working on a large watercolour of it.[23]

23 LT 270, volume 2, 167.

This lengthy commentary gives valuable information about his intentions in this watercolour and for work still to be done. He infused the scene with social comment, seeing the waiting people as living a life of drudgery and hardship and giving them expressions that prompted an assessment of the relationship between the poor and money. He described how he passed the scene and sketched it on the spot, but that the importance of the scene demanded that he make a large watercolour, presumably in his studio, for possible wider consumption and distribution.

Working in his studio, van Gogh could turn to his print collection in order to analyse how his favourite illustrators had tackled similar scenes. Two prints van Gogh must have consulted were Small's *A Queue in Paris* (Figure 31) and Fitzgerald's *A Pawn Office at Merthyr-Tydfil* (Figure 32).

Both of these artists were on van Gogh's mind at the time, as revealed in letters to van Rappard, in which he described Small as 'astonishingly clever'[24] and, four months later, works by Fitzgerald as 'strikingly beautiful'.[25] Thematically both illustrations conform to van Gogh's concern with the poor and money. Small depicts a queue of poor people waiting with empty baskets and jugs to receive rations; hunched over, they stand patiently in the rain. Fitzgerald captures a crowd of the poor hoping to pawn objects in order to survive. However, it is in style and composition that the greatest similarities are found. In common with van Gogh's *The Poor and Money*, these two prints have a strong horizontal dimension, being almost frieze-like in their construction, and the crowd is funnelled towards a dark interior. Van Gogh's central figure, a bent-over old woman, leans towards the dark doorway, guiding the viewer's eye towards the entrance. Small and Fitzgerald both use similar visual devices: a curved figure in Small's illustration, and the curved outline of the woman with a child on her back in Fitzgerald's. All three images have a shallow foreground, inviting the viewer into the action. Mindful of not bringing the wall of figures too close, van Gogh incorporated triangular pockets of space in the foreground, which help to give a sense of movement to the crowd shuffling towards the entrance. Van Gogh noted that in the two prints some figures looked directly at the viewer and added this to his own composition, albeit only a single figure, drawn poorly and with almost indistinguishable facial features. Some of van Gogh's figures were dressed in ways that replicated examples from the prints, especially in the use of white headwear, most evident with the woman on the far right. Van Gogh has drawn and placed her in a position similar to a woman on the far right in Small's work, whose white headwear serves as a visual resting point in both

24 LT 273, volume 2, 173.

25 LT 314, volume 2, 272.

works. Finally, to mark the scene's location, van Gogh placed a sign on the wall identifying the building the crowd are entering as the state lottery office, emulating a narrative device used by Small and Fitzgerald.

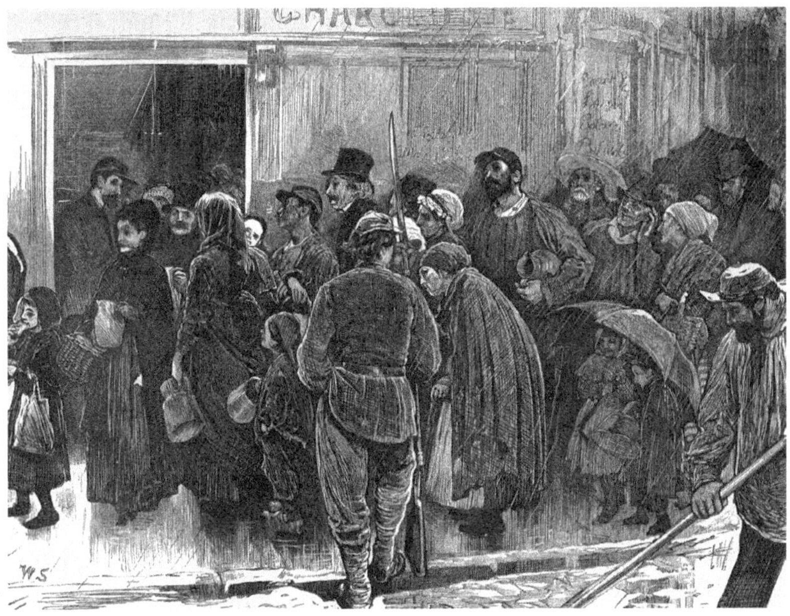

Figure 31. William Small, *A Queue in Paris* (*The Graphic*, 11 March 1871).

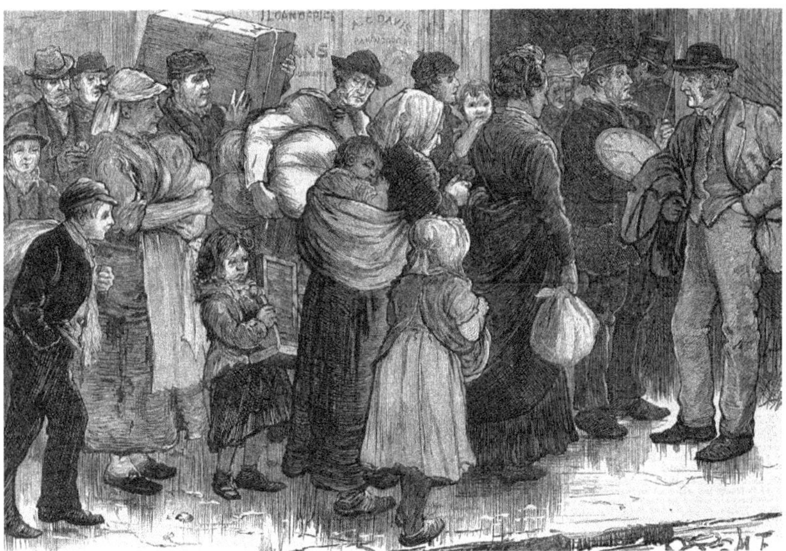

Figure 32. Patrick Michael Fitzgerald, *A Pawn Office at Merthyr-Tydfil* (*The Illustrated London News*, 20 February 1875).

Although van Gogh aspired to become a draughtsman and would, therefore, have used his prints intensively in producing drawings, there are strong indications that he also used them for the construction of his paintings. One of his earliest paintings, *A Girl in a Wood* (1882), is an example;[26] it is the third known version of the subject and, although painted *en plein air*, it seems that this particular composition was inspired by several prints in van Gogh's collection. The first iteration of this painting is reversed compositionally in comparison to the final version; the figure is on the right, painted in black and side on to the picture plane.[27] The closest tree trunk is on the left and the line of trees moves into the distance towards the right. The next painting of this subject is in portrait rather landscape format and has two figures dominating the composition, instead of the landscape.[28] The final version was painted outdoors as van Gogh told Theo:

> The other study from the woods is of big green beech trunks on a ground with dead leaves, and the small figure of a girl in white.
>
> The great difficulty there was to keep it clear and bring in space between the tree-trunks, which stand at different distances – and the place and relative thickness of the trunks altered by the perspective. To ensure, in short, that one can breathe and wander about in it – and smell the woods.[29]

It is unlikely that van Gogh had access to a model, as he would have mentioned it to Theo if he did. He does discuss returning to the studio and it is most likely there that he amended and finished the painting, referring to some of his prints as he did. The work has striking similarities with Helen Paterson's *Innocent – A Tale of Modern Life* and Macquoid's *Reflections*.[30] Both of these images have a single female, leaning against a tree, wearing a full-length, flowing dress that dominates the composition. Macquoid's figure is in white, because of the dominant darkness of the composition, which van Gogh noted and emulated, making his landscape similarly dark. The

---

26 Vincent van Gogh, *A Girl in a Wood*, 1882 (Kröller-Müller Museum, Otterlo. F0008/JH0182).

27 Vincent van Gogh, *A Girl in a Wood*, 1882 (private collection. F0008a/JH0180).

28 Vincent van Gogh, *Two Women in a Wood*, 1882 (private collection. F1665/JH0181).

29 LT 258, volume 2, 138.

30 H. Paterson, *Innocent – A Tale of Modern Life* (*The Graphic*, 11 January 1873); P. Macquoid, *Reflections* (*The Illustrated London News*, Christmas number 1874). For a visual comparison of these works, see Ronald Pickvance, *English Influences on Vincent van Gogh* (London: Arts Council of Great Britain, 1974), 37.

remainder of van Gogh's painting, however, seems to be based on Paterson's work. The trees move away in the same direction creating a strong perspective line; the figure faces the viewer, and the background has a similar high horizon line, with a strong vertical presence in the distance. Van Gogh's painting is his own original creation, painted outdoors and emphasising the rich reddish-brown soil.[31] After attempting the scene several times, however, he needed to turn to his print collection to create a harmonious and well-balanced composition.

Throughout his career van Gogh reworked scenes before settling on a definitive version, as he did with his first great genre painting *The Potato Eaters* (PLATE 4). He completed the painting in April–May 1885, but preliminary drawings date back to March. In late February, Theo had asked van Gogh if he had any work to enter in the Paris Salon. Although pleased, van Gogh declined: 'I don't have anything that I would care to send in'. He had been working steadily on paintings of heads, but saw them only as studies 'meant for the studio'.[32] Soon after, though, he began using these studies for a group composition. Choosing an easily identifiable subject van Gogh aimed to create a work that would sit in the pantheon of peasant art. The outcome was *The Potato Eaters*. As his first great genre painting, it was the climax of his work in the Netherlands. Its subject – a peasant family eating around a table – was not new, having been, for example, the subject of paintings by The Hague artist Jozef Israëls, whom van Gogh knew and admired. For van Gogh *The Potato Eaters* was of utmost importance. He wished, as Louis van Tilborgh puts it, to 'prove himself to the world after five years of study'.[33] The painting developed through various manifestations in oil, beginning as a sketch, and concluding as the Amsterdam painting. Van Gogh described the lengthy and sometimes troubling process: 'I've had the threads of this fabric in my hands the whole winter long, and searched for the definitive pattern – and if it's now a fabric that has a rough and coarse look, nevertheless the threads were chosen with care and in accordance with certain rules'.[34]

---

31 In numerous letters van Gogh wrote about works he completed in the woods at this time; he focused his discussion of the soil and surrounding landscape; see LT 258 and 260.

32 LT 484, volume 3, 209.

33 Louis van Tilborgh (ed.), *The Potato Eaters by Vincent van Gogh* (Zwolle: Waanders, 1993), 9.

34 LT 497, volume 3, 231.

The initial sketches for *The Potato Eaters* reveal van Gogh's intention to depict four peasants at a table eating from a central dish. The first sketch, from March to April 1885, shows the hunched-over figures. Another sketch from the same period reveals a more open composition and introduces a ceiling lamp – a detail that would remain throughout the work's multiple manifestations. Van Gogh obviously intended the bowl of potatoes to be a key component of the composition, placing the table on an angle in both sketches in order to focus the viewer's attention on the bowl. He also intended to give the figures identities by seating them upright with their faces exposed, another detail that persisted through the painting's development. Soon after executing the initial black chalk sketches van Gogh produced his first oil sketch, *Study for the Potato Eaters* (1885).[35] Unlike the second chalk sketch, he rearranged the figures, closing off the open space on the table in the earlier image, perhaps to create a halo effect around the central figure who faces away from the viewer in front of the rising steam. This figure, however, suffers from a lack of shape and definition; it is block-like and dark in comparison to the other figures and seems not to be participating in the meal in an immediate sense. In his next study, also painted but with more detail, van Gogh introduced another figure, which changed the dynamic but created new problems with the central figure.[36] While the other four figures had previously modelled for van Gogh, so he could use his drawings and oil studies to assist with their depiction, the newly introduced figure of a young girl was drawn from his imagination and positioned so that it would not upset the composition's balance. As in the earlier oil sketch, van Gogh turned the figure away from the viewer to the left, thus creating a sight line towards the potatoes. The weakness in this painting and in the preceding oil sketch seems to be the figure's silhouetted appearance, which gives the impression of a cut-out figure rather than a fleshed human being. The silhouetted body and the head are block-like shapes that give no impression of a rounded and sculpted face. In addition, there is no allusion to a relationship between this additional figure and the other peasants.

Rather than continuing with this canvas, van Gogh told Theo that after three days of constant reworking the paint had become muddy, so he had begun afresh on a new canvas. The slightly larger and final version of *The*

35 Vincent van Gogh, *Four Peasants at a Meal*, 1885 (Van Gogh Museum, Amsterdam (Vincent van Gogh Foundation). JH686, F77).

36 Vincent van Gogh, *Five Persons at a Meal (The Potato Eaters)*, 1885 (Kröller-Müller Museum, Otterlo. F0078/JH0734).

Potato Eaters (Plate 4) is more finished, having benefited from van Gogh's many struggles in trying to compose a harmonious and ambitious piece of art. Although essentially the same as the previous painting, van Gogh made slight alterations; the two figures on the right were placed closer together and the woman pouring the coffee was turned towards the viewer, exposing additional cups on the table. The troubling central figure was also amended. Returning to the concept in the original oil study, van Gogh placed the figure in front of the rising steam. More importantly, the figure's head was now more sculpted and the cheek more rounded and reflecting the shine of the suspended lamplight.

Van Tilborgh has commented that this figure of the young girl 'would be difficult to identify [from] any specific precedent'.[37] We can now see, however, that the precedent lies buried in van Gogh's collection of black-and-white prints. Of all of the existing prints from van Gogh's collection only one has evidence of a trace mark on the reverse – *Chris Ferrum, The Blacksmith of Locksley Green, and His Workman* (Figure 33). The trace mark is only around the head, shoulder and upper arm of the right figure, suggesting that van Gogh may have used this print in order to resolve the many problems the central figure in *The Potato Eaters* had caused. It would be logical for van Gogh to refer to an image whose environment paralleled that of his own work. In both, the setting is an interior lit by a central light source – a lamp in the painting and molten metal in the print. The light that falls on the face and upper body of van Gogh's figure replicates the traced area of the worker in the print. The young girl's cheekbone is more pronounced and, like her neck and shoulder, reflects the light, while a soft glow highlights her upper arm. The size of van Gogh's figure and that in the print is very similar, further indicating the possibility that van Gogh may have transferred the image directly onto the canvas. More probable, however, is that van Gogh referred to this print when applying final touches to the canvas. An x-ray photograph of the work reveals van Gogh's added final touches, including the highlighting of the young girl's cheek and shoulder.[38] When we consider the importance of this work and the difficulty this figure posed throughout the composition's development, it is understandable that van Gogh would turn to his print collection for assistance – an aid that he had used on many previous occasions.

---

37 Van Tilborgh, *The Potato Eaters*, 19.

38 Van Tilborgh, *The Potato Eaters*, 55.

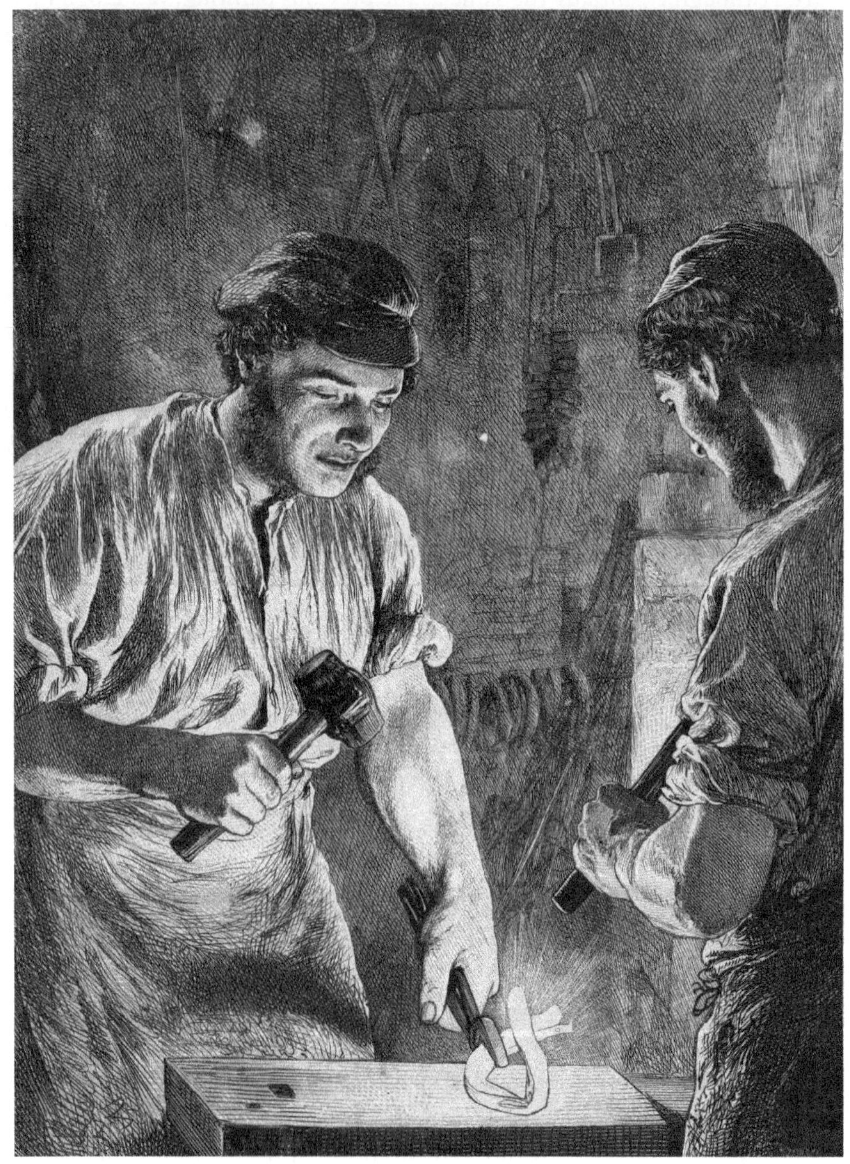

Figure 33. J. Knight, *Chris Ferrum, the Blacksmith of Locksley Green, and His Workman*
(date and source not known).

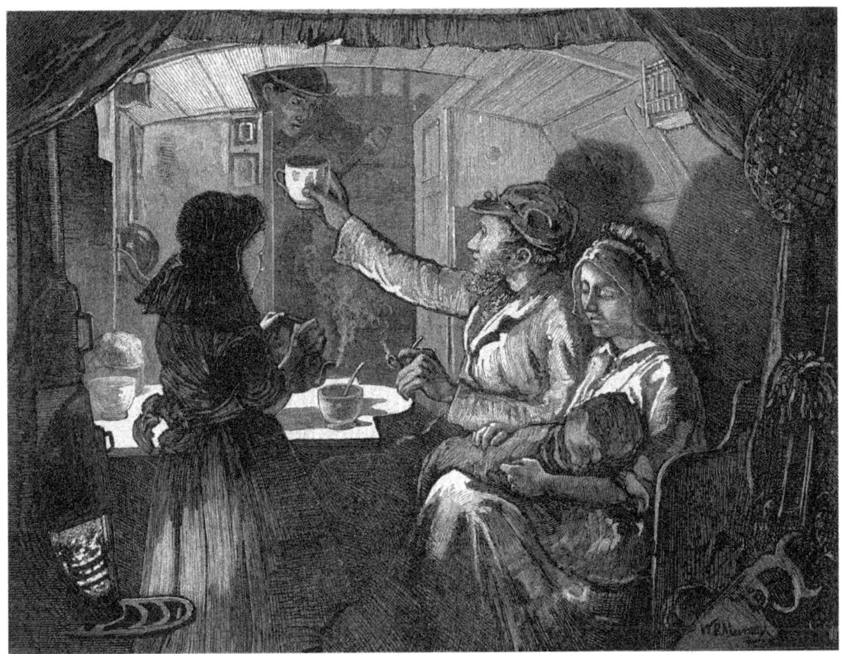

Figure 34. W.B. Murray, *Canal Life: Tea-time on a "Monkey Boat"* (*The Illustrated London News*, 10 October 1874).

It would appear that van Gogh referred to a further print in his collection to assist with the overall construction of the final composition. In a letter sent just after he had completed the second canvas he told Theo that he had seen an illustration by Belgian artist Xavier Mellery – 'a bargee's family in the little deckhouse on their barge – husband, wife, children – round a table'.[39] Although van Gogh did not own a copy of this illustration, he had in his collection an equivalent – Murray's *Canal Life: Tea-time on a "Monkey Boat"* (Figure 34). Van Gogh knew his collection intimately and Mellery's illustration may have reminded him of Murray's print to which he had easy access. Strong parallels between the final version of *The Potato Eaters* and Murray's print suggest that van Gogh used compositional rules from *Canal Life: Tea- time on a "Monkey Boat"* in finalising his painting. In both, the figures are crowded and the small intimate light reflects off the ceiling and the walls. The inclusion of a lowered ceiling was one of the major changes from the very first oil sketch and is comparable with the composition

39 LT 493, volume 3, 225.

of Murray's print.[40] The beams lining the ceiling in both works move away from the viewer to give a sense of perspective, while two strong diagonals at the top corners of both images create an arch-like effect over the respective groups. On the right side of van Gogh's painting the female figure sits in an alcove, closed off by a strong vertical beam. Her placement is similar to the placement of the husband and wife in Murray's print. The empty space in the bottom right corner of the earlier painting was now filled with an object, adding balance to the composition, a lesson taken from Murray. Both images include various hanging objects, suggesting the modest belongings of the families and the limited space they had to store them. Other similarities include the offering of the cup, the emphasis on the faces, only half-length and three-quarter-length figures and a young girl standing.

The final version of *The Potato Eaters* was the culmination of months of work and was finally realised only after various sketches and trials. The argument here is that van Gogh had turned to his print collection, as he had done in the past and would continue to do so in the future, to solve the problems that this ambitious project presented. The prints he most likely used – *Canal Life: Tea-time on a "Monkey Boat"* and *Chris Ferrum, The Blacksmith of Locksley Green, and His Workman* – were not actually peasant scenes, but had parallels with van Gogh's subject; both were set in intimately lit interiors and one included the sharing of a meal. The first print aided with the structure and balance of the final composition, while the other assisted in solving the most difficult problem in the painting, that of the central figure standing in front of the rising steam. Although *The Potato Eaters* was derided by many of van Gogh's peers, it remained special to him. It is the most recognisable painting from his Dutch period, is central to his œuvre, and was the most important and ambitious painting he had attempted to this point in his career. He declared it 'a real peasant painting'.[41] Two years later he wrote to his sister Wil: 'What I think about my own work is that the painting of the peasants eating potatoes that I did in Nuenen is after all the best thing I did'.[42] His fondness for this work above others he produced is understandable given that it took over two months of work from the initial sketch to the completion of the third and final painting. It summarises many of van Gogh's interests, is a reflection of his moral and ethical compass, and realised his aim of making works of the

40 Van Tilborgh (*The Potato Eaters*, 20) has noted that the ceiling height in peasant cottages at the time was not as low as van Gogh depicted.

41 LT 497, volume 3, 231: 'And it might well prove to be a real peasant painting. I know that it is'.

42 LT 574, volume 3, 370.

people for the people in an honest and direct fashion, referencing and recalling the popular black-and-white prints of which he was so fond.

It is difficult to assess van Gogh's usage of his prints after he left the Netherlands. In a letter from July 1888 he wrote to his sister Wil about junk that he had left in Breda, some of which was his prints. While he writes that 'Theo brought a whole batch of woodcuts with him last year' and that a 'few of the best portfolios are missing and the rest isn't as good precisely because it's no longer complete', it is unclear exactly which of the prints Theo had brought with him and where he brought them to.[43] Did van Gogh leave a number in Paris when he left in 1888 which Theo decided to return to the family home in the Netherlands? Or did Theo collect some of the prints, returning with them to Paris after visiting the family? Alternatively, did Theo deliver part of the collection on a visit and was van Gogh hoping to receive more? Unfortunately, the letters shed no light on these questions. While by this stage in his career van Gogh was a highly competent artist, able to draw without aids like perspective frames, and paint complete canvasses without the need to sketch or use preliminary under-drawings, there are traces that he could at least remember certain prints, assuming he didn't have any on hand, as is evident in the painting *Gauguin's Chair* (Plate 5).

Gauguin's Chair, a homage to his friend and peer Paul Gauguin and a matching pendant to a painting of his own chair, has a striking resemblance to Fildes' illustration *The Empty Chair, Gad's Hill – Ninth of June 1870* (Figure 35). Fildes, who conceived the illustration just after the death of Charles Dickens, referenced the renowned author by drawing his empty chair in his study. Van Gogh recalled the image:

> Edwin Drood was Dickens's last work, and Luke Fildes, having got in touch with D. through those small illustrations, comes into his room on the day of his death – sees his empty chair standing there, and so it was that one of the old Nos. of The Graphic had that striking drawing.[44]

Van Gogh greatly admired this print and would have remembered its composition and finer details. Dickens' chair was a comfortable and luxurious armchair, behind which, in the shadows, sits a simple armless chair that places Dickens' visitors in a subordinate position. Van Gogh conceived the two paintings of his and Gauguin's chairs similarly, where Gauguin is represented by an authoritative and comfortable armchair while his own is a simple straw chair,

43 LT 626, volume 4, 130.

44 LT 293, volume 2, 220.

indicating Gauguin's leading role in the establishment of a Studio of the South.[45] On van Gogh's chair one sees the items of a worker – a tobacco pouch and pipe; by contrast, on Gauguin's chair are a candle and books, confirming van Gogh's view that Gauguin was worldlier, more intelligent and a greater artist.

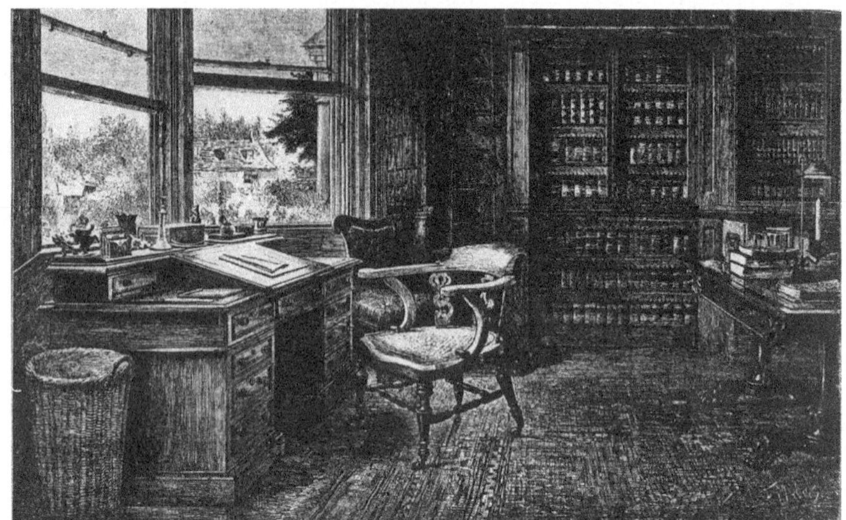

Figure 35. Luke Fildes, *The Empty Chair, Gad's Hill - Ninth of June 1870* (*The Graphic*, Christmas number 1870).

These two paintings also represent the declining state of the relationship between van Gogh and Gauguin, which had become strained after months of living together. Years earlier van Gogh had professed in the context of the Fildes' print: '*Empty chairs* – there are many, more will come, and sooner or later instead of Herkomer, Luke Fildes, Frank Holl, William Small &c. there will only be *Empty chairs*'.[46] His time with Gauguin, whom he revered, was coming to an end, so it was logical for him to reference one of his favourite illustrations to depict his similar situation of losing a great artist. While there are symbolic and sentimental parallels between them, a comparison of the works of van Gogh and Fildes reveals even more obvious stylistic parallels. Van Gogh may not have had the illustration on hand, but he was able to remember its composition to assist with his painting of Gauguin's chair. In both the Fildes print and van Gogh's painting, the chairs face in the same

45 Vincent van Gogh, *Vincent's Chair*, 1888 (The National Gallery, London. F0498/JH1635).

46 LT 293, volume 2, 220.

direction and the light falling on Dickens' chair through the large bay window is replicated by candlelight in van Gogh's painting. The arms and back of the chairs are similarly curved, with only the seat and legs different. The simple and perhaps unnoticeable detail of a lack of shadow is also consistent in both images – an aspect that van Gogh could have only been aware of through comparison.

As we have seen, when van Gogh was struggling with his own work he referred to his collection of prints to help him resolve complex composition issues, regardless of whether they had a thematic parallel. His collection was central in teaching him how to construct images and ultimately enabled him to resolve, refine and complete ambitious works like *The Potato Eaters*. It also gave van Gogh direction in regard to subject matter, best demonstrated in his admiration for *The Graphic*'s 'Heads of the People' series and its influence on his view and production of portraits throughout his career.

Van Gogh's 'Heads of the People' Series: Intentions and Legacies

In December 1882 van Gogh wrote to his brother Theo justifying the subject matter that had been a part of the focus of his art up to that time.

> *See, Theo, old chap – I can't make any* TYPES OF BEAUTY – *but I will do my best for* HEADS OF THE PEOPLE. See, Theo, I would like to do the same as those who began The Graphic (though I don't consider myself their equal), that is to take a chap or woman or child from the street and do that in my studio.[47]

Van Gogh was deeply rooted in the tradition of the peasant painters, such as Millet, Lhermitte and Israëls and thought the 'Types of Beauty' of which he wrote, *The Graphic*'s series of portraits of members of the upper and middle classes, did not fit his œuvre or what he considered to be worthwhile subject matter. Van Gogh's preference was to produce a series of portraits based on the 'Heads of the People' series published in *The Graphic* during the 1870s, which depicted universal types rather than identifiable people, with a focus on workers and labourers. Although two drawings in this series represented types from the middle and upper classes, one of a barrister and the other of a young upper-class woman, which were precursors of the newspaper's later 'Types of Beauty' series, the remaining works were of types from the lower

47 LT 293, volume 2, 222.

and working classes and included a miner, a farm labourer, a city worker and a street urchin. These works reinforced *The Graphic*'s social realist leanings and appealed to van Gogh's sensibilities and career aspirations.

Central to these drawings of types was the now discredited practice of physiognomy – the assessment of a person's character by their facial characteristics. As Mary Cowling points out, physiognomy was 'all but universally believed in' at the time. For the Victorians, facial features had specific meanings and by reading myriad signs one could learn about a person's intellect, disposition and social class; faces in art 'were read as they were in life'.[48] It was, therefore, possible in the nineteenth century to produce a body of work of 'types', knowing that it would be understood by the masses. Van Gogh was aware of the new science, having read extracts from Johann Lavater's writing.[49] He also discussed his own physiognomic traits with Theo, indicating an unwavering belief in the theory.[50] Like so many others, he could easily interpret the works from *The Graphic*. He also believed that an understanding of physiognomy was required in order to become an artist and his work on depicting heads was guided by this principle. Van Gogh's intense fascination with *The Graphic* series spanned just over four years, culminating in what was arguably his first masterpiece, *The Potato Eaters*. During these four years he painted and drew hundreds of heads, some merely as studies, while others were done as a series that followed in the tradition of *The Graphic* illustrations.

Van Gogh refers explicitly to the 'Heads of the People' series for the first time in December 1882, although he was aware of it much earlier. In January 1882 he had acquired a copy of *The Graphic Portfolio*, which contained Herkomer's *The Agricultural Labourer – Sunday* (Figure 37). By January 1883 he had acquired a complete run of twenty-one volumes of *The Graphic*, which contained all seven works that made up the series.[51] A later addition to the

48 Mary Cowling, *The Artist as Anthropologist: The Representation of Type and Character in Victorian Art* (Cambridge: Cambridge University Press, 1989), 9.

49 LT 160, volume 1, 260.

50 LT 405, volume 3, 63.

51 William Small, *Heads of the People I: The British Rough* (*The Graphic*, 26 June 1875); Hubert Herkomer, *Heads of the People II: The Agricultural Labourer* (*The Graphic*, 9 October 1875); W. Small, *Heads of the People III: At Court* (*The Graphic*, 23 October 1875); H. Herkomer, *Heads of the People IV: The Brewer's Drayman* (*The Graphic*, 20 November 1875); W. Small, *Heads of the People V: The Barrister* (*The Graphic*, 11 December 1875); M.W. Ridley, *Heads of the People VI: The Miner* (*The Graphic*, 15 April 1876); H. Herkomer, *Heads of the People VII: The Coastguardsman* (*The Graphic*, 20 September 1879). Of the seven prints, only Herkomer's *The Brewer's Drayman* is not currently among the remnants of van Gogh's collection at the Van Gogh Museum.

series, Arthur Hopkins' *A Cornish Fisher Lad*, appeared in June 1883, but was probably not collected by van Gogh, as his collecting had diminished by this stage and he usually mentioned any prints he found in his letters.

In order to portray types in his own work, van Gogh sought out items of clothing with which to dress his models, which tended to negate their personalities by drawing attention to their clothing and signifying their type. As early as 1881, while living in Brussels, van Gogh was already discussing acquiring such a wardrobe. To his parents he wrote:

> As regards that other suit, I have another objective apart from wearing it myself for as long as possible, for the fact is that when it's a bit older it will serve me in another way. You see, I'll gradually need a small collection of work-clothes with which to dress the models for my drawings.
>
> The blue smock of Brabant, for example, the grey linen suit that the miners wear and their leather hat, also a straw hat and clogs, a fisherman's costume of brown fustian and a sou'wester. And most definitely the clothing made of that kind of black or brown velvet that's very picturesque and characteristic – furthermore, a red doublet or vest. Likewise, a couple of women's costumes, such as that of Kempen and the area of Antwerp with the Brabantian cap and that of Blankenberge, for example, or Scheveningen or Katwijk.[52]

Van Gogh began to acquire these necessary 'costumes' while in The Hague and they soon began appearing in his drawings. One newly acquired item, a sou'wester, appeared in as many as ten drawings, eight of which are of heads only.[53] He was convinced that purchasing these items was essential for his success in producing work that would lead to his employment as a draughtsman:

52 LT 163, volume 1, 264.

53 *Fisherman with Sou'wester, Head*, 1883 (Van Gogh Museum, Vincent van Gogh Foundation. F1017/JH0302); *Fisherman with Sou'wester, Pipe and Coal Pan*, 1883 (Van Gogh Museum, Vincent van Gogh Foundation. F1016/JH0304); *Fisherman with Sou'wester, Sitting with Pipe*, 1883 (Van Gogh Museum, Vincent van Gogh Foundation. F1013/JH0305); *Fisherman with Sou'wester, Sitting with Pipe*, 1883 (Kröller-Müller Museum, Otterlo. F1010/JH0306); *Fisherman with Sou'wester, Smoking a Pipe*, 1883 (Van Gogh Museum, Vincent van Gogh Foundation. F1015/JH0307); *Fisherman with Sou'wester, Head*, 1883 (Private Collection. F1012/JH0308); *Fisherman with Sou'wester, Head*, 1883 (Kröller-Müller Museum, Otterlo. F1011/JH0309); *Fisherman with Sou'wester, Head*, 1883 (Van Gogh Museum, Vincent van Gogh Foundation. F1014/JH0310); *Fisherman in Jacket with Upturned Collar*, 1883 (F.A.C. Guépin Estate, London. F1049/JH0312); *Fisherman with Basket on His Back*, 1883 (Location unknown. F1083/JH0313).

'this is the only true way to succeed', he wrote.[54] He also possessed many farm tools and props such as old chairs and lanterns. Reminiscing about his time with van Gogh, amateur artist Anton Kerssemakers recalled farm tools 'in all corners' of the artist's Nuenen studio.[55] Dutch landscape painter and illustrator L.W.R. Wenkebach remembered the Nuenen studio being littered with 'old chairs without seats, rickety and broken, and in a corner all sorts of working tools'.[56] Van Gogh continued to use his props and assorted costumes in his attempts to produce drawings that would appeal to the illustrated magazines. They enabled him to use a small number of sitters to produce a wide range of physiognomies, advertising to prospective employers the range of his artistic skills and his cache of ready-to-use models.

Having drawn a number of portraits, van Gogh attempted to create his own version of the 'Heads of the People' series on two occasions: once in The Hague and again while living with his parents in Nuenen. The drawings from both periods were influenced by his newly established black-and-white print collection. When he first began to work on his 'head' drawings he told van Rappard: 'I've been working on Black and White drawings … [particularly] heads – Heads of the People – including fishermen's heads with sou'westers'.[57] He wrote the words 'Heads of the People' in English, confirming the influence of *The Graphic* illustrations and placing van Gogh's own drawings in a similar context, thus indicating the direction he wished to take his own newly created portraits.

Between January 1882 and September 1883, while living in The Hague, van Gogh produced thirty-two drawings that were influenced by the 'Heads of the People' series. Most were created between December 1882 and April 1883, during which time he also purchased the twenty-one volumes of *The Graphic*. In three letters in late December 1882 van Gogh wrote of making drawings with a focus on depicting types. In the first he mentioned two new drawings: 'one is a man reading the Bible and the other is a man saying his prayers before his midday meal'.[58] Four days later he told Theo he was working on 'two large heads of an orphan man, with his white beard and old-fashioned,

54 LT 163, volume 1, 264.

55 'Letter from Anton Kerssemakers to Johan Briedé on van Gogh's studio in Nuenen, 23 June 1914', in Susan Alyson Stein (ed.), *Van Gogh: A Retrospective* (Sydney and London: Bay Books, 1986), 56.

56 'Ludwig "Willem" Reijmert Wenkebach, interviewed by Mrs. Johan de Meester (1936)', quoted in Stein, *Van Gogh: A Retrospective*, 67.

57 LT 302, volume 2, 235.

58 LT 294, volume 2, 223.

old top hat',[59] and in the third letter he told him he was 'occupied with large heads'.[60] The first two drawings he mentioned – a man reading a Bible and another saying grace (Figure 36) – are similar in sentiment to Herkomer's *The Agricultural Labourer – Sunday* (Figure 37).[61]

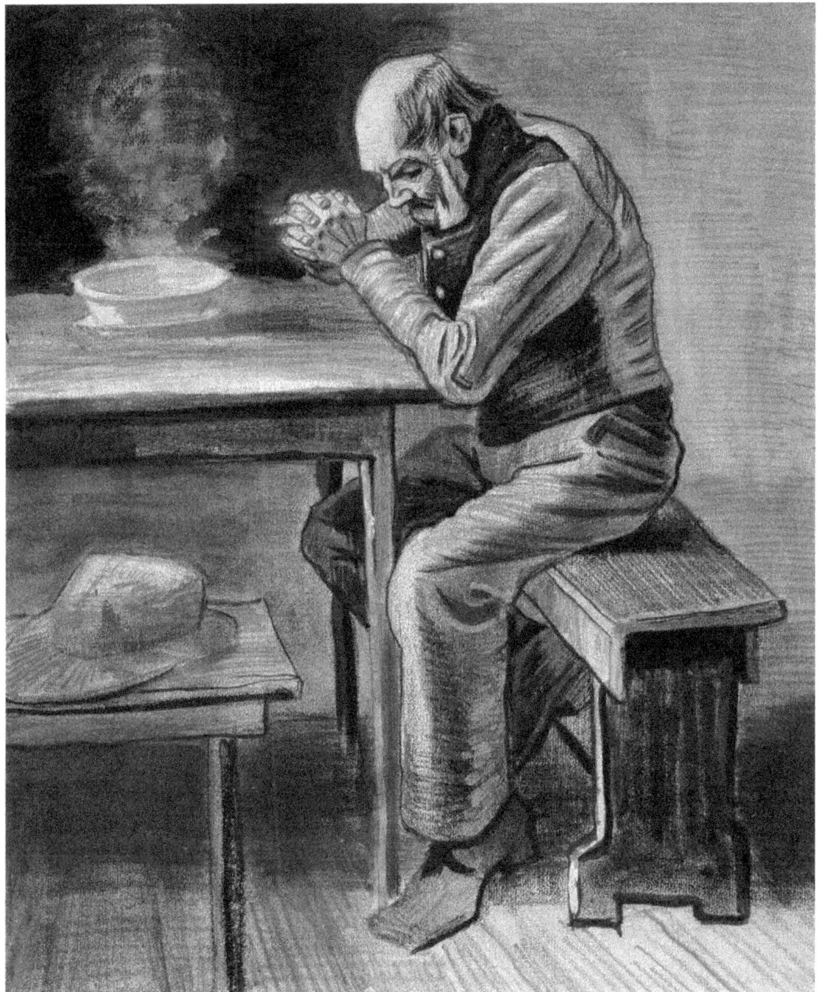

Figure 36. Vincent van Gogh, *Prayer Before the Meal*, 1882 (private collection).

59 LT 295, volume 2, 224.

60 LT 296, volume 2, 226.

61 Vincent van Gogh, *Man, Sitting, Reading a Bible*, 1882 (Kröller-Müller Museum, Otterlo. F1001/JH0278).

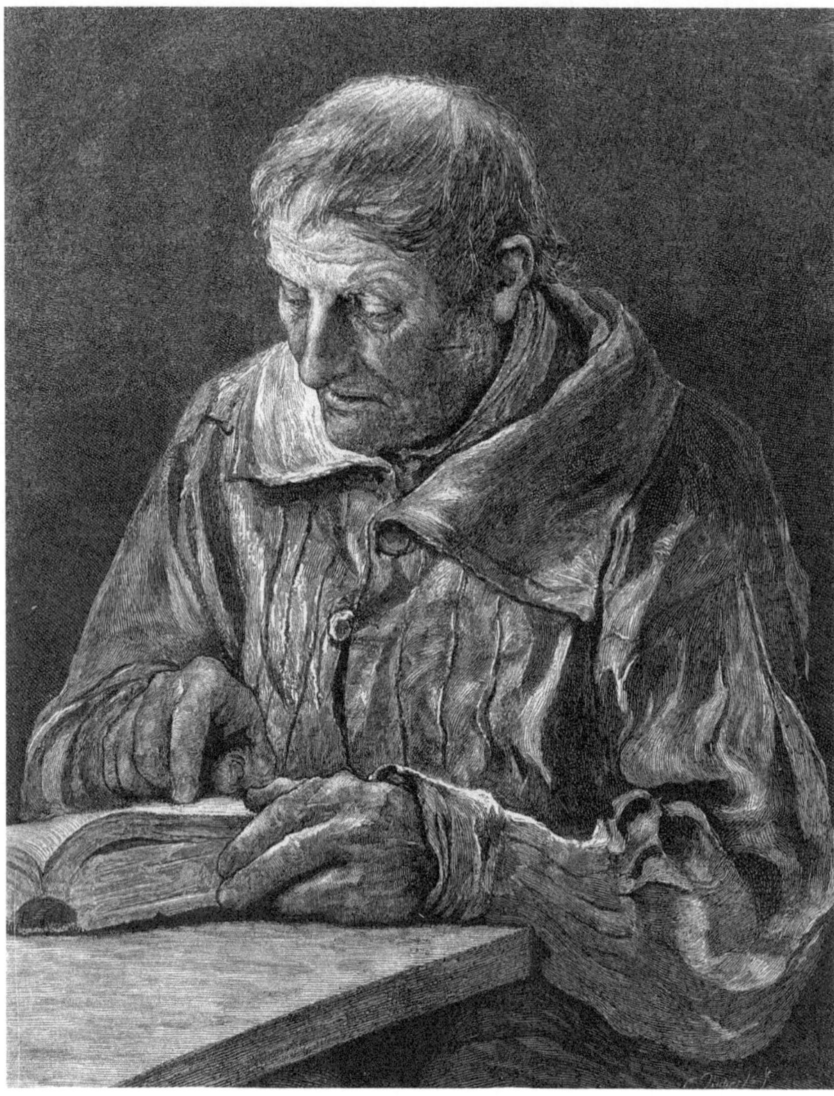

Figure 37. Hubert Herkomer, *Heads of the People: The Agricultural Labourer - Sunday* (*The Graphic*, 19 October 1875).

In both, van Gogh portrays a farm labourer as a simple noble worker who earns his daily crust through hard work, a sentiment emphasised by *The Graphic*: 'there are no more worthy men to be found in the world than some of our farm labourers'.[62] In the second drawing (Figure 36) van Gogh placed his subject sitting at a simple wooden table, replicating the environment

62 *The Graphic*, 9 October 1875, 351.

depicted by Herkomer and reinforcing the modesty and simplicity of this man's existence and conveying a message of dignified frugality by placing a simple meal of steaming soup before the praying man. These two works by van Gogh and Herkomer are deeply religious, capturing an act of sharing with God, either in prayer or reading the Bible. In Herkomer's work the figure, the Bible and the finger that guides the reading are bathed in light. In van Gogh's *Prayer Before the Meal* the old man is placed against a dark background, his bald head highlighted, creating a halo effect, and his clasped hands bathed in light, emphasising deep prayer. While *The Graphic* stated that the labourer's family Bible provided 'lessons of cheerfulness and contentment',[63] van Gogh went further, declaring that he hoped to express in his drawings the sentiment of Christmas and New Year and 'a feeling of belief in something on high'.[64]

In a more accomplished drawing from this period, *Orphan Man in Sunday Clothes with Eye Bandage* (1882), van Gogh aimed to render a further type – an old soldier ravaged by time and war.[65] The war medal pinned to his lapel helped the viewer read the work and recognise the 'type' depicted. Similar visual keys can be found in Herkomer's *The Coastguardsman*[66] and Ridley's *The Miner* (Figure 39). In the former the short telescope and sailor's uniform denote his life watching over the sea. In the latter the miner's face and hands show signs of a tough life and the pick slung over his shoulder, easily interpreted as a crucifix, representing his daily burden, indicates his employment. Of his plan for these drawings, van Gogh wrote to Theo that his 'intention would be to find a large number like these to try to form a sort of entity that wouldn't be entirely unworthy of the title 'heads of the people''.[67] This was the first time van Gogh explicitly drew a parallel between his own work and the famous series published by *The Graphic.* Over the next few months his letters were littered with references to drawings of heads. Even in a letter discussing Theo's moral dilemma and social obligation of caring for a sick and homeless woman, van Gogh mentioned in the closing line, 'I'm busy with work, still doing various Heads'.[68]

---

63 *The Graphic*, 9 October 1875, 351.

64 LT 294, volume 2, 223.

65 Vincent van Gogh, *Orphan Man in Sunday Clothes with Eye Bandage*, 1882 (Fogg Art Museum, Harvard University, Cambridge, Massachusetts. F1003/JH0285).

66 Hubert Herkomer, *Heads of the People: The Coastguardsman* (*The Graphic*, 20 September 1879).

67 LT 298, volume 2, 229.

68 LT 301, volume 2, 234.

In late January 1883 van Gogh reported excitedly that he had acquired a sou'wester[69] – a Scheveningen fishermen's hat – which he could use to transform his models into a new type. The sou'wester, rather than the model, made the drawings into depictions of a fisherman.[70] Over the next two months van Gogh drew six different versions of heads wearing a sou'wester and four full-length portraits of a figure wearing the same hat.[71] He confirmed that the drawings of the heads formed part of his intended 'Heads of the People' series in a February letter to van Rappard, whom he told he was working almost exclusively on 'heads – *Heads of the people* – including fishermen's heads with sou'westers'.[72] Van Rappard, who was just as familiar with English black-and-white illustrations, would have recognised the reference. By using the English phrase 'Heads of the people', van Gogh did not need to discuss the drawings in detail, as van Rappard was aware of their context, composition and their place in a wider body of work.

Three of these drawings – *Fisherman with Sou'wester, Head* (1883), *Fisherman with Sou'wester, Pipe and Coal Pan* (1883) and *Fisherman with Sou'wester, Head* (1883) – reveal van Gogh's increasing competency.[73] All are similar and indicate the care van Gogh took to produce high-quality works. The headwear and the fishermen's faces are emphasised by rendering parts of the background in a deep black to bring the faces and the sou'westers to the fore. In *Fisherman with Sou'wester, Head* (1883), the area under the sou'wester and the fisherman's smock just under the chin of white whiskers is a dense black. In *Fisherman with Sou'wester, Pipe and Coal Pan* (1883) van Gogh used this heavy darkening technique in the top right corner, emphasising the brim of the hat and the fisherman's white beard. He also used lithographic crayon to darken the left sleeve, highlighting the hand that holds the coal pan. This

---

69 'Tomorrow I'll be getting a *sou'wester* for the heads. Heads of fishermen, old and young, that's what I've been thinking about for a long time and I had already done one, but then later I couldn't get hold of a sou'wester again. Now I'm going to have one of my own, an old one that many gales and seas have swept over' (LT 301, volume 2, 235); and 'I'm still very happy with my sou'wester. I'm curious to know whether you'll find anything good in the heads of fishermen. The last one I did this week was of a chap with a white fringe of beard' (LT 305, volume 2, 252).

70 Laura Soth, 'Fantasy and Reality in The Hague Drawings', in Joseph J. Rishel *et al.*, *Van Gogh Face to Face: The Portraits* (New York: Thames and Hudson, 2000), 66.

71 For the titles of these drawings, see footnote 53 in this chapter; of the four full-length figures, two (F1049/JH0312 and F1083/JH0313) seem to have slightly different headgear; drawn in an outdoor setting, they appear not to be of the same model wearing van Gogh's sou'wester.

72 LT 302, volume 2, 234.

73 F1017/JH0302; F1016/JH0304; F1014/JH0310, of which details are given in footnote 53 in this chapter.

clever use of chiaroscuro emphasised key indicators in the drawing that the figure was a fisherman. Van Gogh achieved these effects by experimenting with lithographic crayon, a development that had its origins in his earlier attempts at making lithographs. The medium produced a velvety black, resembling the printed images found in newspapers, and van Gogh hoped 'that drawings done in this way will be suitable for reproduction'.[74]

Over the next few months van Gogh's letters were dominated by news of his purchase of twenty-one volumes of *The Graphic*. He compiled endless lists for van Rappard and Theo and was preoccupied with cataloguing his new prints into folios. Even with all the activity of organising his new collection, van Gogh continued to draw fishermen's heads as well as other types of heads, notably women with shawls and bonnets and men with top hats and caps. If van Gogh was going to produce a successful 'Heads of the People' series, he needed to expand the range of types he drew. He needed to capture as many different types as possible and he encouraged van Rappard to follow a similar path, urging him to draw blind men and later suggesting he draw Scheveningen women. Ironically, it was at about this time that van Gogh's own practice of drawing heads began to diminish, until it disappeared while he travelled through remote Drenthe.[75] He also stopped referring to drawings of heads in his letters, until he discussed the making of portraits in a letter to Theo in early December 1884 sent from Nuenen.[76]

Van Gogh arrived in Nuenen in December 1883 and stayed until November 1885. During that time he produced 115 studies of heads, not including those in sketchbooks and letters. From December 1884 to February 1885 he worked on these images exclusively, returning to the subject in May 1885, when he completed the genre painting *The Potato Eaters*. His letter to Theo in early December 1884 confirmed his intention to return to the depiction of heads and clearly outlined his objectives. The series, unlike the one he had suggested in The Hague would include paintings. Further, it was to be more ambitious; van Gogh aimed to complete at least fifty heads by the end of January. The project dominated his practice and correspondence, as evident in a letter from mid-December: 'I have to make 50 of these heads – while I am still here and

74 LT 297, volume 2, 228.

75 Of all the known works from Van Gogh's Drenthe period, only one is of a head. It is a pen drawing, measures only 21 x 13.5cm, of a woman with a dark cap (*Head of a Woman with Dark Cap*, October 1883, F1073/JH0404). A sheet of sketches (ca. October 1883 F1095/JH405) sent with a letter to Theo also has a tiny 'scratch' of a woman's head.

76 LT 470, volume 3, 188–9.

can get models of all types relatively easily during the winter months'.[77] A few days later he confirmed he was working on the project and the possibility that some works would be in watercolour, but he was adamant that he must 'paint them first'.[78] In his next letter to Theo he said he was sending twelve little pen-and-ink drawings of heads, complemented with extra sketches sent a few weeks later in January 1884.[79] This group of pen-and-ink drawings are of interest because they most closely resemble a series produced with the illustrated magazines in mind. Fifteen drawings still exist, five of which stand out as being more ambitious than the rest.[80] They are larger in size, measuring 14 x 10cm, and were carefully executed, having been underdrawn with a pencil before they were completed in ink. They are constructed mainly of lines, with extensive use of cross-hatching; four of them are framed with a border around the image, a device used previously to give drawings the appearance of magazine illustrations. Most importantly, all five of the more ambitious drawings are signed, indicating that they were more than mere indicative and experimental sketches for Theo.

Two of these works, *Head of a Man* (Figure 38) and *Head of a Woman* (1884–85),[81] reveal van Gogh's experimentation in order to make works that resembled black-and-white illustrations and stylistic parallels with works from the original *Graphic* series. In these works, van Gogh incorporated small spots of ink, seen to the right of the man's head and to the left of the woman's. Although not explicitly mentioned, van Gogh may have developed the technique, believing that it would assist engravers when preparing illustrations for printing. A comparison between *Head of a Man* (1884–85) and Ridley's *The Miner* (Figure 39) also reveals how van Gogh used compositional and stylistic cues from the English print in his own work. Van Gogh's copy of *The Miner*, now in the Van Gogh Museum, is marked in each corner with small pinholes and has yellowed from exposure to light, suggesting it had hung in his studio. If this was the case, it is easy to accept it as a source for this and other drawings. In both Ridley's and van Gogh's work the face is the focus – highlighted by a lamplight in *The Miner* and by a light source entering from

77 LT 475, volume 3, 196.

78 LT 476, volume 3, 197.

79 LT 477 and 479.

80 Although van Gogh mentions sending twelve in his correspondence, van Heugten has argued that up to twenty may have been sent over a short period (Sjraar van Heugten, *Vincent van Gogh Drawings*, vol, 2: *Nuenen 1883–1885* (Amsterdam: Van Gogh Museum, 1997), 124).

81 Vincent van Gogh, *Head of a Woman*, 1884–85 (Van Gogh Museum, Amsterdam (Vincent van Gogh Foundation).

the left in *Head of a Man* (1884–85). The similarities extend to the chiselled appearance of the cheekbones and the distinctly drawn lapels of the jackets. When viewed in the context of van Gogh's desire to be a professional draughtsman, this drawing, as well as the other four in the group sent to Theo, seem to have been intended for the general public viewing, either through the gallery system or the editors of the illustrated newspapers.

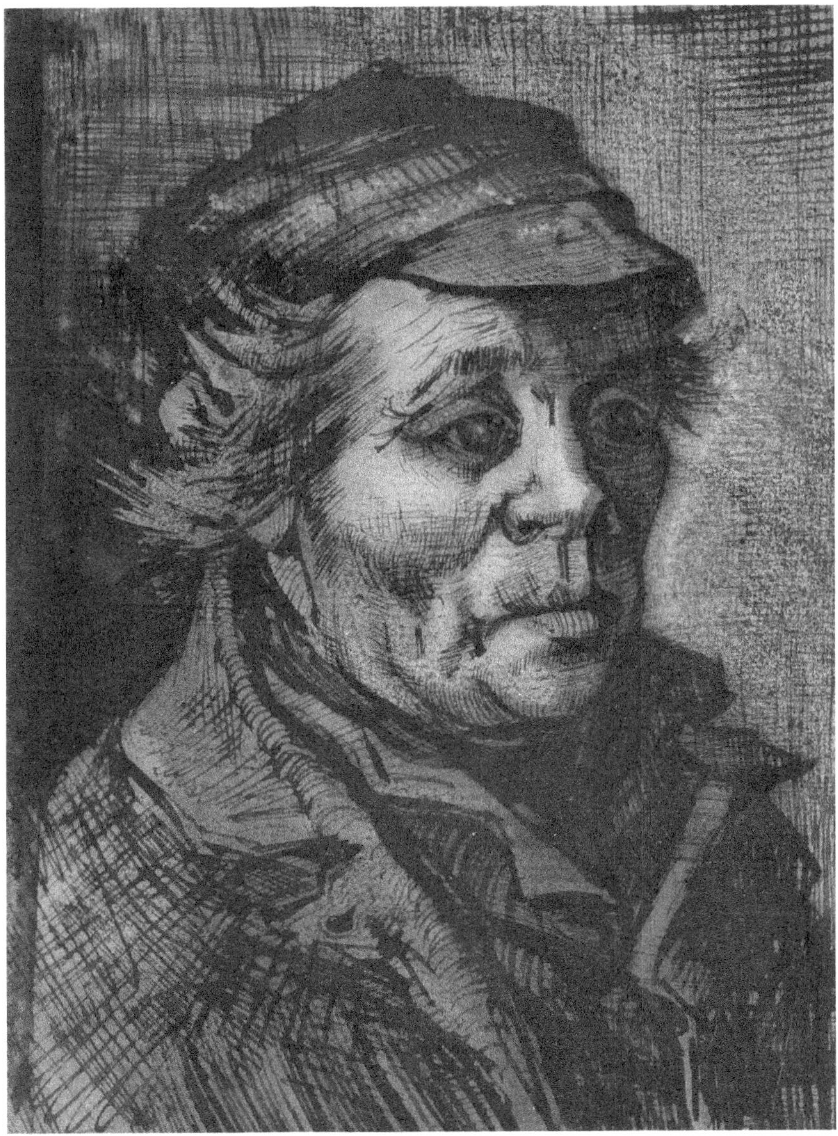

Figure 38. Vincent van Gogh, *Head of a Man*, 1884–85 (Van Gogh Museum, Amsterdam (Vincent van Gogh Foundation)).

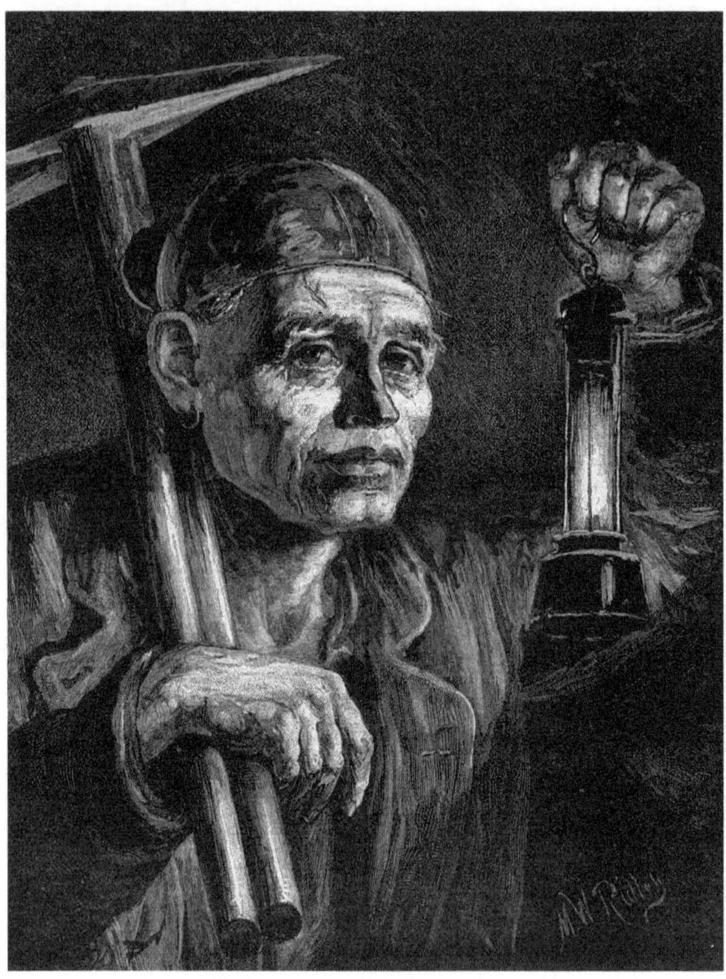

Figure 39. Matthew Ridley, *Heads of the People VI: The Miner* (*The Graphic*, 15 April 1876).

In due course van Gogh reproduced the drawing of *Head of a Man* (1884–85) and a number of other drawings from this series as paintings, following in the footsteps of illustrators like Herkomer and Holl, who often reimagined their illustrations in oil on canvas. This and other paintings maintained the stylistic, compositional and conceptual parallels with the work in *The Graphic*. Bold outlines are used, the sitters are rendered with well-defined and structured faces, and in *Peasant, Head* (1884–85)[82] van Gogh retains a halo-like

82 Vincent van Gogh, *Peasant, Head*, 1884–85 (Art Gallery of New South Wales, Sydney. F0160a/JH0563).

glow on the sitter's face that is reminiscent of Ridley's miner. In a number of other works van Gogh also dressed his sitters with headwear denoting their employment and social position, as in *Peasant Woman, Head* (1885), where the model wears a red morning cap, indicating that she is indoors and at home (rather than the white day cap she would have put on when leaving her house), and *Peasant, Head* (1885), which shows a male wearing his evening cap and jacket, indicating that he was resting after a long day's work, a sentiment also depicted in Herkomer's *The Agricultural Labourer – Sunday* (Figure 37).[83] With these works van Gogh aimed to produce 'illustrations of types' and to represent 'the very incarnation of primitive rural life', which had been the agenda of *The Graphic*'s 'Heads of the People' series.[84]

In May 1885 van Gogh's project of depicting heads culminated with the completion of *The Potato Eaters*. Although a work of a family set in an identifiable space – the figures in the painting have been identified as the De Groot-Van Rooijen family – he intended it to be a depiction of a universal type, in this case a representation of a peasant family. Nothing in the image is unique to or representative of the particular family, but it has many generic references, such as to the type of cottage, the frugal meal the family survives on, the piety of their social class, their dress, and the simplicity of their existence. In order to achieve success in representing peasants, van Gogh wanted the focus to remain on the depiction of the heads. Van Tilborgh and Vellekoop argue for such a position, writing that 'he confined himself to half-length figures, and could thus concentrate all his energy on the heads – a motif he had been hard at work on since the winter'.[85] Van Gogh confirmed this in a letter to Theo in April 1885.

> Just wanted to tell you that I'm hard at work on the potato eaters.
>
> I've started it again on a new canvas and painted new studies of the heads; changed the hands, in particular, a great deal. Above all, I'm doing my best to put life into it…
>
> Still, it's coming along, and I think there'll be something very different in it from what you can ever have seen by me. At least that clearly.

83 Vincent van Gogh, *Peasant Woman, Head*, 1885 (Van Gogh Museum, Amsterdam (Vincent van Gogh Foundation) F0160/JH0722); *Peasant, Head*, 1885 (Musées Royaux des Beaux-Arts de Belgique, Brussels. F163/JH687). For information about traditional headwear styles, see Louis van Tilborgh and Marije Vellekoop (eds.), *Vincent van Gogh Paintings*, Vol. 1 *Dutch Period 1881–1885* (Amsterdam: Van Gogh Museum, 1999), 86.

84 van Tilborgh and Vellekoop, *Vincent van Gogh Paintings*, Vol. 1, 86.

85 van Tilborgh and Vellekoop, *Vincent van Gogh Paintings*, Vol. 1, 138.

> I mean the *life* especially. I'm painting this FROM MEMORY *on the painting itself.*
>
> But you know yourself how many times I've painted the heads![86]

This sentiment was further echoed four months later in a letter to van Rappard written after they had disagreed about the painting's merit, with van Gogh stressing that his focus had been the depiction of the heads:

> Heads and hands were done with great care, though, and – since these were the most important and the rest almost entirely dark (so *really quite different* in effect from the lithograph), it may perhaps be more excusable of me than you think to have painted it as I did.[87]

Van Gogh was understandably defensive about this work. Not only was it his first major painting, but it was also the conclusion of months of hard work painting and drawing heads. The bold aim of making fifty such works was a grand project in the mould of the famous *Graphic* series, with which van Rappard was familiar. Van Gogh believed he had succeeded and therefore proven to his peer that he was on his way to equalling the skill of the artists and illustrators whom they both so admired. It also indicated the beginning of his transition from would-be illustrator to committed painter and artist.

Van Gogh only produced a handful of paintings and drawings of heads immediately after finishing *The Potato Eaters*. He turned his focus towards depicting peasants in the fields and still lifes. By November 1885 he had decided to leave Nuenen, travelling first to Antwerp and Brussels before arriving in Paris in February 1886, where his art would take on a radically different aesthetic. Writing to his sister Wil after twenty months in Paris, he declared that even after all his exposure to the influences of the modern painters he had encountered, what he hoped to achieve was 'to paint a good portrait'.[88] This remained a central preoccupation and during the productive period from his arrival in Paris in 1886 to his death in Auvers in 1890, van Gogh produced more than 130 portraits, including a substantial body of self-portraits. Many of these were single works and most were painted, thus differing from the concept of the series that had been his focus during his Dutch years. Nevertheless, the influence of *The Graphic*'s 'Heads of the People' series persisted.

86 LT 496, volume 3, 230.

87 LT 528, volume 3, 278.

88 LT 574, volume 3, 369.

What differentiated the portraits van Gogh did after he had left The Netherlands from his earlier ones was the fact that many of the sitters were identifiable. Van Gogh was not necessarily interested, however, in portraying the sitter as an individual, and he persisted in producing a universal type of portrait in which specific traits, clothing and accessories classified the sitter. *Woman at a Table in the Café du Tambourin* (1886–87) depicts a very modern Parisian woman, whose modernity was confirmed by her clothes and the objects placed before her.[89] Van Gogh's first portrait from Arles, of a woman, encapsulated the stereotype of the region.[90] She wears the traditional dress of the province: a black headdress and a blue shawl over a white lace top. A portrait of an Arlésian peasant, *The Old Patience Escalier* (1888), which van Gogh declared 'absolutely a continuation of certain studies of heads done in Holland', is exaggerated so as to transform the individual into a representation of a peasant type.[91] The withered face, expression of tiredness, and potential ugliness were all considered; the peasant was, as van Gogh wrote to Emile Bernard, 'a wild animal'.[92] The colour combination of golden yellow and deep blue reinforced that the image be viewed as depicting the peasantry; it suggested 'the scorched air of harvest time at midday' under which the local peasants worked.[93]

L'Arlésienne (Madame Ginoux), with Books (1888), reveals the modern nature of this rural sitter.[94] Although Madame Ginoux is dressed in local traditional clothing, she sits at a table in the café she runs with her husband, a pile of modern books before her. In this sense the composition is similar in sentiment to *The Agricultural Labourer – Sunday*. Just as the Bible denotes the piety of the farmer, van Gogh's use of modern literature affirms the modern qualities of Madame Ginoux and women like her who could be found in French bars at the time. Joseph Roulin, the local postman, described by van Gogh as 'a raging republican' and 'a more interesting man than many people', also proved to be a great model.[95] Van Gogh made nine paintings and drawings of Roulin, every

89 Vincent van Gogh, *Woman at a Table in the Café du Tambourin*, 1886–87 (Van Gogh Museum, Amsterdam (Vincent van Gogh Foundation). F0370/JH1208).

90 Vincent van Gogh, *An Old Woman of Arles*, 1888 (Van Gogh Museum, Amsterdam (Vincent van Gogh Foundation). F0390/JH1357).

91 Vincent van Gogh, *The Old Patience Escalier, Head*, 1888 (Norton Simon Museum, Pasadena California. F0443/JH1548); see LT 665, volume 5, 241.

92 LT 665, volume 5, 241.

93 LT 665, volume 5, 241.

94 Vincent van Gogh, *The Arlésienne (Madame Ginoux), with Books*, 1888 (Metropolitan Museum of Art, New York. F0488/JH1624).

95 LT 652, volume 4, 204.

one depicting him as a postman.[96] He is always shown wearing his royal blue and gold uniform and cap, with the word '*POSTES*' clearly visible, emulating Herkomer's use of a uniform and telescope to indicate the occupation of the sitter in *The Coastguardsman*. Roulin's wife, Augustine, also the subject of a number of portraits, eventually became the universally renowned *La Berceuse* (1889).[97] With a rope in her hand she gently rocks a cradle beyond the picture frame, van Gogh transforming her from humble mother into what Kristin Hoermann Lister has described as 'a serene high priestess' offering consolation to the broken-hearted.[98] Van Gogh believed *La Berceuse* (1889) would not be out of place on an Icelandic fishing boat where the sailors 'at once children and martyrs ... would experience a feeling of being rocked, reminding them of their own lullabies'.[99] Later, while recuperating in the asylum at Saint Rémy, he remembered the work fondly, wishing he had the strength to further his experiments with making 'portraits of saints and of holy women from life', using models who were 'citizens of the present day'.[100]

Beyond Arles, van Gogh's portraits continued in a similar tradition. In Saint Rémy he painted a young gardener wearing a slouch hat within the grounds of the asylum.[101] He also painted an inmate; not a friend or even an acquaintance, but rather a stereotype of those with whom he was living.[102] Van Gogh's portraits, although of individuals, were also representative of many people in society. With the portraits of the local postman, the peasant, and the Arles woman, and a further work of a gypsy woman from Arles, for example, van Gogh created a series of the people one might meet in his neighbourhood.

The idea of capturing a type also applied to van Gogh's self-portraits. He produced almost forty self-portraits, all painted during his time in France where he depicted himself as an artist, a member of the Parisian avant-garde, a cosmopolitan, a farmer, and, late in his career, a monk-like figure. These

96 The only variations in the images are a change between three-quarter length and bust composition and the inclusion of a flowered background in the last three versions, produced between February and April 1889.

97 Vincent van Gogh, *La Berceuse*, 1889 (Kröller-Müller Museum, Otterlo. F0504/JH1655).

98 Kristin Hoermann Lister, 'Tracing a Transformation: Madame Roulin into La Berceuse', *Van Gogh Museum Journal* (2001), 70.

99 LT 743, volume 4, 399–400.

100 LT 801, volume 5, 92.

101 Vincent van Gogh, *Portrait of a Gardener*, 1889 (Galleria Nazionale d'Arte Moderna e Contemporanea, Rome. F0531/JH1779).

102 Vincent van Gogh, *Portrait of a Patient*, 1889 (Van Gogh Museum, Amsterdam (Vincent van Gogh Foundation). F0703/JH1832).

works form part of his wider œuvre of portraits, and as such were made in the context of his earlier experiments after *The Graphic*'s 'Heads of the People' series. His first self-portrait, dating from early 1886, shows him as a respectable Parisian immersed in city life. Although it is still dark and reminiscent of his earlier Dutch works, it reveals him, according to Hulsker, 'trying to adapt to his brother's environment'.[103] Other works from Paris depict a similar persona. There are self-portraits with van Gogh wearing the clothes of the Parisian middle-class (hat, jacket, vest and tie), while others show him smoking a pipe, giving him an air of distinction and reinforcing his self-image as belonging to the cosmopolitan bourgeoisie. Others offer a contrast to the middle-class city man. *Self-Portrait with Straw Hat* (1887), for instance, although painted in Paris depicts van Gogh as from rural stock; he wears a bright yellow straw hat and a matching smock.[104] The painting is a composition in yellow, emphasising the glowing sun, which the farmers not only worked under but also relied on for bountiful harvests. This theme was taken up later, again in Paris, with van Gogh painting himself with a similar hat and smock, the key features glowing in a golden hue against a non-descript background.[105]

Van Gogh's time in Paris begins and ends with two self-portraits as an artist. The first, from early 1886, is austere: this artist is in the mould of the great Dutch Masters.[106] The painting is dark and sombre, and the artist looks out towards the viewer with a serious expression. The palette of just a handful of colours – red, green, orange, white and a small amount of dark blue – reinforces the classical nature of the artist depicted. The later self-portrait – the last from Paris, painted just before he left for Arles – shows a different type of artist (Plate 6), who is no longer of the Dutch School but of the French avant-garde. Gone are the hat and traditional artist's smock. Instead, van Gogh presents himself wearing a heavy blue worker's jacket and with short-cropped red hair. The palette reflects the change in van Gogh's approach and, more importantly, a multitude of colours – a range of greens, reds, blues, yellows and whites – informs the viewer that this work is part of

103 Vincent van Gogh, *Self Portrait with Dark Felt Hat*, 1886 (Van Gogh Museum, Amsterdam (Vincent van Gogh Foundation). F0208a/JH1089); Jan Hulsker, *The New Complete van Gogh: Paintings, Drawings, Sketches: Revised and Enlarged ed.* (Amsterdam: J.M. Meulenhoff: Philadelphia: John Benjamins, 1996), 236.

104 Vincent van Gogh, *Self-Portrait with Pipe and Straw Hat*, 1887 (Van Gogh Museum, Amsterdam (Vincent van Gogh Foundation). F0469/JH1310).

105 Vincent van Gogh, *Self-Portrait with Straw Hat*, 1887 (Van Gogh Museum, Amsterdam (Vincent van Gogh Foundation). F0524/JH1565).

106 Vincent van Gogh, *Self-Portrait with Dark Felt Hat in Front of the Easel*, 1886. (Van Gogh Museum, Amsterdam (Vincent van Gogh Foundation). F0181/JH1090).

a modern artist's practice. Moreover, with its lightness of colour and shimmering technique, the work emphasises that the artist depicted is part of a contemporary vanguard, not one from academic traditions.

One of van Gogh's most interesting self-portraits, dated September 1888, has often been referred to as a depiction of him as a devotee of Buddhism.[107] The first bust-type self-portrait from Arles, it shows him with cropped hair and a cleanly shaven beard, truly representing his appearance at the time. Writing to his sister Wil, van Gogh said he looked 'like a Japanese'.[108] In two later letters, one to Theo and the other to Gauguin, he expanded on this likeness. To Gauguin he wrote, 'exaggerating my personality also, I looked more for the character of a bonze, a simple worshipper of the eternal Buddha',[109] and a day later to Theo, 'I had conceived this portrait as being that of a bonze, a simple worshiper of the eternal Buddha'.[110] Representing himself as such was in keeping with his belief that Arles was like Japan, strategically reinforcing his wish to create a studio of the south, a haven for modern artists living and creating together, as he believed the great Japanese artists had done. The portrait also was intended to confirm the influence of Japanese prints on modern painting and painters, of which he was one, by being a portrait not only of himself but of 'an Impressionist in general'.[111] It depicted a universal type of which van Gogh was an example.

While van Gogh continued to explore the notion of depicting types in his portraits, he also maintained the stylistic lessons learnt from the 'Heads of the People' series, even after he had left The Netherlands for Belgium and then France. A strong illustrative foundation underpins many of his portraits; bold outlines, cross-hatching, especially in the drawings, and the juxtaposition of dark and light spaces persisted as stylistic features. The composition of many of the portraits, both bust-style and three-quarter length, also followed rules van Gogh had learnt from the black-and-white prints. One of the first portraits of the postman Roulin, a three-quarter length painting (Plate 7), reveals a striking resemblance to Herkomer's *The Brewer's Drayman* (Figure 40).

107 Vincent van Gogh, *Self-Portrait*, 1888 (Fogg Art Museum, Harvard University, Cambridge, Massachusetts. F0476/JH1581).

108 LT 678, volume 4, 265. In that letter van Gogh recommended that Wil familiarise herself with Japanese prints so as to understand 'the direction that painting has taken at present. Colourful and bright'. He told her he no longer needed such prints 'because I'm always saying to myself that I'm in Japan here'.

109 LT 695, volume 4, 304.

110 LT 697, volume 4, 308.

111 LT 697, volume 4, 308.

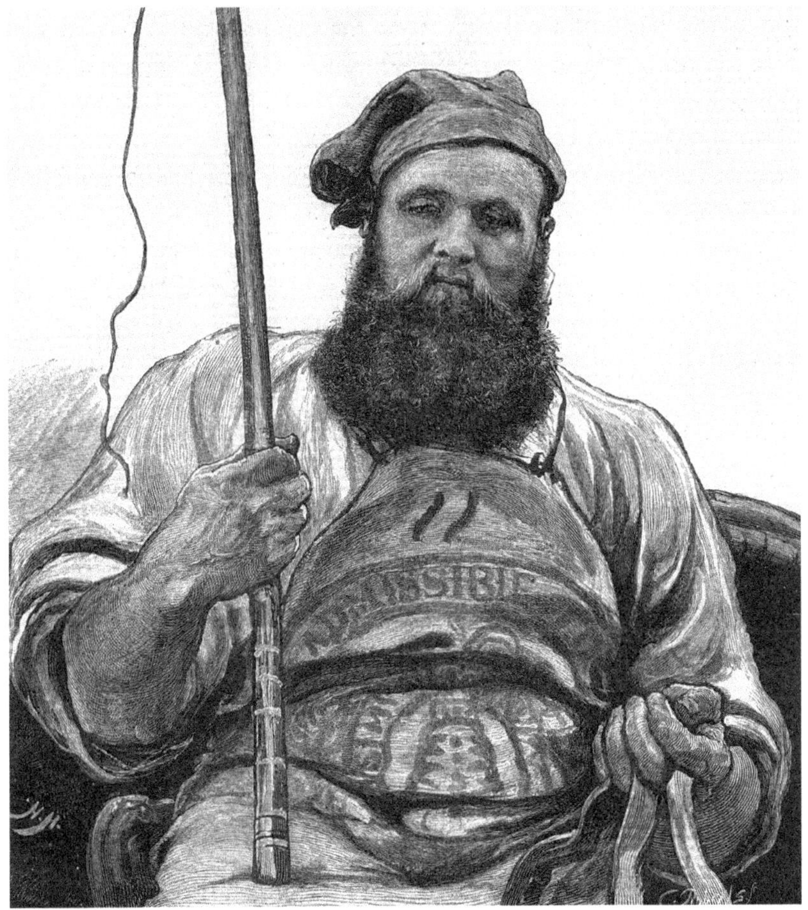

Figure 40. Hubert Herkomer, *The Brewer's Drayman* (*The Graphic*, 20 November 1875).

In both works the sitter is square to the picture plane, staring directly at the viewer. The background from the chest up is plain, emphasising each sitter's facial features. Although more by coincidence than design, the similar full-length beards become central anchor points, as do the hands, clearly depicted with bold outlines. The use of strong outlines is consistent in both images; the clothing, the hats, the facial features, and the accompanying furniture are all encased in a strong line. A drawing from July to August 1888, although showing only Roulin's head, reveals further similarities.[112] It is constructed of

112 Vincent van Gogh, *Joseph Roulin, Head*, 1888 (J. Paul Getty Museum, Los Angeles, California. F1458/JH1536).

strong cross-hatching and bold outlines. There are large areas of darkness, such as in the jacket, cap and beard. Placed against a light background, the head clearly becomes the focus. Drawn for the artist John Russell, it continued van Gogh's process of producing drawings after paintings, a habit copied from the example set by the draughtsmen whose work van Gogh collected and admired.

Although van Gogh's later portraits were influenced by new trends in art and his wish to be identified as one of the avant-garde, they were, as we have seen, underpinned by the lessons and aims that shaped his early works of heads. His collection of prints was central to this early education and played a wider role in shaping the way he made and thought about this work. His substantial body of portraiture was not conceived in the grand and noble traditions of the genre, but rather in the context of what he had learnt and taken from black-and-white illustrations, particularly *The Graphic*'s 'Heads of the People' series. The portraits and self-portraits he did after he left The Netherlands have a direct lineage from this series and, although he did not attempt to create a unified body of portraits or heads as he had done in the past, van Gogh still believed that the aim of portraiture was to epitomise a universal type rather than to be just an accurate depiction of the appearance of the sitter.

Looking for Employment and Discovering the Series

In organising his print collection in seventeen folios, van Gogh ensured that he had easy access to its contents to help with his own compositions. He designated some folios for artists, types of workers, animals and landscapes, and general military and shipping scenes. Two folios contained prints from particular series, one with portraits from *The Graphic*'s 'Heads of the People' series and the other with sketches of London life and similar illustrations of Paris and New York. Neither the 'Heads of the People' prints nor the images of cities were a haphazard collection of random drawings. They were particular series, appearing in the illustrated newspaper over multiple issues that told a story. Van Gogh also had in his other folios many illustrations that similarly constituted a series. He had a number of works from the 'American Sketches' and 'The State of Ireland' series from *The Illustrated London News*, about which he was enthusiastic, declaring they 'form a series together'.[113] He had a very large number of illustrations from the series 'Les enfants assistés', produced in *L'Illustration*, the

113 LT 275, volume 2, 182.

Pictorial World's 'How the Poor Live' and two series documenting prison life – *L'Illustration*'s 'The Prisons of Paris' and *The Illustrated London News*'s 'Prison Life on Blackwell's Island'. He had copies of Millet's series. 'The Labours of the Field' and 'The Four Times of the Day', which he copied both at the beginning and the end of his career.

As well as those he sourced from the illustrated newspapers, van Gogh also knew of, and sometimes collected, prints associated with novels and books.[114] He collected almost all of the illustrations that accompanied Victor Hugo's serialised novel, *Ninety-Three*,[115] referencing one of its images, *Dolorosa*, in his correspondence.[116] He strongly recommended Mahoney's illustrated version of Dickens' *Oliver Twist* to van Rappard.[117] He admired Gavarni's illustrations of 'London drunkards and beggars' found in *Gavarni in London: Sketches of Life and Character* and in *The Illustrated London News*,[118] and wrote glowingly of Doré's illustrations in *London: a Pilgrimage*, describing them as 'splendidly beautiful and noble in sentiment'.[119] These illustrations, like those in the newspapers, told a story across a series; they formed a narrative in pictures. A major development during the nineteenth century, the concept of the series enhanced the experience of the written word and, more importantly, presented narratives visually for the illiterate. In this sense series of images were truly inclusive and produced for the masses. For van Gogh they constituted a powerful medium that told the story of places and their people; they were art of and for everybody.

As his confidence increased, van Gogh began executing drawings as cohesive groups. For instance, the two commissions he completed for his Uncle Cor were drawings depicting several areas of The Hague, while the third commission, which never eventuated, was to be of a number of drawings of the seaside hamlet of Scheveningen. His ventures into printmaking were conceptually similar. On two occasions he suggested producing a publication of 'types' in a venture with Theo and van Rappard, which would be made available to the lower classes. All of these projects had at their core two key drivers; the first

114 For a list of the novels and publications van Gogh read, see Fieke Pabst and Evert van Uitert, 'A Literary Life, With a List of Books and Periodicals Read by Vincent van Gogh', in Evert van Uitert and M. Hoyle (eds.), *The Rijksmuseum Vincent van Gogh* (Amsterdam, Van Gogh Museum, 1987), 68–83.

115 Instalments appeared in *The Graphic*, 28 February–8 August 1874.

116 Helen Paterson, *"Ninety-Three" – Dolorosa* (*The Graphic*, 3 June 1874).

117 LT 273, volume 2, 174.

118 LT 356, volume 2, 361.

119 LT 267, volume 2, 160.

was van Gogh's intention of becoming a draughtsman, and the second was his wish to create works in the context of a series – an idea he had derived from the illustrated newspapers.

While the content of many of van Gogh's series of drawings reflected subjects found in his print collection, one series, images of humble weavers, differed. He had conceived of the series because he noticed they were not represented in any illustrated newspapers. In September 1880, remembering his trip to Courrières six months earlier, he recalled visiting weavers' villages in the area.[120] Although he had just begun making drawings, he stated his intentions and ambition:

> The miners and the weavers are something of a race apart from other workmen and tradesmen, and I have a great fellow-feeling for them and would count myself happy if I could draw them one day, so that these types, as yet unpublished or almost unpublished, could be brought to notice.[121]

His interest in these people was reignited in September 1882 after receiving a letter from his sister Wil: 'I don't know whether I told you that I've had a letter from Wil in which she gives a quite charming description of the countryside at Nuenen...I've asked her for more information on one or two points about the weavers, who especially interest me'.[122] Van Gogh maintained an interest in the subject throughout the following year, but it was not until January 1884, in Nuenen and living with his parents, that he had the opportunity to realise his earlier aim of using these artisans as subjects of his work. Arriving in Nuenen in December 1883, he quickly acquainted himself with the district's weavers and wrote to Theo: 'I've been studying the weavers while I've been here. Do you know many drawings of weavers? I only very few'. He told Theo he had completed three watercolours of them as a means of rectifying the situation.[123] During his stay in Nuenen van Gogh produced ten paintings and sixteen finished drawings of weavers. Of the drawings, eleven were signed, indicating his belief that there was a market for them.[124]

Van Gogh's watercolours were his first works depicting the weavers, but, in due course, he would produce a number of drawings, which he considered

120 For more on van Gogh's travels through these villages, see Sjraar van Heugten (ed.), *Van Gogh: The Birth of an Artist* (Brussels: Mercatorfonds, 2015), 30–5.

121 LT 158, volume 1, 256.

122 LT 261, volume 1, 147.

123 LT 419, volume 2, 92.

124 van Heugten, *Vincent van Gogh Drawings*, vol. 2, 50.

a coherent series. Surprisingly, it seems that Theo, rather than van Gogh, initiated the plan. In late January van Gogh wrote to Theo: 'I think those things of the looms with that quite complicated machinery, in the middle of which sits the little figure, will also lend themselves to pen drawings, and I'll make some as a result of the tip you give me in your letter'.[125] By mid-February, he had confirmed completing the project:

> Just a word to tell you that – partly in response to your letter in which you mentioned pen drawings – I have five weavers for you which I've made after my painted studies and are slightly different – and I think livelier – in execution than the pen drawings of mine you've seen so far.[126]

Early in March van Gogh told Theo he was planning to send a further work, slightly larger than the others, so as to make 'this little series of drawings more complete'. He also declared that the drawings of the weavers would be the foundation of a group that represented 'Brabant artisans'.[127] All of these drawings depict the weaver at the loom; the machine is the focus in all but one. Van Gogh wanted the viewer to hear the machine, to see its parts moving back and forward. He also wanted to portray through a number of drawings the life of the weaver, as demonstrated in a drawing showing the weaver at work in the company of his young child.[128] Van Gogh's portrayal was a romantic one, in which the father passed his craft on to his son; those born weavers remain weavers, as Carol Zemel posited: 'The baby protectively enclosed in the chair will inherit the traditional craft of his father enclosed in his loom, a continuity sanctioned by the institutional presence of the church seen through the window'.[129] Through van Gogh's eyes the life of the weaver was idyllic and protected from the ills of progress; for him it was a craft yet to be industrialised, performed by artisans rather than in large factories, although at the time this was not true. The weavers were for van Gogh, who was aware of the poverty of their existence, part of that noble uncultivated race who did not know much of the 'civilised

125 LT 428, volume 3, 105.

126 LT 430, volume 3, 107.

127 LT 434, volume 3, 121.

128 Vincent van Gogh, *Weaver Facing Right, Interior with One Window and High Chair*, 1884 (Van Gogh Museum, Amsterdam (Vincent van Gogh Foundation). F1118/ JH0452).

129 Carol Zemel, 'The 'Spook' in the Machine: Van Gogh's Pictures of Weavers in Brabant', *Art Bulletin*, 67 (1985), 125.

world'.[130] They were the people he felt most comfortable with and deserved to be enshrined in pictures.

That van Gogh would produce a cohesive series of images of a central subject in the early years of his development was to be expected, as it fits with his aim of becoming a draughtsman. The impact of doing so, however, was far reaching. When he decided that he would become an artist with a focus firmly on painting, he did so in the context of all that he had learnt in his early years of toiling away over his drawings. The habit of documenting a site or illustrating a given subject in a series persisted in his artistic endeavours in Paris, Arles and Saint-Rémy.

When van Gogh told Theo in March 1886 that he had arrived in Paris, he advised him that he could be found at the Louvre.[131] Paris was not only home to a great number of works by the great masters, but was also the epicentre of contemporary art and the home of radicals like the Impressionists. Paris offered van Gogh the opportunity to acquaint himself with many of the new painters, especially now that the lure of the black-and-white illustrators had diminished. During this period, and over the next four and half years, van Gogh's art changed dramatically. Gone were the earthy colours of his Dutch years. Instead, he was to develop into one of the great colourists of the late nineteenth century. Nevertheless, the education he had derived from the illustrated newspapers stayed with him, and the notion and concept of series of images endured as a fundamental aspect of his œuvre.

In summer 1887, a year after arriving in Paris, van Gogh ventured to the outer suburbs and executed a series of drawings of defunct military fortifications.[132] The fortifications, which where thirty kilometres long and encircled the city of Paris, had become a popular spot for the working class on Sundays and public holidays, while at night they attracted criminals and prostitutes.[133] Van Gogh's drawings depict people using the areas, such as at the Port de Clichy, for recreational purposes, rather than depicting them as historical sites. Always comfortable among the working and lower classes, van Gogh would have undoubtedly been attracted to the area as a subject, creating images that

130 LT 419, volume 3, 92.

131 LT 567, volume 3, 362.

132 Vincent van Gogh, *Road Running Beside the Paris Ramparts*, 1887 (Van Gogh Museum (Vincent van Gogh Foundation) F1400/JH1283); *Gate in the Paris Ramparts*, 1887 (Van Gogh Museum (Vincent van Gogh Foundation) F1401/JH1284); *The Ramparts of Paris*, 1887 (private collection) F1402/JH1280); *The Ramparts of Paris*, 1887 (Whitworth Art Gallery, University of Manchester) F1403/JH1281).

133 Marije Vellekoop & Sjraar van Heugten, *Vincent van Gogh Drawings*, vol. 3: *Antwerp and Paris 1885–1888* (Amsterdam: Vincent van Gogh Museum, 2001), 295.

reflected contemporary society and were consistent with his earlier views of depicting the common world. Van Gogh initially became acquainted with the fortifications on his walks to Asnières, Clichy and Saint-Ouen, but may have been inspired to create a series of them after seeing the work of other artists. In his collection of prints Van Gogh had a nocturnal scene of the fortifications, *Escaping from Paris by Night*.[134] He would have also been aware of their depiction in French illustrations and paintings, such as on the cover of *Le Mirliton* in June 1887.[135]

Although finished in colour, the four works in this series are essentially line drawings. *Gate in the Paris Ramparts* (Plate 8), for example, was first completed as a pen drawing with colour added at a later stage, most likely in his studio.[136] In this regard they mirror many drawings van Gogh had done earlier in his career. The Paris drawings also employ compositional devices from many of van Gogh's earlier drawings, especially from some of The Hague drawings he had done for Uncle Cor. *Gate in the Paris Ramparts* employs the same elevated viewpoint and a fence line to guide the viewer through the picture, as in *Carpenter's Yard and Laundry* (Plate 2). Another of the Paris drawings uses a wide road to lead the viewer through the composition – a device used in The Hague drawings *Ditch along the Schenkweg* (1882) and *Country Road in Loosduinen near The Hague* (1882).[137] For all the parallels, the Paris drawings were unique in that van Gogh made preparatory sketches, the only time he did so for works on paper, as Vellekoop and Van Heugten have noted.[138] After his time in Paris van Gogh moved to the south of France where he created perhaps his greatest paintings. While painting had taken priority, he still continued to draw, sometimes with the clear intention of selling the drawings as a series, as in Arles and in Saint-Rémy, both of which were produced with Theo's prompting.

Three miles northeast of Arles the ancient ruined abbey of Montmajour rises above the plains of La Crau. Van Gogh discovered the abbey soon after he arrived in Arles, but did not attempt to draw or include it as a major detail

134 *Escaping from Paris at Night* (*The Graphic*, 6 May 1871).

135 For a review of the fortifications in French art at the time, see Richard Thomson, 'Van Gogh in Paris: The Fortifications Drawings of 1887', *Jong Holland*, 3/3 (1987), 20–2.

136 For an analysis of the drawing, see Vellekoop & van Heugten, *Vincent van Gogh Drawings* vol. 3, 300–3.

137 Vincent van Gogh, *The Ramparts of Paris*, 1887 (Whitworth Art Gallery, University of Manchester) F 1403/JH1281); *Ditch along the Schenkweg*, 1882 (Kröller-Müller Museum, Otterlo F0921/JH116); *Country Road in Loosduinen near The Hague*, 1882 (Van Gogh Museum, Amsterdam (Vincent van Gogh Foundation) F1089/JH0124).

138 Vellekoop & van Heugten, *Vincent van Gogh Drawings* vol. 3, 289.

in any of his early works. It was not until the middle of May 1888, after a letter from Theo, that he began to capture it and its immediate surroundings in his work. Theo invited van Gogh to send drawings to the second exhibition of the Dutch Etching Society, to which Van Gogh responded positively, producing seven drawings for the exhibition, all signed and six with French titles: *Bruyère* (1888); *Vue de la Crau* (1888); *Vue Prise à Montmajour* (1888); *Vue d'Arles* (1888); *Ruine de Montmajour* (1888); and *Montmajour* (1888).[139] They are all similar in size, ranging from 29 x 47cm to 31 x 48cm. Five are composed horizontally, two are vertical, and they depict the ruins as well as the views from and around the landmark.[140] They tell a story and need to be viewed together. They are, as Pickvance describes, like 'illustrations to an article'.[141] This initial series of Montmajour was never exhibited at the Dutch Etching Society as intended, as van Gogh decided against it after sending them to Theo. Nevertheless, it did not prevent him from producing another series of drawings of the same subject, this time with the clear intention of selling them.

As with the first series of drawings, Theo also prompted the second; however, it seems that on this occasional it was done so indirectly. Theo had just written to tell his brother that Gauguin had agreed to travel to Arles, but that the cost of his travel remained a concern. On three separate occasions over a short period, van Gogh suggested selling work to the art supplier George Thomas, including this second series of drawings, in order to raise the funds. On 8 July 1888 he wrote:

> I'd like to send you the 30 studies at this moment, so that it may perhaps help with the costs to be found in order for Gauguin to come…And *père* Thomas – he really ought to buy from me or from Gauguin for a hundred francs – then we'd nearly be there.[142]

---

139 Unfortunately, because of the type of ink used, many of the seven drawings have faded and their titles are barely visible; they are: Vincent van Gogh, *Ruins of Montmajour*, 1888 (Van Gogh Museum (Vincent van Gogh Foundation) F1417/JH1434); *Landscape with Tree in the Foreground*, 1888 (private collection. F1418/JH1431); *The Plain of La Crau*, 1888 (Museum Folkwang, Essen. F1419/JH1430); *Ruins of Montmajour*, 1888 (Van Gogh Museum (Vincent van Gogh Foundation) F1423/JH1433); *The Plain of La Crau*, 1888 (location not known) F1448/JH1432); *Landscape with Arles in the Background*, 1888 (Museum Boymans-van Beuningen, Rotterdam) F1475/JH1435); *Hill with Bushes*, 1888 (Van Gogh Museum (Vincent van Gogh Foundation). F1493/JH1436).

140 Two drawings show the ruined abbey, four are panoramic views around the abbey, and the last captures a view of the rock face.

141 Johannes van der Wolk, Ronald Pickvance and E.B.F. Pey, *Vincent van Gogh: Drawings* (Otterlo: Kröller-Müller Museum, 1990), 222.

142 LT 637, volume 4, 166.

Less than a week later van Gogh again referred to Thomas buying a number of the recently completed Montmajour drawings: 'As I see it, the two views of the Crau and the countryside along the banks of the Rhône are the best I've done with my pen. Should Thomas by chance want them? He can't have them for less than 100 francs each'.[143] In the next letter, dated 15 July 1888, van Gogh told Theo he had sent him a roll of drawings, again with a number depicting Montmajour, which he should take to Thomas so that they could raise the funds required for Gauguin's travel:

> I've sent you a roll of drawings. If you went to see Thomas with these, and added the (I believe there are 4 of them) other drawings in the same format, perhaps we'd pick up a few sous from *père* Thomas if you explain to him the rather exceptional reasons there are at this moment for our wanting to do a deal.[144]

This second series, which van Gogh believed was saleable, consisted of six drawings, all larger in scale than those in the first series and all in a horizontal format, ensuring consistency and cohesiveness.[145] Every drawing in the series was signed and two had French captions: *La Crau vue prise a Montmajour* (1888) and *La campagne du côte des bords du Rhône* (1888). They were drawn on more expensive heavy wove paper, which Van Gogh only used for drawings intended for the art market rather than for private use in his studio.[146] As with the first series, van Gogh did not concentrate solely on depicting the ruins, which are only in one drawing, but on the area surrounding the abbey and the view seen from the hilltop. It was his intention to capture multiple views in order to give a complete picture of the area: 'If the other 4 drawings I have in my head are like the first two I have', he informed Theo, 'then you'll have the epitome of a very beautiful corner of Provence'.[147] Although these works were more complex than any drawings from the past and can almost

143 LT 639, volume 4, 172.

144 LT 640, volume 4, 174–5.

145 Each drawing measured either 48 x 59cm or 49 x 61cm. Vincent van Gogh, *Olive Trees, Montmajour*, 1888 (Musée de Beaux-Arts, Tournai) JH addenda 3; *La Crau, Seen from Montmajour*, 1888 (Van Gogh Museum, Amsterdam (Vincent van Gogh Foundation)) F1420/JH1501; *Landscape near Montmajour with Train*, 1888 (British Museum, London) F1424/JH1502; *Hill with the Ruins of Montmajour*, 1888 (Rijksmuseum Museum, Amsterdam) F1446/JH1504; *Rocks with Trees*, 1888 (Van Gogh Museum, Amsterdam (Vincent van Gogh Foundation)) F1447/JH1503; *View of Arles from a Hill*, 1888 (Nasjonalgalleriet, Oslo) F1452/JH1437.

146 Liesbeth Heenk, 'Revealing van Gogh: An Examination of his Papers', *Paper Conservator*, 18 (1994), 31.

147 LT 637, volume 4, 166.

be considered as paintings in ink, they nevertheless conform to van Gogh's early attempts at producing a series of works focusing on a unified subject available to the public at an affordable cost.

After the Montmajour drawings, van Gogh executed thirty-two drawings after painted studies. Each group of drawings was done with three intended recipients in mind – his artist friends, Émile Bernard and John Russell, and Theo. Through them van Gogh aimed to inspire, inform and encourage transactions. The fifteen drawings for Bernard, of which six were sent on 1 July and a further nine soon after, were meant to inform him of his current output and with an offer to exchange works.[148] The drawings sent to Russell, as Susan Alyson Stein notes, were to 'win over the recalcitrant Russell as a prospective patron for Gauguin'.[149] This was the culmination of van Gogh's long campaign to get Russell to support Gauguin by raising the funds to get him to Arles. Van Gogh produced twelve drawings that he knew would appeal to Russell – landscapes, seaside vistas and three portraits.[150] The series

148 Vincent van Gogh, *Drawbridge with Lady with Parasol*, 1888 (Los Angeles County Museum of Art) JH1420; *Haystacks near a Farm*, 1888 (Art Museum, Budapest) F1426/JH1514; *Fishing Boats at Sea*, 1888 (Kupferstichkabinett. Staatliche Museen zu Berlin) F1430/JH1505; *Streets in Saintes-Maries*, 1888 (Museum of Modern Art, New York) F1435/JH1506; *Sower with Setting Sun*, 1888 (private collection) F1442/JH1508; *Canal with Women Washing*, 1888 (Kröller-Müller Museum, Otterlo) F1444/JH1507; *Newly Mowed Lawn with Weeping Tree*, 1888 (private collection) F1450/JH1509; *Wheat Field*, 1888 (Metropolitan Museum of Art, New York) F1481/JH1515; *Zouave, Half Figure*, 1888 (Metropolitan Museum of Art, New York) F1482/JH1487; *Harvest Landscape*, 1888 (Kupferstichkabinett. Staatliche Museen zu Berlin) F1485/JH1540; *Wheat Field with Sheaves*, 1888 (location not known) F1488/JH1517; *Wheat Field with Sheaves and Arles in the Background*, 1888 (National Gallery of Art, Washington) F1491/JH1516; *View of a River, Quay and Bridge*, 1888 (Metropolitan Museum of Art, New York) F1507/JH1469; *Wheatfield with Setting Sun*, 1888 (Kunstmuseum, Winterhur. F1514/JH1546); *Rocks with Trees*, 1888 (private collection) F1554/JH1518.

149 Colta Ives *et al.*, *Vincent van Gogh: The Drawings* (New Haven and London: Yale University Press, 2005), 266.

150 Vincent van Gogh, *Haystacks near a Farm*, 1888 (Philadelphia Museum of Art) F1427/JH1525; *Fishing Boats at Sea*, 1888 (Guggenheim Museum, New York) F1430a/JH1526; *Zouave Sitting, Whole Figure*, 1888 (Van Gogh Museum, Amsterdam (Vincent van Gogh Foundation)) F1443/JH1485; *Lawn with Weeping Tree*, 1888 (location unknown) F1449/JH1534; *Garden with Flowers*, 1888 (private collection) F1454/JH1532; *Joseph Roulin, Head*, 1888 (Getty Museum, California) F1458/JH1536; *Zouave Sitting, Half Figure*, 1888 (Guggenheim Museum, New York) F1482a/JH1535; *Harvest Landscape*, 1888 (private collection) F1486/JH1527; *Wheat Field with Sheaves*, 1888 (private collection) F1489/JH1530; *Wheat Field with Sheaves and Arles in the Background*, 1888 (private collection) F1490/JH1529; *The Road to Tarascon*, 1888 (Guggenheim Museum, New York) F1502a/JH1531; *Mousme, Half Figure*, 1888 (Thomas Gibson Fine Art, Ltd, London) F1503/JH1533.

sent to Theo was simply to inform him of current work.[151] Like those sent to Bernard and Russell, van Gogh included drawings after his paintings from the seaside village of Les Saintes-Maries-de-la-Mer, a view of Arles from the wheat fields, and a corner of the garden in the Place Lamartine. That each body of work was conceived as a series is evident in a number of details. The drawings in each are uniform in size, except for one sheet sent to Russell.[152] The technique used is consistent across all the illustrations. Completed in reed pen, the drawings are not the hasty sketches seen in many of van Gogh's letters, but are complex and indicative of his increasing technical competence, with a collage of lines and dots invoking the spirit and rhythm of the original paintings. The drawing for Bernard made after *Fishing Boats at Sea* (1888) (Plate 9) demonstrates this complexity, ambition and attention to detail in reproducing the liveliness of the painting (Plate 10). The painting, with a higher horizon-line has the sea divided in two planes, of which the lower is heavily mixed with varying shades of white, and the upper is a composition in blue. In order to recreate this in the drawing van Gogh used thick, closely placed, parallel strokes in the upper plane of the sea, rendering the area darker, while the lower is a combination of parallel vertical, horizontal and diagonal strokes, swirls of varying lengths and groupings of dots spaced to create the foam-like appearance of the white crested waves. The sails of the boats offer the viewer resting points throughout the drawing, just as the flat areas of colour do in the painting. Although by this stage Japanese woodblock prints were an influence on van Gogh's technique, the recreation of his paintings in a purely monotone format grew out of his admiration for and collecting of black-and-white prints. The use of parallel lines and pen strokes of varying sizes strongly reflect the marks of etchers attempting to recreate an artist's vision on a woodblock. Van Gogh's contemporaries, Paul Signac and Georges Seurat, had already begun reproducing some of their paintings in black-and-white for illustrated magazines and the projects van Gogh conceived for Bernard, Russell and Theo, shared a similar logic.[153]

---

151 Vincent van Gogh, *Fishing Boats at Sea*, 1888 (Musée d'Art Moderne, Musées Royaux des Beaux-Arts de Belgique, Brussels) F1430b/JH1541; *A Fishing Boat at Sea*, 1888 (location not known) F1431/JH1542; *Sower with Setting Sun*, 1888 (Van Gogh Museum, Amsterdam (Vincent van Gogh Foundation)) F1441/JH1543; *Newly Mowed Lawn with Weeping Tree*, 1888 (Menil Collection, Houston) F1451/JH1545; *Wheat Field with Sheaves and Arles in the Background*, 1888 (The National Gallery, London) F1492/JH1544.

152 Some sheets vary by 50mm to 1cm, but are consistently 24.0 x 31.0cm. The only exception is a sheet measuring 52.0 x 66.0cm sent to Russell.

153 Ives et al., *Vincent van Gogh: The Drawings*, 267.

For the drawings sent to Bernard, van Gogh created two cover pages, emphasising that these works were to be viewed as a set. The first cover page created was for the initial six drawings. Van Gogh added a marbled paper border to the image *Newly Mowed Lawn with Weeping Tree* (1888), mirroring the use of drawn borders by the illustrated papers for the works chosen for the front page of their weekly issues.[154] The second cover page, *Zouave* (1888), was the only drawing in colour and was intended to precede the second lot of drawings.[155] The added colour and a dedication in the top right-hand corner – '*à mon cher copain / Emile Bernard / Vincent*', indicating their close friendship – distinguished this drawing from the others that followed. If the series were bound, as Bernard later did, it would serve as an introduction to the story in pictures contained within. Indirectly, by assembling these drawings as an album and later exhibiting and publishing them, Bernard realised van Gogh's long-standing intention to produce a collection of works that could be shown and perhaps purchased as a single entity.

Although van Gogh's focus remained on painting, he turned to drawing once more while recuperating at the Saint-Paul asylum in Saint-Rémy-de-Provence. On the 3 May 1889, before leaving for the asylum, he expressed his desire to pick up his reed pen to Theo: 'I'm thinking of beginning to draw more with the reed pen again which, like last year's views of Montmajour, is less expensive and distracts me just as much … [drawing] could even become a means of earning a livelihood'.[156] His early days in the asylum were dominated by drawing, as his physician, Dr. Théophile-Zacharie-Auguste Peyron confirmed to Theo: 'He spends the day drawing in the park here'.[157] During a frantic two-week period of work while van Gogh was confined to the asylum, he produced seven brush drawings of the asylum's gardens.[158] The drawings

154 Vincent van Gogh, *Newly Mowed Lawn with Weeping Tree*, 1888 (private collection) F1450/JH1509.

155 Vincent van Gogh, *Zouave, Half-Figure*, 1888 (Metropolitan Museum of Art, New York) F1482/JH1487.

156 LT 768, volume 4, 443.

157 Quoted in Ronald Pickvance, *Van Gogh in Saint-Rémy and Auvers* (New York: The Metropolitan Museum of Art, 1986), 31.

158 Vincent van Gogh, *Flowering Shrubs*, 1889 (location not known) F1526/JH1707; *Flowering Shrubs*, 1889 (Kröller-Müller Museum, Otterlo) F1527/JH1708; *Trees and Shrubs*, 1889 (Van Gogh Museum, Amsterdam (Vincent van Gogh Foundation)) F1533/JH1710; *Trees and Shrubs*, 1889 (location not known) F1534/JH1709; *Stone Steps in the Garden at the Asylum*, 1889 (Van Gogh Museum, Amsterdam (Vincent van Gogh Foundation)) F1535/JH1713; *Trees in the Garden at the Asylum*, 1889 (location not known) F1536/JH1712; *Stone bench in the Garden at the Asylum*, 1889 (Van Gogh Museum, Amsterdam (Vincent van Gogh Foundation)) F1537/JH1711.

present a multi-faceted impression of van Gogh's surroundings and constitute a unified series, in which each drawing concentrates on a particular aspect of the garden: a tree with bushes; the garden stairs; a stone bench; or a clump of blossoming shrubs. They are constructed with an array of short broad marks, washes of colour and occasionally cross-hatching. The images are pushed to the outer edges of the paper, creating a density and vibrancy not seen in his previous drawings. They are also macro views of the garden and as such have a short depth of field. This consistency in technique, subject, format, approach, size and materials reinforces the notion of them forming a cohesive group.

Unfortunately, van Gogh makes no detailed reference to these drawings in his correspondence, thus making it difficult to fully understand his intentions. They may have been created with the aim of earning money from their sale, as van Gogh had expressed before being admitted to the asylum, but none of the works are signed, suggesting that they were deemed inappropriate for a commercial audience. Van Gogh did not send them to Theo immediately, further supporting this view of them. Pickvance has suggested that they were possibly drawn as illustrations to accompany van Gogh's descriptions of the asylum in his letters to Theo, but they seem too complex and finished for such use.[159] Moreover, van Gogh had previously drawn in the letters or sent accompanying sketches for such purposes. What is perhaps most likely is that they were conceived as a stand-alone series to inform Theo and friends of his new environment, as the illustrations depicting different corners of the garden gave the viewer a panoramic view of van Gogh's new home.

In early June 1889, van Gogh was given permission to work beyond the asylum walls. Naturally, his efforts went into creating a number of new paintings of the local landscape, including wheat fields, cypress trees, olive groves and the surrounding mountain range. As he had done in Arles, van Gogh produced a collection of drawings after these new paintings.[160] He

159 Van der Wolk, Pickvance and Pey, *Vincent van Gogh Drawings*, 284.

160 It is unclear how many belonged to this group; van Gogh's correspondence suggests between ten and sixteen (LT 784, 785 and 790). The ten that survive are: Vincent van Gogh, *Trees with Ivy*, 1889 (Van Gogh Museum, Amsterdam (Vincent van Gogh Foundation)) F1522/JH1695; *Cypresses*, 1889 (Art Institute of Chicago) F1524/JH1749; *Cypresses*, 1889 (Brooklyn Museum, New York) F1525/JH1747; *Wild Vegetation in the Mountains*, 1889 (Van Gogh Museum, Amsterdam (Vincent van Gogh Foundation)) F1532/JH1742; *Wheat Field* with *Cypresses*, 1889 (Van Gogh Museum, Amsterdam (Vincent van Gogh Foundation)) F1538/JH1757; *The Starry Night*, 1889 (Museum of Architecture, Moscow) F1540/JH1732; *Olive Trees in a Mountain Landscape*, 1889 (Museum of Modern Art, New York) F1544/JH1741; *Enclosed Wheat Field with Reaper*, 1889 (Kupferstichkabinett. Staatliche Museen zu

sent these to Theo as an indication of his most recent output, as he indicated in a letter before sending them: 'so that you may have an idea of what I have on the go I'm sending you ten or so drawings today, all after canvases'.[161] All of these drawings are made on identical smooth wove paper and are all of a similar size.[162] Unlike the previous series of the asylum gardens, these drawings were monotone and completed predominantly with reed pen; in this sense they relate most closely to the earlier drawings made for Bernard, Russell and Theo. The drawings are constructed with a combination of short strokes of various widths and lengths, dotted areas and a clever use of vacant space, which gives tonal variation and a sense of depth. Like the previous projects for Bernard, Russell and Theo, these drawings capture the rhythm and intensity of the original paintings. Van Gogh was able to reproduce his paintings in a black-and-white visual language because of the lessons he had learnt many years earlier when collating and studying his print collection. Throughout his hospitalisation at Saint-Rémy van Gogh continued to draw, as he did when he discharged himself and relocated to Auvers-sur-Oise. After arriving in Auvers, however, he turned to printing, a medium he had not used since leaving Nuenen.

Van Gogh had gone to Auvers to be treated by the physician Dr. Gachet who introduced him to etching, which van Gogh had not used in the past. Gachet was an amateur artist and art collector who owned a printing press, making the medium convenient and attractive to van Gogh. Years later Gachet's son Paul recalled van Gogh's first attempt at etching:

> After lunch in the open air in the courtyard, and with their pipes lit, Vincent was given an etching needle and a prepared copper plate, and accepted with enthusiasm that his new friend should be the motif. As soon as it was drawn, the plate was bitten – under the supervision of van Ryssel [Dr. Gachet] – as was the case seventeen years earlier with the plates of Cézanne. Thus was born *L'Homme à la pipe*, van Gogh's only etching. The operation was not yet finished: the printing must have amused Vincent still more. He pulled *illico* [on the sly] several proofs, which came muddy, because the plate had not been wiped. He

---

Berlin) F1546/JH1754; *Mountain Landscape Seen Across the Walls*, 1889 (Van Gogh Museum, Amsterdam (Vincent van Gogh Foundation)). F1547/JH1724; *Wheat Field with Cypresses*, 1889 (Pierpont Morgan Library, New York) F1548/JH1726.

161 LT 784, volume 5, 49.

162 The average sheet size is 47.0 x 62.0cm with a 0.5cm variation in some drawings. Only one drawing, *Enclosed Wheat Field with Reaper* (1889), has a greater variation, measuring 45 x 58.5cm.

> himself found them 'a little dirty', too black, and willingly agreed to pull some more in *sanguine*; in this way, it was necessary to wait and see what happened: other colors were tried: yellow ochre, red ochre, gray, greenish, orange; they all pleased him enormously by their diversity. Vincent was thrilled and talked only of continuing engraving, especially to reproduce some of his canvasses.[163]

Paul Gachet's recollection indicates van Gogh's enthusiasm for the new medium and also his experimental nature. It also reflects van Gogh's confidence in being able to draw directly on the plate without any preparatory sketches. Theo commented on the draughtsmanship, describing it as 'a real painter's etching' and praising van Gogh for the lack of 'refinement in the procedure, but a drawing done on metal', concluding 'I like this drawing very much'.[164] This would have pleased van Gogh no end, because it placed him in the context of the great painters who had the capacity to make drawings for reproduction and because he intended to produce a series of etchings after his canvasses.

In the middle of June 1890, at the same time that van Gogh produced his first etching, he wrote to Theo and Gauguin about creating a series of etchings after some of his paintings from Provence. In a letter to Gauguin, which was never sent, he outlined his plans: 'I'll probably make etchings of this one, and of other landscapes and subjects, reminiscences of Provence, and then I'll look forward to giving you an ensemble, a rather deliberate and studied summary'.[165] The letter to Theo elaborated on details for the proposed project and suggested etchings not only of van Gogh's works but also some of Gauguin's.

> I really hope to do a few etchings of subjects from the south, let's say 6, since I can print them free of charge at Mr Gachet's; he's very willing to run them off for nothing if I do them. It's certainly a thing that must be done, and we'll act in such a way that in some way it forms a sequel to the Lauzet-Monticelli publication, if you approve. And Gauguin will probably engrave a few of his canvases in combination with me. His painting which belongs to you, and especially for the rest of the Martinique things.

163 Pickvance, *Van Gogh in Saint-Rémy & Auvers*, 229.

164 LT 890, volume 5, 267.

165 LT RM23, volume 5, 322.

> Which plates Mr Gachet will also print off for us. Of course we'll leave him free to run off copies for himself. Mr Gachet will come one day to see my canvases in Paris, and then we'd choose the ones to be engraved.[166]

Van Gogh clearly states his intention to produce the etchings as an album, and his suggestion to work with Gauguin echoes in concept the proposal he put forward years earlier for a publication of his works and those of van Rappard. While the earlier idea had been inspired by the illustrated newspapers, this project had its foundation in Theo's venture with Paris-based artist Auguste Lauzet to prepare an album of lithographs after works by Adolphe Monticelli.[167] Theo was financing the Monticelli album and van Gogh may have thought he would do likewise for his suggested project of etchings after paintings made in Provence.

Several sketches in one of van Gogh's sketchbooks indicate the paintings earmarked for etching. In his analysis of van Gogh's seven sketchbooks, Johannes van der Wolk highlighted sketches after six canvasses that van Gogh wished to etch, describing them as forming *Souvenirs de Provence*.[168] Van der Wolk argued that van Gogh made the sketches 'to describe for Gachet the paintings in Paris he should look out for', as Gachet was going there and would have the chance to see many of van Gogh's paintings.[169] As the 'partner' in the project and the expert in the medium, it was essential for Gachet to view and assess their viability for etching. The paintings chosen for reproduction – three made in Arles and another three in Saint-Rémy – were evenly split between landscapes and still lifes. The still lifes, all flowers in vases, could well have been printed in colour, which may be why van Gogh chose them. The landscapes were very complex, but, as he had demonstrated in the past in the series of drawings for Bernard, Russell and Theo, van Gogh was able to translate elaborate paintings into line drawings. Like the van Rappard album, this new printing project was never realised; it was a failure, an unrealised dream. The only etching he conceived was that of Dr. Gachet, which was produced in a large edition after van Gogh's death.[170] Many

---

166 LT 889, volume 5, 265.

167 For the making of the Monticelli album, see Aaron Sheon, 'Theo van Gogh, Publisher: The Monticelli Album', *Van Gogh Museum Journal* (2000), 53–61.

168 Johannes van der Wolk, *The Seven Sketchbooks of Vincent van Gogh: A Facsimile Edition* (London: Thames and Hudson, 1987), 302–9.

169 van der Wolk, *The Seven Sketchbooks*, 303.

170 Vincent van Gogh, *Portrait of Dr Gachet with Pipe*, 1890 (various collections) F1664/JH2028. There are more than seventy known impressions, only some of which were printed before van Gogh died (see Sjraar Van Heugten & Fieke Pabst, *The Graphic Work of Van Gogh* (Zwolle: Waanders, 1995), 79–86 and 99–106.

were given to museums and to artists as gifts, posthumously fulfilling van Gogh's desire to have his work produced in a graphic format and known by the public at large. His only etching, produced cheaply, distributed his work to the masses and, most importantly, beyond the gallery walls.

Throughout his career van Gogh believed that a group of drawings would be more representative of his ideas than a single work, but the underlying motivation for making these series shifted throughout his career. Early in his career as an artist, he did so with the intention of becoming an illustrator, and the first works he did that constituted a series were influenced by the examples in his collection of black-and-white prints. At this early stage of his career, van Gogh collected and admired scenes of London, Paris, New York, America and Ireland, gravitating in particular to images of working class people in these locations. The two commissions completed for his Uncle Cor in 1882 of scenes from The Hague, therefore, reflect these newspaper series, as do the drawings of the Paris fortifications. Van Gogh also took as his example the notion of depicting types, intending to create a series of thirty lithographs of 'types' from The Hague. He created a large body of works of heads while in The Hague and in Nuenen, inspired by *The Graphic*'s 'Heads of the People' series. He made a series of images of weavers while in Nuenen in 1884, driven by the fact that weavers had not been presented in the illustrated newspapers.

These early drawings presented the possibility of sales and the chance to find employment. Eventually the need for employment diminished, but the need to sell did not. Both the Montmajour series were conceived with hopes of commercial gain and a selection of drawings for the Australian painter John Russell were made in the hope that they would raise the necessary funds for Gauguin to travel to Arles. After leaving Paris, van Gogh shifted his focus to his painting, but the lessons he learned from black-and-white illustrators stayed with him. In Arles for the first time, he produced a series of drawings after his paintings for Bernard, Russell and Theo, completing another for Theo and Bernard while in Saint-Rémy. Completed as monotone drawings these series are comparable to the practice of wood-block engravers who reproduced paintings for publication in the illustrated newspapers. In Auvers the planned, but never completed, album of etchings was conceived with the same mindset. All of these drawings were made to inform others of van Gogh's œuvre and current practice. Van Gogh had learnt from his extensive collection of prints that making a series of works could inform others of his new surroundings. The drawings of Montmajour, although intended for a commercial market, apprised Theo of the landscape around van Gogh's new home; the drawings he did in the asylum gardens achieved the same purpose. Both sets of drawings were made soon after van Gogh had arrived in his new surroundings. Even though he was far from the examples in his print collection, they are consistent with the notion of capturing a place across a number of works. Van Gogh could only have conceived these drawings, and others that constituted a series, with the knowledge he had gained from collecting and admiring so many prints.

CONCLUSION

> Anyway, some paintings in their huge frames look very substantial, and later one is surprised when they actually leave behind such an empty and dissatisfied feeling. On the other hand, one overlooks many an unpretentious woodcut or lithograph or etching now and then, but comes back to it and becomes more and more attached to it with time, and senses something great in it.[1]

Throughout his artistic career van Gogh returned to the art of simple wood engraving time and again. He became 'more and more attached to them'. Introduced to the visual arts as a young art dealer with Paris-based firm Goupil & Cie, van Gogh was surrounded by the graphic arts, and the grand paintings of both masters and promising artists. Years later his ultimate artistic pursuit was to produce paintings that would speak to others and that represented the many ideas and influences that had shaped him as a person and an artist. That he maintained an interest and the utmost admiration for the humble black-and-white print speaks volumes. It was an honest, accessible and democratic art form that, above all, was of the people and for the people.

Van Gogh's collection of black-and-white prints, most of which was amassed in the first few years of his artistic career, has long been underused and under-referenced by van Gogh scholars. It is, however, of utmost importance as it played a fundamental role in shaping van Gogh the artist and creator of paintings now so universally loved. It was the basis of his drawing style and the source of his subject matter and influenced his thinking about life and art in significant ways. His obsession with black-and-white illustrations occupied him for the first five years of his artistic development and was a common thread in his first long artistic dialogue with an artist, fellow Dutchman Anthon van Rappard. It influenced his career aims, initially as he aspired to become an illustrator of drawings for newspapers and magazines and, later, as his radical and expressive painting style emerged. Thus it helped transform

1 LT 290, volume 2, 213.

twentieth-century modernist art. English black-and-white prints were, quite simply, central to what van Gogh believed constituted the essence of great art.

Van Gogh amassed the bulk of his collection of black-and-white prints over three years and it is comparable in importance and definitely in size to his collection of Japanese prints, works by other artists, his own works and his letters. The collection contains significant works from French, Dutch, German and American publications and engravings, such as those produced by Goupil & Cie., but is dominated by works from the two most important English illustrated publications, *The Illustrated London News* and *The Graphic*, the torch-bearers and pace-setters of illustrated journalism and social-realist mass-produced images. *The Illustrated London News* was the great publishing pioneer, while *The Graphic* was a great innovator and champion of artistic merit. They delivered print after print of outstanding quality and quenched the thirst of a public clamouring for quality mass-produced images. Developments in printing technologies throughout the Industrial Revolution were fully embraced by the newspaper publishing industry, enabling the rapid rise of a new mass visual culture through the regular publication of consistently high-quality illustrations, which democratised the predominantly upper-class activity of fine art appreciation. The democratisation of the visual arts had special appeal for van Gogh. In his eyes the black-and-white illustrations represented art that was more popular and accessible. It represented art that was of the people and for the people, and he wished to embrace it and replicate it in his own practice, initially as a draughtsman and later as one of the most radical avant-garde artists of his generation.

In terms of its themes, van Gogh's collection was shaped by his beliefs and moral values, established by his upbringing, his experience of England, his religious pursuits and fervour, and the time he spent in the Borinage mining district, where he experienced first-hand the many faces of a changing industrialising world. Newspapers across all countries sought to document contemporary society in all of its nuanced beauty and challenges. While van Gogh was familiar with the many images of royal families and dignitaries, travel expeditions and imperial exploration, fashion and leisurely pursuits, there are very few of these images in his collection; rather, he chose works portraying weightier themes. In simple terms, he admired, responded to and remained most interested in works that belonged within the great artistic genre of social realism, which, in England at least, was intricately linked with popular black-and-white illustrations. While the term 'social realism' remains an apt umbrella term for the sentiment of his collection, greater investigation reveals van Gogh's deeper thinking that helped shape it. It is a collection that represented the dichotomy of city and rural life, which was a reflection of van Gogh's own experience, as he was of rural stock and pined for simplicity, but as an adult he experienced the wonder of city life and all its offerings, from new art to literature, philosophy and progressive world views. The collection mirrors van Gogh's evangelical mindset, which was founded in his upbringing in a religious family and further shaped by his direct experience of organised religion, the mature spirituality derived from the texts of John Bunyan and Thomas à Kempis, and his belief in loving and supporting one's fellow man as honestly, sincerely and directly as possible. Lastly, the collection speaks of van Gogh's belief in a democratic art that is of the people and for the people and can be shared and appreciated equally among peasants and workers in their humble cottages and among middle- and upper-class people decorating their family homes.

Stylistically the collection is uniform in character because the images he selected for it are best described as weighty and serious. Van Gogh was not interested in the simple line drawings expediently produced to accompany news articles; rather, he gravitated towards ambitious single- and double-page illustrations that were dark and moody, compositionally complex, and reflecting a monotone high-art aesthetic. Poster-like, they were intended to grace the walls of the homes of ordinary people; everyone could have an artwork in their home to appreciate and enjoy.

The project of amassing such a large collection was driven in the first instance by van Gogh's early aim of becoming a draughtsman for one of the illustrated newspapers, preferably, as he frequently declared in his letters, with one of the leading English publications. This idea was born out of his failure to become a clergyman, having been encouraged by Theo to find some form of employment and level of respectability. It became his priority as he abandoned the pulpit for his pencil in a bid to be productive while still promulgating his view of how people should treat each other. The collection ultimately embodied the criteria that van Gogh believed he needed to meet to join the ranks of his artistic heroes among the black-and-white illustrators in London. It served to shape his views on the nature and purpose of art. In November 1882, after reading an article by Herkomer that argued for greater acknowledgement and respect for illustrators, he instructed his fellow collector and artistic peer van Rappard to focus his attention 'on the work and on the men of the past'; to do otherwise, van Gogh asserted and has already be noted, would result in both of them being 'counted among the decadent fellows'.[2]

2 LT 279, volume 2, 191.

Like so many artists before and after him, van Gogh built his artistic practice upon knowledge and experience gained from multiple sources. His print collection was more than an aesthetic library; it became, as we have seen, a permanent visual catalogue of artistic reference. He used it to learn his craft, copying from it as one would from plaster casts in an art academy, and in due course the collection would play an important role in helping him solve problems of complex composition. Van Gogh was able to analyse many of his prints to establish what made them read successfully. He could take what he needed from any of the many examples and implement the lessons learnt in his own work. Early in his career as an artist, it helped him choose subjects that could provide direction on his path towards employment as a draughtsman. Ultimately, later in his career, the lessons and skills he had learnt from his collection allowed him to make works without needing to underdraw or to refer to external examples, all while creating works of art that resonated and aligned with his conceptual aspirations. His decision to produce images of heads based on *The Graphic*'s 'Heads of the People' series is one such example; the knowledge he gained from his appropriation of the series had a telling effect on his development as an avant-garde artist. The notion of the series, thoroughly explored in his attempt at making heads, became a central preoccupation throughout his career. He often produced a 'series' of works to fully illustrate a subject, describe a location or document his own work for peers and friends. Such a method was neither revisionist in approach nor revolutionary; it had its foundations in a long-standing tradition demonstrated in the pages of the illustrated newspapers, copious examples of which were found in van Gogh's collection of black-and-white prints.

Van Gogh, one the leading avant-garde artists of the late nineteenth century, found his artistic voice because of many influences. One that has been seriously undervalued, however, is perhaps the influence of his collection of prints, which was central to his development. An analysis of the collection – what was collected, how it was organised, and how it was used by van Gogh – reveals an aspiring artist who worked at his craft purposefully and systematically. Van Gogh was not the mad genius, as he is often portrayed. He was an artist who made informed decisions in a logical manner to assist in his development. If we read his letters from the early 1880s as he collated thousands of these prints and provided list after list of what he had bought and swapped, we can develop a deeper understanding of why he described them as 'a kind of Bible'.[3] More importantly, we realise that he was very serious

3 LT 311, volume 2, 266.

in advising van Rappard 'to have them in the studio once and for all'.[4] Van Gogh really believed in this mantra. It was how he created his unique modus operandi and a visual language that was revolutionary, unique, influential and, to do this day, much loved.

4 LT 311, volume 2, 266.

APPENDIX
OF VAN GOGH'S COLLECTION OF BLACK-AND-WHITE PRINTS

During the research for this book I was able to reconstruct Vincent van Gogh's collection of black-and-white prints using multiple sources. A significant number of prints are held in the collection of the Van Gogh Museum, Amsterdam (Vincent van Gogh Foundation), which formed the basis of this appendix. The remaining prints were identified by examing references in van Gogh's letters and referring to important existing scholarly work on the collection. This listing was too long to include as an appendix in this book. As such a dedicated website has been created at doi.org/10.26181/5e700281e05d2 which will be updated as further research identifies new works from the original collection.

BIBLIOGRAPHY

Allingham, Philip V., 'Robert Barnes' Illustrations for Thomas Hardy's *The Mayor of Casterbridge* as Serialised in *The Graphic*', *Victorian Periodicals Review*, 28/1 (1995), 27–39.

Altick, Richard, *The English Common Reader: A Social History of the Mass Reading Public 1800–1900* (Chicago and London: University of Chicago Press, 1967).

Anderson, Patricia, '"A Revolution in Popular Art": Pictorial Magazines and the Making of a Mass Culture in England, 1832–1860', *Journal of Newspaper and Periodical History*, 7 (1991), 16–27.

Bailey, Martin, *Young Vincent: The Story of van Gogh's Years in England* (London: Alison & Busby, 1990).

Bailey, Martin, 'Van Gogh and *The Illustrated London News*', *The Illustrated London News – Royal Issue* (1990), 80–5.

Bailey, Martin, (ed.), *Van Gogh in England: Portrait of the Artist as a Young Man* (London: Barbican Art Gallery, 1992).

Bailey, Martin, 'Van Gogh in London', *The Antique Collector*, March 1992, 74–7.

Bargue, Charles, *Exercices au fusain, pour préparer à l'étude de l'Académie d'après nature* (Paris: Goupil & Cie, 1871).

Barker, Hannah, *Newspapers, Politics and English Society, 1695–1855* (Harlow: Longman, 2000).

Bishop, James, 'The Story of the *ILN*', *The Illustrated London News*, 30 May 1992, 29–34.

Bliss, Douglas P., *A History of Wood Engraving* (London: Spring Books, 1964).

Booth, William, *In Darkest England and the Way Out* (London: International Headquarters of the Salvation Army, 1890).

Boyce, George, J. Curran & P. Wingate (eds), *Newspaper History: From the 17th Century to the Present Day* (London: Constable, 1978).

Bradley, Ian, *The Call to Seriousness: The Evangelical Impact on the Victorians* (London: Jonathan Cape, 1976).

Brouwer, Jaap, L. Siesling and J. Vis, *Anthon van Rappard: Companion and Correspondent of Vincent van Gogh, His Life and All His Works* (Amsterdam: Van Gogh Museum, 1974).

Buser, Thomas, 'Van Gogh as a Religious Artist', *Gazette des Beaux-Arts*, 114 (1989), 41–50.

Chadwick, Owen, *The Victorian Church*, 2 volumes (London: Adam & Charles Black, 1970).

Chapman, Stanley, *The History of Working Class Housing: A Symposium* (Newton Abbot: David and Charles, 1971).

Chatto, William A. & John Jackson. *A Treatise on Wood Engraving: Historical and Practical* (London: Henry G. Bohn, 1861).

Chetham, Charles, *The Role of Vincent van Gogh's Copies in the Development of his Art* (New York: Garland Publishing, 1976).

Codell, Julie F., 'The Aura of Mechanical Reproduction: Victorian Art and the Press, *Victorian Periodicals Review*, 24/1, (1991), 4–10.

Colley, Linda, *Britons: Forging the Nation 1707–1837* (London: Vintage, 1996).

Cowling, Mary, *The Artist as Anthropologist: The Representation of Type & Character in Victorian Art* (Cambridge: Cambridge University Press, 1989).

Dalziel, Gilbert, 'Wood-engraving in the "Sixties" and Some Criticism of To-day', *Print Collectors' Quarterly*, 15 (1928), 81–4.

de la Faille, J.B., *The Works of Vincent van Gogh: His Paintings and Drawings* (Amsterdam: Meulenhoff International, 1970).

de Vries, Leonard, *Panorama, 1842–1865: The World of the Early Victorians as Seen Through the Eyes of The Illustrated London News* (London: John Murray, 1967).

Dewsnup, Ernest Ritson, *The Housing Problem in England: Its Statistics, Legislation and Policy* (Manchester: University of Manchester, 1907).

Dickens, Charles, *The Works of Charles Dickens, Volume XIX* (London: Gresham Publishing Co., 1854).

Dickens, Charles, *Dombey and Son* (London: Oxford University Press, 1974).

Dickens, Charles, *Hard Times* (Ware, Herts: Wordsworth Classics, 1995).

Doré, Gustave, *Doré's London: All 180 Illustrations from London, A Pilgrimage* (London: Dover, 2004).

Dyos, Harold James, 'The Slums of Victorian London', *Victorian Studies*, 11 (1967–8), 5–40.

Dyos, Harold James & Michael Wolff, *The Victorian City: Images & Realities* (London: Routledge & Kegan Paul, 1973).

Edwards, Cliff, *Van Gogh and God: A Creative Spiritual Quest* (Chicago: Loyola University Press, 1989).

Edwards, L.M., *Herkomer: A Victorian Artist* (Aldershot: Ashgate, 1999).

Ellenius, Allan, 'Reproducing Art as a Paradigm of Communication: The Case of the Nineteenth Century Illustrated Magazines', *Figura*, 21 (1984), 69–92.

Ensor, Robert, *England: 1870–1914* (The Oxford History of England) (London: Oxford University Press, 1936).

Erickson, Kathleen Powers, *At Eternity's Gate: The Spiritual Vision of Vincent van Gogh* (Grand Rapids, MI; W.B. Eerdmans, 1998).

Fowlie, W., 'The Religious Experience of van Gogh', *College Art Journal,* 9/3 (1950), 317–24.

Fyfe, Paul "A Great Exhibition of Printing: *The Illustrated London News* Supplement Sheet (1851), *Cahiers Victoriens & Édouardiens*, Issue 84 (Autumn 2016), 1–16.

Goldman, Paul, *Victorian Illustration: The Pre-Raphaelites; The Idyllic School and the High Victorians* (Aldershot: Scolar Press, 1996).

The Graphic (London: Illustrated Newspapers Ltd, 1869–1932).

Heenk, Liesbeth, 'Revealing Van Gogh: An Examination of his Papers', *Paper Conservator*, 18/1 (1994), 30–39.

Herkomer, Hubert, 'Drawing & Engraving on Wood', *The Art Journal* (1882), 133–6 & 165–8.

Hibbert, Christopher, *The Illustrated London News: Social History of Victorian Britain* (London: Angus & Robertson, 1975).

Hogarth, Paul, *The Artist as Reporter* (London: Gordon Fraser, 1986).
Hulsker, Jan, 'Van Gogh's First and Only Commission as an Artist', *Vincent: Bulletin of the Rijksmuseum Vincent van Gogh*, 4 no. 4 (1976), 5–19.
Hulsker, Jan, *The New Complete van Gogh: Paintings, Drawings, Sketches: Revised and Enlarged ed.* (Amsterdam: J.M. Meulenhoff: Philadelphia: John Benjamins, 1996).
The Illustrated London News (London: Herbert Ingram, 1842–2003).
Irwin, Michael, *Picturing: Description and Illusion in the Nineteenth-Century Novel* (London: Allen & Unwin, 1979).
Ives, Colta *et al.*, *Vincent van Gogh: The Drawings* (New Haven and London: Yale University Press, 2005).
Jackson, Mason, *The Pictorial Press: Its Origins and Progress* (London: Hurst and Blackett, 1885).
Jerrold, Blanchard & Gustave Doré, *London, a Pilgrimage* (New York: Benjamin Blom, 1968). Originally published London: Grant, 1872.
Jones, Aled, *Powers of the Press. Newspapers, Power and the Public in Nineteenth-century England* (Aldershot: Scolar Press, 1996).
Jones, Gareth Stedman, *Outcast London* (Oxford: Clarendon Press, 1971).
Klingender, Francis, *Art and the Industrial Revolution* (London: Noel Carrington, 1968).
Kodera, Tsukasa, *Vincent van Gogh from Dutch Collections: Religion – Humanity – Nature* (Osaka: National Museum of Art, 1986).
Kodera, Tsukasa, 'Van Gogh and the Dutch Theological Culture of the Nineteenth Century', *Vincent Van Gogh, International Symposium* (Tokyo: Tokyo Shimbun, 1988), 141–70.
Kodera, Tsukasa, *Vincent van Gogh: Christianity versus Nature* (Amsterdam: J. Benjamins, 1990).
Kodera, Tsukasa & Yvette Rosenberg (eds), *The Mythology of Vincent van Gogh*, (Amsterdam: John Benjamins, 1993).
Kranzberg, Melvin & C.W. Pursell Jnr. (eds.), *Technology in Western Civilization,* Volume 1 (New York: Oxford University Press, 1967).
Lindley, Kenneth, *The Woodblock Engravers* (Newton Abbot: David & Charles, 1970).
Lister, Kristin Hoermann, 'Tracing a Transformation: Madame Roulin into *La Berceuse*', *Van Gogh Museum Journal* (2001), 62–85.
Mackay, James Hutton, *Religious Thought in Holland during the Nineteenth Century* (London: Hodder and Stoughton, 1911).
Masheck, Joseph (ed.), *Van Gogh 100* (Westport, Conn: Greenwood Press, 1996).
Mitchell, Sally, *Daily Life in Victorian England* (Westport, Conn: Greenwood Press, 1996).
Mountjoy, Peter R., 'Thomas Bywater Smithies, Editor of the *British Workman*', *Victorian Periodicals Review*, 18/2 (1985), 46–56.
The Penny Magazine (London: Society of the Diffusion of Useful Knowledge, 1832–1845).
Perkin, Harold, *The Age of the Railway* (London: Panther Books, 1970).

Pickvance, Ronald, *English Influences on Vincent van Gogh* (London: Arts Council of Great Britain, 1974).

Pickvance, Ronald, *Van Gogh in Saint-Rémy & Auvers* (New York: Metropolitan Museum of Art, 1986).

Reynolds, Ada, *The Life and Work of Frank Holl* (London: Methuen, 1912).

Rishel, Joseph J. *et al.*, *Van Gogh Face to Face: The Portraits* (New York: Thames and Hudson, 2000).

Shattock, Joanne & Michael Wolff (eds), *The Victorian Periodical Press: Samplings and Soundings* (Leicester: Leicester University Press, 1982).

Sheon, Aaron, 'Theo van Gogh, Publisher: the Monticelli Album', *Van Gogh Museum Journal*, (2000), 53–61.

Sinnema, Peter W., *Dynamics of the Pictured Page: Representing the Nation in The Illustrated London News* (Aldershot: Ashgate, 1998).

Smith, A. (ed.), *Gavarni in London: Sketches of Life and Character* (London: David Bogue, 1849).

Stein, Susan Alyson (ed.), *Van Gogh: A Retrospective* (Sydney and London: Bay Books, 1986).

Stolwijk, Chris & Richard Thomson, *Theo van Gogh 1857–1891: Art Dealer, Collector and Brother of Vincent* (Zwolle: Waanders, 1999).

Stolwijk, Chris, Sjraar van Heugten, Leo Jansen and Andreas Blühm (eds.), *Vincent's Choice: The Musée Imaginaire of Van Gogh* (Amsterdam: Van Gogh Museum, 2003).

Sund, Judy, *True to Temperament: Van Gogh and French Naturalist Literature* (Cambridge; New York: Cambridge University Press, 1992).

Thomas, William Luson, 'The Making of *The Graphic*', *Universal Review*, 2/5 (1888), 80–93.

Thompson, Edward Palmer, 'Time, Work-Discipline, and Industrial Capitalism', *Past and Present*, 38/1 (1967), 56–97.

Thompson, Flora, *Lark Rise to Candleford: A Trilogy* (London: Oxford University Press, 1945).

Thomson, Richard, 'Van Gogh in Paris: The Fortifications Drawings of 1887', *Jong Holland*, 3/3 (1987), 14–25.

Tralbaut, Marc Edo, *Vincent van Gogh* (London: Macmillan, 1969).

Treuherz, Julian (ed.), *Hard Times: Social Realism in Victorian Arts* (Manchester: Manchester City Art Galleries, 1987).

van der Veen, Wouter, *Van Gogh: A Literary Mind* (Zwolle: Waanders, 2009).

van der Wolk, Johannes, *The Seven Sketchbooks of Vincent van Gogh*, Facsimile ed. (London: Thames and Hudson, 1987).

van der Wolk, Johannes, Ronald Pickvance and E.B.F. Pey, *Vincent van Gogh Drawings* (Otterlo: Kröller-Müller Museum, 1990).

van Gogh, Vincent, *The Complete Letters of Vincent van Gogh* (Boston: Bulfinch Press, 2000).

van Gogh, Vincent, *Vincent van Gogh: The Letters: The Complete Illustrated and Annotated Edition*, edited by Leo Jansen, Hans Luijten and Nienke Bakker (Brussels: Mercatorfonds, 2009), 6 volumes.

van Gogh, Vincent, *Vincent van Gogh on England* (Amsterdam: Rijksmuseum Vincent van Gogh, 1968).

van Heugten, Sjraar, *Vincent van Gogh Drawings*. Volume 1: *The Early Years 1800–1883* (Amsterdam: Van Gogh Museum, 1996).

van Heugten, Sjraar, *Vincent van Gogh Drawings*. Volume 2: *Nuenen 1883–1885* (Amsterdam: Van Gogh Museum, 1997).

van Heugten, Sjraar, *Van Gogh: Master Draughtsman* (New York: Harry N. Abrams, 2005).

van Heugten, Sjraar, (ed.), *Van Gogh: The Birth of an Artist* (Amsterdam: Van Gogh Museum; Brussels: Mercatorfonds, 2015).

van Heugten, Sjraar, & Fieke Pabst, *The Graphic Work of Vincent van Gogh* (Zwolle: Waanders, 1995).

van Tilborgh, Louis, *et al. The Potato Eaters by Vincent van Gogh* (Zwolle: Waanders, 1993).

van Tilborgh, Louis & Marije Vellekoop, *Vincent van Gogh Paintings*. Volume 1: *Dutch Period 1881–1885* (Amsterdam: Van Gogh Museum, 1999).

van Uitert, Evert (ed.), *Van Gogh in Brabant* (Zwolle: Waanders, 1987).

van Uitert, Evert & M. Hoyle (eds.), *The Rijksmuseum Vincent van Gogh* (Amsterdam: Van Gogh Museum, 1987).

Vellekoop, Marije, *Vincent van Gogh Drawings*. Volume 4: *Arles, Saint-Rémy & Auvers-sur-Oise 1888–1890* (Amsterdam: Van Gogh Museum, 2007).

Vellekoop, Marije & Sjraar Van Heugten, *Vincent van Gogh Drawings*. Volume 3: *Antwerp and Paris 1885–1888* (Amsterdam: Van Gogh Museum, 2001).

Vizetelly, Henry, *Glances Back Through Seventy Years* (London: Kegan Paul, Trench, Trübner & Co., 1893).

Warner, Malcolm, *The Victorians: British Painting 1837–1901*, with contributions by Anne Helmreich and Charles Brock (Washington: National Gallery of Art, 1996).

White, Jerry, *London in the 19th Century* (London: Vintage Books, 2007).

Williams, Raymond, *Culture and Society 1780–1950* (Harmondsworth: Penguin Books, 1963).

Williams, Raymond, *The Country and the City* (London: Chatto & Windus, 1973).

Williamson, Charles Norris, 'Illustrated Journalism in England: Its Development', *Magazine of Art*, 13 (1890), 297–301, 334–40 and 391–6.

Zemel, Carol, 'The "Spook" in the Machine: Van Gogh's Pictures of Weavers in Brabant', *Art Bulletin*, 67/1 (1985) 123–137.

LIST OF IMAGES

Note for all Vincent van Gogh works: F numbers refer to J.B. De la Faille's cataloguing index in *The Works of Vincent van Gogh: His Paintings and Drawings*, (Amsterdam: Meulenhoff International, 1970); JH numbers refer to Jan Hulsker's cataloguing index in *The New Complete Paintings of Vincent van Gogh*, (Amsterdam/Philadelphia: J.M. Meulenhoff/John Benjamins, 1996).

Figures

Plates

Plate 4

Vincent van Gogh, *The Potato Eaters*, 1885.
Oil on canvas, 82.0 x 114.0 cm.
Van Gogh Museum, Amsterdam (Vincent van Gogh Foundation).
F0082/JH0764

Plate 5

Vincent van Gogh, *Gauguin's Chair*, 1888.
Oil on canvas, 90.5 x 72.7 cm.
Van Gogh Museum, Amsterdam (Vincent van Gogh Foundation).
F0499/JH1636

Plate 6

Vincent van Gogh, *Self-Portrait as a Painter*, 1887–88.
Oil on canvas, 65.0 x 50.5 cm.
Van Gogh Museum, Amsterdam (Vincent van Gogh Foundation).
F0522/JH1356

Plate 7

Vincent van Gogh, *Postman Joseph Roulin*, 1888.
Oil on canvas. 81.3 x 65.4 cm.
Museum of Fine Arts, Boston. Gift of Robert Treat Paine, 2nd.
Photograph © 2019 Museum of Fine Arts, Boston. F0432/JH1522

Plate 8

Vincent van Gogh, *Gate in the Paris Ramparts*, 1887.
Pencil, pen and ink, watercolour, on paper, 24.1 x 31.6 cm.
Van Gogh Museum, Amsterdam (Vincent van Gogh Foundation).
F1401/JH1284

Plate 9

Vincent van Gogh, *Fishing Boats at Sea*, 1888.
Reed pen on paper, 24.0 x 32.0 cm.
Kupferstichkabinett, Staatliche Museen zu Berlin. F1430/JH1505

Plate 10

Vincent van Gogh, *Fishing Boats at Sea*, 1888.
Oil on canvas, 44.0 x 53.0 cm.
Pushkin Museum, Moscow. F0417/JH1453

IMAGE CREDITS

All images have been reproduced with permission.

*

Figures 1–10, 14, 16, 17, 19, 20, 25, 26, 28, 31, 32, 34, 35, 37, 39 and 40: State Library of Victoria.

Figures 11, 15, 18, 24 and Plate 2: Kröller-Müller Museum, Otterlo, the Netherlands; photography by Rik Klein Gotnik, Harderwijk.

Figures 12, 13, 21–23, 29, 33, 38 and Plates 3–6 and 8: Van Gogh Museum, Amsterdam.

Figure 27: Nasjonalgalleriet, Oslo; photographer: Jaques Lathion.

Figure 30: Charles Dickens Museum, London.

Figure 36: private collection.

Plate 1: P. and N. de Boer Foundation, Amsterdam.

Plate 7: Museum of Fine Art, Bostin.

Plate 9: Kupferstichkabinett, Staatliche Museen zu Berlin.

Plate 10: Pushkin Museum, Moscow.

ABOUT THE AUTHOR

Dr Vincent Alessi is a Senior Lecturer in Visual Arts and Art History at La Trobe University, Melbourne, Australia. His research interests include the life and work of Vincent van Gogh, mid-late 19th-Century European art, 19th-Century popular graphic illustration and Australian contemporary visual art and curatorial practice. Vincent has held numerous positions within cultural institutions including as Artistic Director of LUMA | La Trobe University Museum of Art and Curatorial Manager at the Ian Potter Museum of Art, University of Melbourne. He has curated exhibitions both nationally and internationally on artists as diverse as Mike Brown, Philip Hunter, Juan Ford, Julie Rrap and Brook Andrew and on topics varying from Australian abstractionism and modernism to notions of place and identity in contemporary practice.